A Reader's
Hebrew-English Lexicon
of the Old Testament

A Reader's Hebrew-English Lexicon of the Old Testament

Volume II Joshua-2 Kings

Terry A. Armstrong

Douglas L. Busby

Cyril F. Carr

ZONDERVAN
PUBLISHING HOUSE
OF THE ZONDERVAN CORPORATION
GRAND RAPIDS, MICHIGAN 49506

A Reader's Hebrew-English Lexicon
of the Old Testament. Volume 2
(Joshua–2 Kings)

Copyright © 1982 by The Zondervan Corporation
Grand Rapids, Michigan

First printing, January 1982

Library of Congress Cataloging in Publication Data

Armstrong, Terry A   1944-
    A reader's Hebrew-English lexicon of the Old Testament.

    CONTENTS: v. 1. Genesis–Deuteronomy.—v. 2. Joshua–
2 Kings.
    1. Bible. O.T. Hebrew—Glossaries, vocabularies, etc.   2. He-
brew language—Dictionaries—English.   3. Hebrew language—
Word frequency.
    I. Busby, Douglas L., 1946-   joint author.   II. Carr, Cyril F.,
1949-   joint author.   III. Title.
PJ4833.A69   221.4'4'03   79-13294
ISBN 0-310-37030-2 (v. 2)   AACR1

Printed in the United States of America

CONTENTS

PREFACE

A Reader's Hebrew-English Lexicon of the Old Testament is an attempt to meet the need for an Old Testament translation tool on the level of Sakae Kubo's *Reader's Greek-English Lexicon of the New Testament.* With the student and pastor in view, it has been developed as a means to a more rapid reading of the Hebrew text. The *Reader's Lexicon* should not, therefore, be considered a replacement to a standard lexicon.

The format of the *Reader's Lexicon,* then, serves the purpose of eliminating most of the time-consuming lexical work from basic translation. The appendix contains words occurring over fifty times in the Old Testament. For speed and convenience the reader is encouraged to master this list. In the body of the book, words that occur fifty or fewer times in the Old Testament are listed verse by verse in the order of their occurrence. Nouns and adjectives appear in their vocabulary form. Verbs appear in the perfect third person masculine singular form of the stem used at that point in the text (e.g., וַיַּבְדֵּל appears in Genesis 1:4; in the *Reader's Lexicon* it is listed as הִבְדִּיל). This allows the reader to identify both the root (בדל)and the stem (hiphil). When these verb forms are not pointed, it simply means that the specific form is not extant.

In rare situations, forms other than those described will appear in the *Reader's Lexicon.* In each case clarity is the governing principle. This lexicon does not include numerals or proper nouns.

Along with the definition of the Hebrew words, their respective frequencies are given. For words other than verbs, the first number indicates the frequency of that word in the entire Old Testament. In the case of verbs the first number indicates the frequency of the given stem in the Bible book in which it is being studied. The second number gives the number of occurrences of that stem in the entire Old Testament. The third number gives the frequency of all the stems of a given verb in the entire Old Testament.

Example: Genesis 1:22 פרה (10-22-29)

> 10—The Qal stem occurs ten times in Genesis.
>
> 22—The Qal stem occurs twenty-two times in the Old Testament.
>
> 29—The cumulative occurrence of all stems in the Old Testament is twenty-nine.

Konkordanz zum Hebräischen Alten Testament by Gerhard Lisowsky has been relied on for verb, noun, and adjective frequencies. Frequencies for words in other categories come from *Veteris Testamenti Concordantiae Hebraicae Atque Chaldaicae* by Solomon Mandelkern. Occasionally Lisowsky departs from *A Hebrew and English Lexicon of the Old Testament* by Francis Brown, S. R. Driver, and Charles A. Briggs (hereafter designated BDB) in accepting one root, whereas BDB sees two roots (or vice versa). An example of this is Genesis 3:15. Lisowsky assumes the two occurrences of שׁוּף to be two different words, while BDB lists but one root. When a question mark follows the frequency, it indicates this disharmony.

For the sake of ease in rapid reading, the compound form of particles appears in the *Reader's Lexicon* even when the simple form exists in excess of fifty times (e.g., מִלְמַעְלָה, Genesis 6:16, which occurs only twenty-four times, though its basic part, מַעְלָה, occurs more than fifty times). Thus each compound is treated on its own and the numbers appearing with it indicate the frequency of that particle or compound only.

Definitions have been taken from BDB and checked against the text for meaning in context. Question marks following definitions indicate the interrogative. Suggested meanings are indicated by ''perh.,'' while questionable definitions are designated as [dub.]. The number at the end of the entry gives the page number in BDB carrying a discussion of the word.

As an exegetical tool, this work allows the user to (1) estimate the work involved in any given word study he might wish to pursue, (2) appraise the degree of certainty of a given definition, and (3) go directly to the correct page of a standard lexicon for further investigation. As a translational tool, this lexicon has the primary function of making rapid reading of the Hebrew text possible. Students of Hebrew will be enabled to examine the syntax of the language and, by extensive reading of the text, acquire an understanding of the contexts in which a given word occurs.

It is our prayer that this tool will make Hebrew reading and Hebrew exegesis more delightful and more common among students and pastors who have a high regard for the Word of God as given in the Old Testament.

JOSHUA

Chapter 1

מְשָׁרֵת	1 servant (1·20)	1058
מָבוֹא	4 entering (2·23)	99
הִתִיצֵב	5 to take one's stand (2·48·48)	426
הרפה	to abandon, forsake (2·21·44)	951
אמץ	6 to be strong, bold (5·16·41)	54
אמץ	7 to be strong, bold (5·16·41)	54
מושׁ	8 to depart (1·20[?]·20)	559
הגה	to meditate, muse (1·22·24)	211
אמץ	9 to be strong, bold (5·16·41)	54
ערץ	to tremble (1·11·14)	792
שֹׁטֵר	10 official, officer (5·25)	1009
צֵידָה	11 provision (2·9)	845
בְּעוֹד	within yet (1·20)	728
טַף	14 children (2·41)	381
חמשׁ	ptc.: in battle array (2·4·5)	332
יְרֻשָּׁה	15 possession (3·14)	440
מרה	18 to show rebelliousness (1·22·43)	598
אמץ	to be strong, bold (5·16·41)	54

Chapter 2

מְרַגֵּל	1 spy (1·10)	920
חֶרֶשׁ	silently, secretly (1·1)	361
זוֹנָה	harlot (4·33[?])	275
הֵנָּה	2 hither, here (5·49)	244
חפר	to search (2·22·22)	343
חפר	3 to search (2·22·22)	343
צָפַן	4 to hide (1·23·28)	860
מֵאַיִן	whence? (2·48)	32
אָנָה	5 whence? whither? (2·39)	33
הִשִּׂיג	to overtake (1·48·48)	673
גָּג	roof (3·29)	150
טָמַן	to hide (3·28·31)	380
פֵּשֶׁת	flax, linen (1·16)	833
מַעְבָּרָה	7 ford (1·8)	721

טֶרֶם	8 not yet (2·16)	382
גָּג	roof (3·29)	150
אֵימָה	9 terror, dread (1·17)	33
נָמוֹג	to melt (2·8·17)	556
הֶחֱרִים	10 to devote to destruction (14·46·49)	335
נָמֵס	11 to melt, grow fearful (3·19·21)	587
מִמַּעַל	above, on top of (1·29)	751
חֶבֶל	15 cord (5·49)	286
חַלּוֹן	window (3·30)	319
פָּגַע	16 to fall upon (10·40·46)	803
נֶחְבָּא	to hide oneself, be hidden (2·16·34)	285
נָקִי	17 free, exempt from obligations (3·43)	667
שְׁבוּעָה	oath (3·30)	989
תִּקְוָה	18 cord (2·2)	876
חוּט	cord, thread (1·7)	296
שָׁנִי	scarlet (2·42)	1040
קָשַׁר	to bind (2·36·44)	905
חַלּוֹן	window (3·30)	319
נָקִי	19 free, exempt from obligations (3·43)	667
נָקִי	20 free, exempt from obligations (3·43)	667
שְׁבוּעָה	oath (3·30)	989
קָשַׁר	21 to bind (2·36·44)	905
תִּקְוָה	cord (2·2)	876
שָׁנִי	scarlet (2·42)	1040
חַלּוֹן	window (3·30)	319
נָמוֹג	24 to melt (2·8·17)	556

Chapter 3

טֶרֶם	1 before, before that (2·16)	382
שֹׁטֵר	2 official (5·25)	1009
תְּמוֹל	4 yesterday; ת׳ שִׁלְשׁוֹם = formerly (3·23)	1069
שִׁלְשׁוֹם	aforetime, previously = ש׳ תְּמוֹל	

1

נִפְלָאוֹת 5 wonderful acts (1·43) 810

הֵנָּה 9 hither, here (5·49) 244

מִלְמַעְלָה 13 above (2·24) 752

נֵד heap of waters (2·6) 622

נטבל 15 to be dipped (1·1·16) 371

גְּדְיָה riverbank (2·4) 152

קָצִיר harvest (1·49) 894

צַד 16 side (3·31) 841

מֶלַח salt (5·28) 571

חָרָבָה 17 dry ground (3·8) 351

Chapter 4

מַצָּב 3 standing place (2·10) 662

מָלוֹן lodging place (2·8) 533

שְׁכֶם 5 shoulder (1·22) 1014

זִכָּרוֹן 7 memorial (1·24) 272

מָלוֹן 8 lodging place (2·8) 533

מַצָּב 9 standing place (2·10) 622

חמש 12 ptc.: in battle array (2·4·5) 332

חלוץ 13 equipped one, warrior (4·17[?]) 323

נָתַק 18 to be drawn out (2·10·27) 683

חָרָבָה dry ground (3·8) 351

תְּמוֹל yesterday; ת׳ שִׁלְשׁוֹם = formerly (3·23) 1069

שִׁלְשׁוֹם תְּמוֹל שׁ׳ = aforetime, previously (3·25) 797

גְּדְיָה riverbank (2·4) 152

יַבָּשָׁה 22 dry ground (1·14) 387

Chapter 5

נָמֵס 1 to melt, grow fearful (3·19·21) 587

צֹר 2 flint (2·6) 866

מול to circumcise (6·12·29) 557

צֹר 3 flint (2·6) 866

מול to circumcise (6·12·29) 557

עָרְלָה foreskin (1·16) 790

מול 4 to circumcise (6·12·29) 557

מול 5 to circumcise (6·12·29) 557

יִלּוֹד born (1·5) 409

זוב 6 to flow (1·29·29) 264

חָלָב milk (1·44) 316

מול 7 to circumcise (6·12·29) 557

עָרֵל uncircumcised (1·35) 790

נִמּוֹל 8 to be circumcised (1·17·29) 557

גלל 9 to roll away (2·10·17) 164

פֶּסַח 10 passover (2·48) 820

עָבוּר 11 produce, yield (2·2) 721

מָחֳרָת the morrow (2·32) 564

פֶּסַח passover (2·48) 820

קָלָה to roast, parch (1·3·4) 885

בְּעֶצֶם selfsame, itself (1·17[?]) 783

מָן 12 manna (2·14) 557

מָחֳרָת the morrow (2·32) 564

עָבוּר produce, yield (2·2) 721

תְּבוּאָה product, yield (1·43) 100

לְנֶגֶד 13 in front of, before (1·32) 617

שָׁלַף to draw out (1·24·24) 1025

נָשַׁל 15 to draw off (1·6·7) 675

נַעַל sandal (3·22) 653

Chapter 6

הִקִּיף 3 to go around (2·16·27) 668

יוֹבֵל 4 ram (5·27) 385

מָשַׁךְ 5 to draw out, give a sound (1·30·36) 604

יוֹבֵל ram (5·27) 385

הֵרִיעַ to shout a war cry, alarm of battle (7·40·44) 929

תְּרוּעָה alarm [of war], war cry (2·36) 929

יוֹבֵל 6 ram (5·27) 385

חלוץ 7 equipped one, warrior (4·17[?]) 323

יוֹבֵל 8 ram (5·27) 385

חלוץ 9 equipped one, warrior (4·17[?]) 323

הֵרִיעַ 10 to shout a war cry, alarm of battle (7·40·44) 929

הִקִּיף 11 to go around (2·16·17) 668

2

יוֹבֵל 13 ram (5·27) 385

חָלוּץ equipped one, warrior (4·17[?]) 323

שַׁחַר 15 dawn (1·23) 1007

הֵרִיעַ 16 to shout a war cry, alarm of battle (7·40·44) 929

חֵרֶם 17 devoted thing (13·29) 356

זוֹנָה harlot (4·33[?]) 275

הֶחְבִּיא to hide (2·6·34) 285

חֵרֶם 18 devoted thing (13·29) 356

הֶחֱרִים to devote to destruction (14·46·49) 355

עָכַר to disturb, trouble (3·12·14) 747

הֵרִיעַ 20 to shout a war cry, alarm of battle (7·40·44) 929

תְּרוּעָה alarm [of war], war cry (2·36) 929

הֶחֱרִים 21 to devote to destruction (14·46·49) 355

שֶׂה sheep, goat (1·44) 961

רָגַל 22 to spy (5·14·16) 920

זוֹנָה harlot (4·33[?]) 275

רָגַל 23 to spy (5·14·16) 920

זוֹנָה 25 harlot (4·33[?]) 275

הֶחְבִּיא to hide (2·6·34) 285

רָגַל to spy (5·14·16) 920

יִסַּד 26 to found (1·10·42) 413

צָעִיר young (1·22) 859

שֵׁמַע 27 report (2·4) 1035

Chapter 7

מָעַל 1 to act unfaithfully (4·35·35) 591

מַעַל unfaithful act (5·29) 591

חֵרֶם devoted thing (13·29) 356

רָגַל 2 to spy (5·14·16) 920

שֶׁבֶר 5 perh. quarry (1·45) 991

מוֹרָד descent (2·5) 434

נָמֵס to melt, grow fearful (3·19·21) 587

שִׂמְלָה 6 clothes (1·29) 971

אֲהָהּ 7 alas! (1·15) 13

הוֹאִיל to show willingness (2·18·18) 383

בִּי 8 part. of entreaty: I pray, Oh (1·12) 106

עֹרֶף back of neck (2·33) 791

חֵרֶם 11 devoted thing (13·29) 356

גנב to take by stealth, steal (1·30·39) 170

כָּחַשׁ to deceive (2·19·22) 471

עֹרֶף 12 back of neck (2·33) 791

חֵרֶם devoted thing (13·29) 356

חֵרֶם 13 devoted thing (13·29) 356

חֵרֶם 15 devoted thing (13·29) 356

נְבָלָה disgraceful folly (1·13) 615

תּוֹדָה 19 thanksgiving, praise (1·32) 392

כָּחַד to hide (1·15·30) 470

אָמְנָה 20 truly, indeed (1·3) 53

אַדֶּרֶת 21 cloak (2·12) 12

מִשְׁקָל weight (1·48) 1054

חמד to desire (1·16·21) 326

טָמַן to hide (3·28·31) 380

טָמַן 22 to hide (3·28·31) 380

אַדֶּרֶת 24 cloak (2·12) 12

עָכַר 25 to disturb, trouble (3·12·14) 747

רגם to kill by stoning (1·15·15) 920

סקל to stone (1·12·22) 709

גַּל 26 heap (2·20) 164

חָרוֹן [burning of] anger (1·41) 354

Chapter 8

בָּזַז 2 to plunder (3·37·40) 102

אֹרֵב liers in wait (6·18[?]) 70

אָרַב 4 to lie in wait (5·20·23) 70

הִתִּיק 6 to draw away (1·2·27) 683

אֹרֵב 7 place of lying in wait, ambush (6·18[?]) 70

הִצִּית 8 to kindle (2·17·27) 428

מַאֲרָב 9 ambush (1·5) 70

גַּיְא 11 valley (3·47) 161

3

אֹרֵב 12 liers in wait (6·18[?]) 70

עָקֵב 13 hinder part, rear (1·14) 784

אֹרֵב 14 liers in wait (6·18[?]) 70

נָתַק 16 to be drawn out (2·10·27) 683

כִּידוֹן 18 javelin (3·9) 475

אֹרֵב 19 liers in wait (6·18[?]) 70

הִצִּית to kindle (2·17·27) 428

עָשָׁן 20 smoke (2·25) 798

הֵנָּה הנה להנה = hither and thither (5·49) 244

אֹרֵב 21 liers in wait (6·18[?]) 70

עָשָׁן smoke (2·25) 798

בִּלְתִּי 22 not, except (4·24) 116

שָׂרִיד survivor (9·28) 975

פָּלִיט fugitive, escaped one (1·19) 812

כִּידוֹן 26 javelin (3·9) 475

הֶחֱרִים to devote to destruction (14·46·49) 355

בַּזַז 27 to plunder (3·37·40) 102

תֵּל 28 mound (2·5) 1068

תָּלָה 29 to execute by hanging (3·23·27) 1067

נְבֵלָה corpse (1·48) 615

גַּל heap (2·20) 164

שָׁלֵם 31 full, perfect (1·28) 1023

הֵנִיף to wield (1·32·34[?]) 631

מִשְׁנֶה 32 copy (1·35) 1041

שֹׁטֵר 33 official, officer (5·25) 1009

אֶזְרָח native (1·17) 280

מוּל in front of (5·33) 557

קְלָלָה 34 curse (1·13) 887

טַף 35 children (2·41) 381

Chapter 9

שְׁפֵלָה 1 lowland (7·20) 1050

חוֹף shore, coast (1·7) 342

מוּל in front of (5·33) 557

עָרְמָה 4 craftily (1·5) 791

הִצְעִיר perh. to form [cause to become] 85 [or alternate root הִצְטִיד] to suppl oneself with provisions (1·1·1) 845

שָׂק sack [for grain] (1·48) 974

בָּלֶה worn out (4·5) 115

נֹאד skin (2·6) 609

נַעַל 5 sandal (3·22) 653

בָּלֶה worn out (4·5) 115

טָלָא to be patched (1·1·1) 378

שַׂלְמָה outer garment (3·16) 971

צֵיד provision (2·5) 845

נִקֻּד crumbs (2·3) 666

אוּלַי 7 perhaps (2·45) 19

מֵאַיִן 8 whence? (2·48) 32

שֵׁמַע 9 report (2·4) 1035

צֵידָה 11 provision (2·9) 845

חָם 12 hot (1·12) 328

הִצְטַיֵּד to take as one's provisions (1·1·1) 845

נִקֻּד crumbs (2·3) 666

נֹאד 13 skin (2·6) 609

שַׂלְמָה outer garment (3·16) 971

נַעַל sandal (3·22) 653

בלה to become old and worn out (1·11·16) 115

צֵיד 14 provision (2·5) 845

נָלוֹן 18 to murmur (1·8·18) 534

קֶצֶף 20 wrath (3·29) 893

שְׁבוּעָה oath (3·30) 989

חֹטֵב 21 cutter or gatherer of firewood (3·6[?]) 310

שֹׁאֵב water drawer (3·5) 980

רִמָּה 22 to deceive (1·8·8) 941

חֹטֵב 23 cutter or gatherer of firewood (3·6[?]) 310

שֹׁאֵב water drawer (3·5) 980

חֹטֵב 27 cutter or gatherer of firewood (3·6[?]) 310

שֹׁאֵב water drawer (3·5) 980

4

Chapter 10

הַחֲרִים	1	to devote to destruction (14·46·49) 355
הרפה	6	to abandon (2·21·44) 951
בִּפְנֵי	8	in the face of (3·17) 816
פִּתְאֹם	9	suddenly (2·25) 837
הָמַם	10	to confuse, rout (1·13·13) 243
מַכָּה		defeat (2·48) 646
מַעֲלֶה		ascent (4·19) 751
מוֹרָד	11	descent (2·5) 434
בָּרָד		hail (1·29) 135
מֵאֲשֶׁר		from [or than] that which (1·17) 84
דמם	12	to be still, silent (2·23·30) 198
יָרֵחַ		moon (2·27) 437
דמם	13	to be still, silent (2·23·30) 198
יָרֵחַ		moon (2·27) 437
נקם		to avenge (1·13·34) 667
אוץ		to hasten (2·8·10) 21
נֶחְבָּא	16	to hide oneself, be hidden (4·16·34) 285
מְעָרָה		cave (9·40) 792
נֶחְבָּא	17	to hide oneself, be hidden (4·16·34) 285
מְעָרָה		cave (9·40) 792
גלל	18	to roll (2·10·17) 164
מְעָרָה		cave (9·40) 792
זנב	19	to cut off or smite the tail = attack in the rear (1·2·2) 275
מַכָּה	20	slaughter (2·48) 646
שָׂרִיד		survivor (9·28) 975
שׂרד		to escape (1·1·1) 974
מִבְצָר		fortification (3·37) 131
חָרַץ	21	to cut, sharpen, decide (1·5·10) 358
מְעָרָה	22	cave (9·40) 792
מְעָרָה	23	cave (9·40) 792
קָצִין	24	chief, commander (1·12) 892
צַוָּאר		neck, back of neck (2·41) 848
אמץ	25	to be strong, bold (5·16·41) 54

כָּכָה		thus (1·34) 462
תָּלָה	26	to execute by hanging (3·27) 1067
מְעָרָה	27	cave (9·40) 792
נֶחְבָּא		to hide oneself, be hidden (4·16·34) 285
הַחֲרִים	28	to devote to destruction (14·46·49) 355
שָׂרִיד		survivor (9·28) 975
שָׂרִיד	30	survivor (9·28) 975
בִּלְתִּי	33	not, except (4·24) 116
שָׂרִיד		survivor (9·28) 975
הַחֲרִים	35	to devote to destruction (14·46·49) 355
שָׂרִיד	37	survivor (9·28) 975
הַחֲרִים		to devote to destruction (14·46·49) 355
הַחֲרִים	39	to devote to destruction (14·46·49) 355
שָׂרִיד		survivor (9·28) 975
שְׁפֵלָה	40	lowland (7·20) 1050
אֶשֶׁד		mountain slope (4·7) 78
שָׂרִיד		survivor (9·28) 975
נְשָׁמָה		breathing thing (3·24) 675
הַחֲרִים		to devote to destruction (14·46·49) 355

Chapter 11

שְׁפֵלָה	2	lowland (7·20) 1050
נפה		height (2·4) 632
חוֹל	4	sand (1·22) 297
נועד	5	to assemble by appointment (1·18·28) 416
עִקֵּר	6	to hamstring (2·5·7) 785
מֶרְכָּבָה		chariot (2·44) 939
פִּתְאֹם	7	suddenly (2·25) 837
בִּקְעָה	8	valley, plain (3·19) 132
בִּלְתִּי		not, except (4·24) 116
שָׂרִיד		survivor (9·28) 975

עָקַר 9 to hamstring (2·5·7) 785

מֶרְכָּבָה   chariot (2·44) 939

הֶחֱרִים 11 to devote to destruction (14·46·49) 355

נְשָׁמָה   breathing thing (3·24) 675

הֶחֱרִים 12 to devote to destruction (14·46·49) 355

תֵּל 13 mound (2·5) 1068

זוּלָה   except that (1·16) 265

בָּזַז 14 to plunder (3·37·40) 102

נְשָׁמָה   breathing thing (3·24) 675

שְׁפֵלָה 16 lowland (7·20) 1050

בִּקְעָה 17 valley, plain (3·19) 132

בִּלְתִּי 19 not, except (4·24) 116

הֶחֱרִים 20 to devote to destruction (14·46·49) 355

תְּחִנָּה   favor (1·25) 337

הֶחֱרִים 21 to devote to destruction (14·46·49) 355

מַחֲלֹקֶת 23 division (3·44) 324

שָׁקַט   to be quiet, undisturbed (2·31·41) 1052

Chapter 12

מֶלַח 3 salt (5·28) 571

תֵּימָן   south (3·24) 412

יְרֵשָׁה 6 possession (3·14) 440

בִּקְעָה 7 valley, plain (3·19) 132

יְרֵשָׁה   possession (3·14) 440

מַחֲלֹקֶת   division (3·44) 324

שְׁפֵלָה 8 lowland (7·20) 1050

אָשֵׁד   mountain slope (4·7) 78

צַד 9 side (3·31) 841

נפה 23 height (2·4) 632

Chapter 13

זָקֵן 1 to be old, become old (4·25·27) 278 165

גְּלִילָה 2 circuit, boundary, territory (4·6[?]) 165

סרן 3 lord (1·21) 710

תֵּימָן 4 south (3·24) 412

מִישׁוֹר 9 plain (5·23) 449

מִישׁוֹר 16 plain (5·23) 449

מִישׁוֹר 17 plain (5·23) 449

אָשֵׁד 20 mountain slope (4·7) 78

מִישׁוֹר 21 plain (5·23) 449

נסיך   prince (1·6[?]) 651

קֹסֵם 22 necromancers, diviners (1·9) 890

חַוָּה 30 tent village (1·7) 295

Chapter 14

קִנְיָן 4 acquisition (1·9) 889

אֹדוֹת 6 cause; עַל א׳ = because of (2·11) 15

רגל   to spy (5·14·16) 920

המסה 8 to melt (1·4·4) 587

מֵאָז 10 from that time, time past (1·18) 23

בָּצוּר 12 fortified (1·25) 130

אוּלַי   perhaps (2·45) 19

שָׁקַט 15 to be quiet, undisturbed (2·31·41) 1052

Chapter 15

תֵּימָן 1 south (3·24) 412

מֶלַח 2 salt (5·28) 571

עַקְרָב 3 scorpion (1·9) 785

מַעֲלֶה   ascent (4·19) 751

תּוֹצָאָה 4 extremity, outgoing (14·23) 426

קדם 5 eastward (4·26) 870

מֶלַח   salt (5·28) 571

נֹכַח 7 opposite to (2·27) 647

מַעֲלֶה   ascent (4·19) 751

תּוֹצָאָה   extremity, outgoing (14·23) 426

גַּיְא 8 valley (3·47) 161

תָּאַר 9 to incline (5·5·8) 1061

מַעְיָן   spring (2·23) 745

תָּאַר 11 to incline (5·5·8) 1061

תּוֹצָאָה extremity, outgoing (14·23) 426

יָלִיד 14 born (1·12) 409

הֵסִית 18 to instigate (1·18·18) 694

צנח to descend (1·3·3) 856

גֻּלָּה 19 basin (3·15) 165

עֶלִי upper (1·2) 751

תַּחְתִּי lower, lowest (1·19) 1066

שְׁפֵלָה 33 lowland (7·20) 1050

מֶלַח 62 salt (5·28) 571

Chapter 16

תַּחְתּוֹן 3 lower, lowest (2·13) 1066

תּוֹצָאָה extremity, outgoing (14·23) 426

פָּגַע 7 to strike, touch (10·40·46) 803

תּוֹצָאָה 8 extremity, outgoing (14·23) 426

מבדלה 9 a separate place (1·1) 95

מַס 10 slave gang(s) (2·23) 586

Chapter 17

חֶבֶל 5 measured portion, lot (5·49) 286

תּוֹצָאָה 9 extremity, outgoing (14·23) 426

פָּגַע 10 to strike, touch (10·40·46) 803

נפת 11 height (1·1) 632

הוֹאִיל 12 to determine (2·18·18) 383

מַס 13 slave gang(s) (2·23) 586

חֶבֶל 14 measured portion, lot (5·49) 286

ברא 15 to cut down, clear (2·5·5[?]) 135

אוץ to be pressed, confined, narrow (2·8·10) 21

לַאֲשֶׁר 16 to those who (2·38) 81

ברא 18 to cut down, clear (2·5·5[?]) 135

תּוֹצָאָה extremity, outgoing (14·23) 426

Chapter 18

נקהל 1 to assemble (2·19·39) 874

נכבש to be subdued (1·5·14) 461

אָנָה 3 whence? whither? (2·39) 33

התרפה to show oneself slack (1·3·44) 951

הֵנָּה 6 hither, here (5·49) 244

יָרָה to throw (1·13·25[?]) 434

פֹּה here, hither (2·44) 805

כְּהֻנָּה 7 priesthood (1·13) 464

פֹּה 8 here, hither (2·44) 805

מַחֲלֹקֶת 10 division (3·44) 324

תּוֹצָאָה 12 extremity, outgoing (14·23) 426

תָּאַר 14 to incline (5·5·8) 1061

תּוֹצָאָה extremity, outgoing (14·23) 426

מַעְיָן 15 spring (2·23) 745

גַּיְא 16 valley (3·47) 161

תָּאַר 17 to incline (5·5·8) 1061

נֹכַח opposite to (2·27) 647

מַעֲלֶה ascent (4·19) 751

מוּל 18 in front of (5·33) 557

תּוֹצָאָה 19 extremity, outgoing (14·23) 426

מֶלַח salt (5·28) 571

גבל 20 to bound, border (1·3·5) 148

קדם eastward (4·26) 870

גְּבוּלָה border, boundary (2·10) 148

Chapter 19

פָּגַע 11 to strike, touch (10·40·46) 803

קדם 12 eastward (4·26) 870

קדם 13 eastward (4·26) 870

תָּאַר to reach to (1·1·8) 1061

תּוֹצָאָה 14 extremity, outgoing (14·23) 426

גַּיְא valley (3·47) 161

פָּגַע 22 to strike, touch (10·40·46) 803

תּוֹצָאָה extremity, outgoing (14·23) 426

פָּגַע 26 to strike, touch (10·40·46) 803

פָּגַע 27 to strike, touch (10·40·46) 803

גַּיְא valley (3·47) 161

מִבְצָר 29 fortification (3·37) 137

תּוֹצָאָה extremity, outgoing (14·23) 426

אֵלוֹן 33 terebinth, tall tree (1·10) 18

תּוֹצָאָה extremity, outgoing (14·23) 426

פָּגַע 34 to strike, touch (10·40·46) 803

מִבְצָר 35 fortification (3·37) 131

מוּל 46 in front of (6·25) 557

גְּבוּלָה 49 border, boundary (2·10) 148

Chapter 20

מִקְלָט 2 refuge (7·20) 886

רָצַח 3 to murder, slay (8·38·43) 953

שְׁגָגָה sin of error, inadvertance (2·9) 993

מִקְלָט refuge (7·20) 886

גֹּאֵל kinsman (3·44[?]) 145

בִּבְלִי without (2·6) 115

גֹּאֵל 5 kinsman (3·44[?]) 145

רָצַח to murder, slay (8·38·43) 953

בִּבְלִי without (2·6) 115

שֹׂנֵא enemy (1·41) 971

תְּמוֹל yesterday; ת׳ שִׁלְשׁוֹם = aforetime (3·23) 1069

שִׁלְשׁוֹם 5 תְּמוֹל שׁ׳ = aforetime, previously (3·25) 1026

רָצַח 6 to murder, slay (8·38·43) 953

מִישׁוֹר 8 plain (5·23) 449

מוּעָדָה 9 cities appointed (1·1) 418

שְׁגָגָה sin of error, inadvertance (2·9) 993

גֹּאֵל kinsman (3·44[?]) 145

Chapter 21

מִקְלָט 13 refuge (7·20) 886

רָצַח to murder, slay (8·38·43) 953

מִקְלָט 21 refuge (7·20) 886

רָצַח to murder, slay (8·38·43) 953

מִקְלָט 27 refuge (7·20) 886

רָצַח to murder, slay (8·38·43) 953

מִקְלָט 32 refuge (7·20) 886

רָצַח to murder, slay (8·38·43) 953

מִקְלָט 38 refuge (7·20) 886

רָצַח to murder, slay (8·38·43) 953

בִּפְנֵי 42 in the face of (3·17) 816

Chapter 22

נֶכֶס 8 riches (1·5) 647

שַׂלְמָה clothes (3·16) 971

גְּלִילָה 10 circuit, boundary, territory (4·6) 165

מוּל 11 in front of (6·25) 557

גְּלִילָה circuit, boundary, territory (4·6) 165

נִקְהַל 12 to assemble (2·19·39) 874

מַעַל 16 unfaithful act (5·29) 591

מָעַל to act unfaithfully (4·35·35) 591

מָרַד to rebel (5·25·25) 597

נֶגֶף 17 plague (1·7) 620

מָרַד 18 to rebel (5·25·25) 597

קָצַף to be angry (1·28·34) 893

מָרַד 19 to rebel (5·25·25) 597

מִבַּלְעֲדֵי apart from, except, without (1·12) 116

מָעַל 20 to act unfaithfully (4·35·35) 591

מַעַל unfaithful act (5·29) 591

חֵרֶם devoted thing (13·29) 356

קֶצֶף wrath (3·29) 893

גָּוַע to expire, die (1·23·23) 157

אֶלֶף 21 thousand (3·12[?]) 48

מֶרֶד 22 revolt (1·1) 597

מַעַל unfaithful act (5·29) 591

דְּאָגָה 24 anxiety, anxious care (1·6) 178

תַּבְנִית 28 construction, structure (1·20) 125

חָלִילָה 29 far be it [from] (2·21) 321

מָרַד to rebel (5·25·25) 597

מִלְּבַד besides (1·33) 94

אֶלֶף 30 thousand (3·12[?]) 48

מָעַל 31 to act unfaithfully (4·35·35) 591

מַעַל unfaithful act (5·29) 591

Chapter 23

זָקֵן 1 to be old, become old (4·25·27) 278

שֹׁטֵר 2 official, officer (5·25) 1009

זָקֵן to be old, become old (4·25·27) 278

מָבוֹא 4 entering (2·23) 99

הדף 5 to thrust out, drive out (1·11·11) 213

עָצוּם 9 mighty, strong (1·31) 783

בִּפְנֵי in the face of (3·17) 816

הִתְחַתֵּן 12 to form a marriage alliance with (1·11·11) 368

פַּח 13 bird trap (1·25) 809

מוֹקֵשׁ lure (1·27) 430

שֹׁטֵט scourge (1·1) 1002

צַד side (3·31) 841

צְנִין thorn, prick (1·2) 856

מְהֵרָה 16 haste (3·20) 555

Chapter 24

שֹׁטֵר 1 official, officer (5·25) 1009

הִתְיַצֵּב to station oneself (2·48·48) 426

נָגַף 5 to smite (1·24·48) 619

מַאֲפֵל 7 darkness (1·1) 66

צִרְעָה 12 hornets (1·3) 864

גרשׁ to drive out (2·34·48) 176

יגע 13 to toil (1·20·26) 388

זַיִת olives, olive tree (1·38) 268

חָלִילָה 16 far be it [from] (2·21) 321

גרשׁ 18 to drive out (2·34·48) 176

קַנּוֹא 19 jealous (1·2) 888

נֵכָר 20 foreignness (2·36) 648

נֵכָר 23 foreignness (2·36) 648

שֹׁטֵר 24 official, officer (5·25) 1009

אַלָּה 26 terebinth (1·17) 18

עֵדָה 27 testimony, witness (1·3) 729

אֹמֶר speech, word (1·48) 56

כָּחַשׁ to deceive (2·19·22) 471

הֶאֱרִיךְ 31 to prolong (1·31·34) 73

חֶלְקָה 32 portion of ground (1·24) 324

קְשִׂיטָה a unit of [unknown] value, perh. weight (1·3) 903

JUDGES

Chapter 1

תְּחִלָּה 1 beginning; 'בַּתְּ = first, at first (3·22) 321

קצץ 6 to cut, hew off (1·9·14) 893

בֹּהֶן thumb, great toe (2·2 [?]) 97

בֹּהֶן 7 thumb, great toe (2·[2[?]) 97

קצץ to be cut or hewn off (1·1·14) 893

לקט to gather (1·21·36) 544

שְׁפֵלָה 9 lowland (1·20) 1050

לְפָנִים 10 formerly (5·21) 815

לְפָנִים 11 formerly (5·21) 815

הסית 14 to incite (1·18·18) 694

צנח to descend (2·3·3) 856

יהב 15 to give (2·27·27) 396

גֻּלָּה basin (pool, well[?]) (3·15) 165

עִלִּי upper (1·2) 751

תַּחְתִּי lower (1·9) 1066

חֹתֵן 16 wife's father (5·21) 368

תָּמָר palm tree, date palm; עִיר הַתְּמָרִים = Jericho (2·12) 1071

הֶחֱרִים 17 to devote to destruction (2·46·49) 355

התיר 23 to make reconnaissance (1·3·22) 1064

לְפָנִים formerly (5·21) 815

מָבוֹא 24 entrance (2·23) 99

מָבוֹא 25 entrance (2·23) 99

הוֹאִיל 27 to resolve, be determined (4·18·18) 383

מַס 28 labor bands (4·23) 586

מַס 30 labor bands (4·23) 586

מַס 33 labor bands (4·23) 586

לָחַץ 34 to press (3·14·15) 537

הוֹאִיל 35 to resolve, persist (4·18·18) 383

מַס labor bands (4·23) 586

מַעֲלֵה 36 ascent; מ' עַקְרַבִּים = Scorpion Pass (2·19) 751

עַקְרָב scorpion (1·9) 785

Chapter 2

הֵפֵר 1 to break, violate (1·41·44) 830

נָתַץ 2 to pull down (7·31·42) 683

גרש 3 to drive out, away (5·34·48) 176

צַד side, prob. = snare, trap (1·1) 841

מוֹקֵשׁ lure (2·27) 430

הֶאֱרִיךְ 7 to prolong; הֶאֱרִיךְ אַחֲרֵי = survive (1·31·34) 73

שֹׁסִים 14 plunderers (2·7) 1042

שסס to plunder (1·3·5) 1042

שֹׁסִים 16 plunderers (2·7) 1042

נאקה 18 groaning (1·4) 611

לָחַץ to oppress (3·14·15) 537

דחק oppressor (1·1[?]) 191

מעלל 19 practice (1·4) 611

קָשָׁה stiff, stubborn (2·36) 904

נָסָה 22 to test (4·36·36) 650

Chapter 3

נָסָה 1 to test (4·36·36) 650

לְפָנִים 2 formerly (5·21) 815

סרן 3 lord (8·21) 710

נָסָה 4 to test (4·36·36) 650

אֲשֵׁרָה 7 Ashera; Canaanite goddess of fortune and happiness; a sacred tree or pole (5·40) 81

מוֹשִׁיעַ 9 savior (3·27) 446

עזז 10 to be strong, prevail (2·9·11) 738

שָׁקַט 11 to be quiet, undisturbed, at peace (6·31·41) 1052

תָּמָר 13 palm tree, date palm; עִיר הַתְּמָרִים = Jericho (2·12) 1071

מוֹשִׁיעַ 15 savior (3·27) 446

10

אָטֵר shut up, bound [of right hand = left handed] (2·2) 32

גֹּמֶד 16 short cubit (1·1) 167

חגר to gird on (4·44·44) 291

מַד garment (2·12) 551

יָרֵךְ thigh (4·34) 437

בָּרִיא 17 fat (1·14) 135

פְּסִיל 19 idol, image (2·23) 820

סֵתֶר secrecy (1·35) 712

הַס interj.: hush! keep silence! (1·6) 245

עֲלִיָּה 20 roof chamber (4·20) 751

מְקֵרָה coolness (2·2) 903

יָרֵךְ 21 thigh (4·34) 437

נְצָב 22 hilt (1·1) 662

לַהַב blade (4·12) 529

שָׁלַף to draw out (10·25·25) 1025

פַּרְשְׁדֹנָה feces [dub.] (1·1) 832

מִסְדְּרוֹן 23 porch [dub.] (1·1) 690

עֲלִיָּה roof chamber (4·20) 751

נָעַל to bar, lock (2·7[?]·8[?]) 653

עֲלִיָּה 24 roof chamber (4·20) 751

נָעַל to bar, lock (2·7[?]·8[?]) 653

הֵסֵךְ to cover (1·5·18[?]) 696

חֶדֶר chamber (4·34) 293

מְקֵרָה coolness (2·2) 903

חִיל 25 to be in anxious longing (1·3·5[?]) 296

עֲלִיָּה roof chamber (4·20) 751

מַפְתֵּחַ key (1·3) 836

הִתְמַהְמֵהַּ 26 to linger, wait (2·9·9) 554

פְּסִיל idol, image (2·23) 820

מַעְבָּרָה 28 ford (3·8) 721

שָׁמֵן 29 stout, robust (1·10) 1032

נִכְנַע 30 to be subdued (3·25·36) 488

שָׁקַט to be quiet, undisturbed, at peace (6·31·41) 1052

מַלְמֵד 31 oxgoad (1·1) 541

Chapter 4

לָחַץ 3 to oppress (3·14·15) 537

חָזְקָה strength, force, forcibly (2·6) 306

נְבִיאָה 4 prophetess (1·6) 612

תֹּמֶר 5 palm tree (1·2) 1071

מָשַׁךְ 6 to proceed, march (4·30·36) 604

מָשַׁךְ 7 to draw, lead along (4·30·36) 604

אֶפֶס 9 אֶפֶס כִּי = save that, howbeit (1·41) 67

נִפְרָד 11 to divide, separate (1·12·26) 825

חֹתֵן wife's father (5·21) 368

אֵלוֹן terebinth, tall tree (3·10) 18

הָמַם 15 to confuse, discomfit (1·13·13) 243

מֶרְכָּבָה chariot (2·44) 939

שְׂמִיכָה 18 rug or thick coverlet [dub.] (1·1) 970

צָמֵא 19 to be thirsty (2·10·10) 854

נֹאד skin bottle, skin (2·6) 609

חָלָב milk (2·44) 316

פֹּה 20 here (3·46) 805

יָתֵד 21 tent peg (6·24) 450

מַקֶּבֶת hammer (1·4) 666

לָאט secrecy, בַּלָּאט = secretly (1·7) 532

רַקָּה the temple of the head (3·5) 956

צנח to go down (1·3·3) 856

נִרְדָּם to be or fall fast asleep (1·7·7) 922

עִיף to be faint (1·5·5) 746

יָתֵד 22 tent peg (6·24) 450

רַקָּה the temple of the head (3·5) 956

הִכְנִיעַ 23 to subdue (1·36) 488

קָשָׁה 24 severe (2·36) 904

Chapter 5

פֶּרַע 2 leader [dub.] (2·2) 828

פרע to act as leader, lead [dub.] (1·13·16) 828

הִתְנַדֵּב to volunteer (2·14·17) 621

הֶאֱזִין 3 to listen, give ear (1·41·41) 24

רֹזְנִים rulers (1·6) 931

11

זָמַר to make music, to sing (1·43·43) 274

צָעַד 4 to step, march (1·7·8) 857

רָעַשׁ to quake, shake (1·21·29) 950

נָטַף to drop (2·9·18) 642

עָב dark cloud (1·30) 728

נָזַל 5 to shake, quake (1·3·4) 272

נְתִיבָה 6 path (1·21) 677

עֲקַלְקַל crooked, i.e., roundabout (1·2) 785

פְּרָזוֹן 7 coll. rural population, rustics [dub.] (2·2) 826

לָחֶם 8 war [dub.] (1·1) 535

רֹמַח spear, lance (1·15) 942

חוקק 9 commander (1·1[?]) 349

הִתְנַדֵּב to volunteer (2·14·17) 621

אָתוֹן 10 she ass (1·35) 87

צָחֹר tawny (1·1) 850

מַד cloth, carpet [dub.] (2·12) 551

שִׂיחַ to talk, sing (1·18·20) 967

חַצַץ 11 archer (1·1·3[?]) 346

מַשְׁאָב place for drawing water [dub.] (1·1) 980

תנה to recount (2·2·2) 1072

פְּרָזוֹן coll. rural population, rustics [dub.] (2·2) 826

שָׁבָה 12 to lead captive (1·29·37) 985

שְׁבִי captivity, captives (1·46) 985

שָׂרִיד 13 survivor (1·28) 975

אַדִּיר majestic one (2·27) 12

שֹׁרֶשׁ 14 root (1·33) 1057

מְחֹקֵק commander (1·7) 349

מָשַׁךְ to proceed, march (4·30·36) 604

פלגה 15 division, section [of tribe] (2·3) 811

מִשְׁפְּתַיִם 16 fire places or ash heaps [dub.] (1·2) 1046

שְׁרִיקָה hissing [whistling, piping] (1·2) 1057

עֵדֶר flock (1·39) 727

פלגה division, section [of tribe] (2·3) 811

חֵקֶר searchings, questionings (1·12) 350

אֳנִיָּה 17 ship (1·31) 58

חוֹף shore, coast (1·7) 342

מִפְרָץ landing place (1·1) 830

חָרַף 18 to reproach, despise, scorn (2·34·38) 357

בֶּצַע 19 gain made by violence (1·23) 130

כּוֹכָב 20 star (1·37) 456

מְסִלָּה highway (5·27) 700

גרף 21 to sweep away (1·1·1) 175

קְדוּמִים dubious (1·1) 870

הלם 22 to hammer, strike down (2·8·8) 240

עָקֵב heel (1·14) 784

דהרה rushing, dashing (2·2) 187

אַבִּיר mighty, valiant (1·17) 7

עֶזְרָה 23 help (2·26) 740

חָלָב 25 milk (2·44) 316

סֵפֶל bowl (2·2) 705

אַדִּיר majestic one (2·27) 12

חֶמְאָה curd, curdled milk (1·10) 326

יָתֵד 26 tent peg (6·24) 450

הַלְמוּת hammer, mallet (1·1) 240

עָמֵל laborer, workman (1·9) 766

הלם to smite (2·8·8) 240

מחק to utterly destroy (1·1·1) 563

מָחַץ to smite through (1·14·14) 563

חָלַף to pass through, i.e., pierce (1·2·2[?]) 322

רַקָּה the temple of the head (3·5) 956

כָּרַע 27 to bow down (4·29·35) 502

בַּאֲשֶׁר in [the place] where (3·19) 84

חַלּוֹן 28 window (1·30) 319

נִשְׁקַף to lean over, look through (1·10·22) 1054

יבב to cry shrilly (1·1·1) 384

אֶשְׁנָב window lattice (1·2) 1039

אָחַר to delay, tarry (1·15·17) 29

מֶרְכָּבָה chariot (2·44) 939

שָׂרָה 29 princess (1·5) 979

אֹמֶר utterance, word (1·48) 56

רֶחֶם 30 a woman (2·33) 933

צֶבַע dye, dyed stuff (2·2) 840

רִקְמָה variegated stuff (2·12) 955

צַוָּאר neck, back of neck (3·41) 848

אֹהֵב 31 friend, lover (1·36[?]) 12

שָׁקַט to be quiet, undisturbed, at peace (6·31·41) 1052

Chapter 6

עזז 2 to be strong, prevail (2·9·11) 738

מנהרה dubious (1·1) 626

מְעָרָה cave (1·40) 792

מְצָד mountain fastness (1·11) 844

יְבוּל 4 produce (1·13) 385

מִחְיָה sustenance (2·8) 313

שֶׂה a sheep or goat (1·44) 961

כְּדֵי 5 according to the abundance of (1·5) 191

אַרְבֶּה locust (2·24) 916

נדלל 6 to be brought low (1·8·8) 195

אדה 7 cause; עַל אֹדוֹת = because of (1·11) 15

לחץ 9 oppressor (2·4) 537

גרש to drive out, away (5·34·48) 176

אֵלָה 11 terebinth, tall tree (2·17) 18

חבט to beat out (1·4·5) 286

חִטָּה wheat (2·30) 334

גַּת wine press (1·5) 387

בִּי 13 part. of entreaty: I pray (3·13) 106

אַיֵּה where? (2·44) 32

נִפְלָאוֹת wonderful acts (1·43) 810

נָטַשׁ to forsake (1·33·40) 643

בִּי 15 part. of entreaty: I pray (3·13) 106

בַּמָּה by what means? (8·29) 552

אֶלֶף thousand (1·12[?]) 48

דַּל weak (1·48) 195

צָעִיר little, insignificant (1·22) 859

מוּשׁ 18 to depart (1·20?·20) 559

גְּדִי 19 kid (5·16) 152

אֵיפָה ephah, a grain measure (1·38) 35

קֶמַח flour, meal (1·14) 887

סַל basket (1·15) 700

מָרָק broth (2·3) 600

פָּרוּר pot (1·3) 807

אֵלָה terebinth, tall tree (2·17) 18

הַלָּז 20 this (1·7) 229

מָרָק broth (2·3) 600

מִשְׁעֶנֶת 21 staff (1·12) 1044

אֲהָהּ 22 alas! (2·15) 13

הָרַס 25 to throw down, tear down (1·30·43) 248

אֲשֵׁרָה Ashera; Canaanite goddess of fortune; a symbol of this goddess — sacred tree or pole (5·40) 81

מָעוֹז 26 place of safety, fastness (1·36) 731

מַעֲרָכָה row (1·18) 790

אֲשֵׁרָה a sacred tree or pole (5·40) 81

נָתַץ 28 to be torn down (1·1·42) 683

אֲשֵׁרָה a sacred tree or pole (5·40) 81

נָתַץ 30 to pull down (7·31·42) 683

אֲשֵׁרָה a sacred tree or pole (5·40) 81

נָתַץ 31 to pull down (7·31·42) 683

נָתַץ 32 to pull down (7·31·42) 683

הַצִּיג 37 to set, place (3·15·16)

גִּזָּה fleece (7·7) 159

צֶמֶר wool (1·16) 856

גֹּרֶן threshing floor (1·34) 175

טַל night mist, dew (4·31) 378

חֹרֶב dryness (3·16) 351

מָחֳרָת 38 the morrow, next day; מִמָּחֳרָת = on the morrow (3·32) 564

זור to press [twist or wring] out (1·3·3) 266

גִּזָּה fleece (7·7) 159

מִצָּה to drain (1·4·7) 594

טַל night mist, dew (4·31) 378

סֵפֶל bowl (2·2) 705

נִסָּה 39 to test (4·36·36) 650

גִּזָּה fleece (7·7) 159

חֹרֶב dryness (3·16) 351

טַל night mist, dew (4·31) 378

חֹרֶב 40 dryness (3·16) 351

גִּזָּה fleece (7·7) 159

טַל night mist, dew (4·31) 378

Chapter 7

הִתְפָּאֵר 2 to glorify oneself (1·7·13) 802

יָרֵא 3 afraid (1·45) 431

חָרֵד trembling (1·6) 353

צפר to depart [dub.] (1·1·1) 861

צָרַף 4 to test (1·18·21) 864

לקק 5 to lap (2·5·7) 545

כֶּלֶב dog (1·32) 476

הִצִּיג to set, place (3·15·16) 426

כָּרַע to bow (4·29·35) 502

בֶּרֶךְ knee (3·25) 139

לקק 6 to lap (2·2·7) 545

כָּרַע to bow (4·29·35) 502

בֶּרֶךְ knee (3·25) 139

לקק 7 to lap (2·2·7) 545

צֵידָה 8 provision (2·9) 845

חמש 11 in battle array (1·4·5[?]) 332

אַרְבֶּה 12 locust (2·24) 916

חוֹל sand (1·22) 297

שֶׁעַל which [is] upon (2·2) 979

חָלַם 13 to dream (1·26·28[?]) 321

שְׂעֹרָה barley (1·34) 972

לְמַעְלָה upwards (1·34) 751

בִּלְתִּי 14 except (1·24) 116

שֶׁבֶר 15 breaking [of dream], i.e,
interpretation (1·45) 991

חָצָה 16 to divide (2·11·15) 345

כַּד jar (4·18) 461

רֵק empty [of vessels] (3·14) 938

לַפִּיד torch (5·13) 542

אַשְׁמֹרֶת 19 watch [div. of time] (1·7) 1038

תִּיכוֹן middle (1·12) 1064

נפץ to shatter (1·5·21) 658

כַּד jar (4·18) 461

כַּד 20 jar (4·18) 461

לַפִּיד torch (5·13) 542

הָרִיעַ 21 to shout a war cry, alarm of battle
(2·40·44) 929

עֹרֵב raven (1·12) 788

זְאֵב 25 wolf [dub.] (1·8) 255

יֶקֶב wine press (1·16) 428

Chapter 8

חָזְקָה 1 force, strength, severe rebuke
(2·6) 306

עֹלְלוֹת 2 gleaning (1·6) 760

בָּצִיר vintage (1·7) 131

רָפָה 3 to relax, abate (2·14·44) 951

עָיֵף 4 faint, weary (2·17) 746

עָיֵף 5 faint, weary (2·17) 746

דּוּשׁ 7 to tread, thresh (1·12·15) 190

קוֹץ thornbush (2·11) 881

בַּרְקָנִים briers (2·2) 140

נָתַץ 9 to pull down (7·31·42) 683

מִגְדָּל tower (9·49) 153

שָׁלַף 10 to draw out (10·25·25) 1025

בֶּטַח 11 securely (2·43) 105

הֶחֱרִיד 12 to drive in terror, rout (1·16·39) 353

מַעֲלֵה 13 ascent (2·19) 751

חֵרֵף 15 to reproach, taunt (2·34·38) 357

יָעֵף weary, faint (1·4) 419

קוֹץ 16 thornbush (2·11) 881

בַּרְקָנִים briers (2·2) 140

מִגְדָּל 17 tower (9·49) 153

נָתַץ to pull down (7·31·42) 683

14

אֵיפֹה 18 where? of what kind? (2·25) 33

תֹּאַר outline, form (1·15) 1061

שָׁלַף 20 to draw out (10·25·25) 1025

פָּגַע 21 to fall upon (3·40·46) 803

שַׂהֲרֹן moon, crescent (2·3) 962

צַוָּאר neck, back of neck (3·41) 848

שְׁאֵלָה 24 request, petition (1·13) 982

נֶזֶם earring (4·17) 633

שִׂמְלָה 25 wrapper, mantle, covering (1·29) 971

נֶזֶם earring (4·17) 633

מִשְׁקָל 26 weight (1·48) 1054

נֶזֶם earring (4·17) 633

שַׂהֲרֹן moon, crescent (2·3) 962

נטיפה pendant (1·2) 643

אַרְגָּמָן purple cloth (1·39) 71

שֶׁעַל which [were] on (2·2) 979

עֲנָק neck pendant [dub.] (1·31) 848

צַוָּאר neck, back of neck (3·41) 848

אֵפוֹד 27 ephod (6·49) 65

הַצִּיג to set (3·15·16) 426

מוֹקֵשׁ lure (2·27) 430

נִכְנַע 28 to be subdued (3·25·36) 488

שָׁקַט to be quiet, undisturbed, at peace (6·31·41) 1052

יָרֵךְ 30 thigh = loins (4·34) 437

פִּילֶגֶשׁ 31 concubine (12·37) 811

שֵׂיבָה 32 old age (1·20[?]) 966

Chapter 9

שָׂכַר 4 to hire (2·17·20) 968

רֵק empty, idle, worthless (3·14) 938

פחז to be wanton, reckless (1·2·2) 808

נֶחְבָּא 5 to hide oneself (1·16·34) 285

אֵלוֹן 6 terebinth, tall tree (3·10) 18

מֻצָּב set up (1·2[?]) 662

זַיִת 8 olive, olive tree (3·38) 268

זַיִת 9 olive, olive tree (3·38) 268

דֶּשֶׁן fatness (1·15) 206

נוּעַ to wave (3·22·38) 631

תְּאֵנָה 10 fig tree (2·39) 1061

תְּאֵנָה 11 fig tree (2·39) 1061

מתק sweetness (1·1) 608

תְּנוּבָה fruit, produce (1·5) 626

נוּעַ to wave (3·22·38) 631

תִּירוֹשׁ 13 must, new wine (1·39) 440

נוּעַ to wave (3·22·38) 631

אָטָד 14 bramble, buckthorn (3·4) 31

אָטָד 15 bramble, buckthorn (3·4) 31

חָסָה to seek refuge (1·37·37) 340

גְּמוּל 16 dealing (1·19) 168

מִנֶּגֶד 17 in front, straight away [i.e., hazarded it] (2·26) 617

שׂרר 22 to rule over (1·5·7) 979

בגד 23 to act or deal treacherously, faithlessly (1·42·42) 93

ארב 25 lier in wait (1·2·23) 70

גָּזַל to tear away, sieze; rob, plunder (2·29·30) 159

בצר 27 to cut off [grapes] (1·7·7[?]) 130

הלולים praise, rejoicing (1·2) 239

פָּקִיד 28 commissioner, deputy (1·13) 824

תָּרְמָה 31 treacherously [dub.] (1·1) 941

צור to incite [dub.] (1·5·5) 848

אָרַב 32 to lie in wait (5·20·23) 70

זָרַח 33 to rise (1·18·18) 280

פָּשַׁט to put off [one's shelter], i.e., make a dash [from a sheltered place] (4·24·43) 833

אָרַב 34 to lie in wait (5·20·23) 70

מַאֲרָב 35 ambush (1·5) 70

טַבּוּר 37 highest part (1·2) 371

אֵלוֹן terebinth, tall tree (3·10) 18

עוֹנֵן to practice soothsaying (1·10·11) 778

אַיֵּה 38 where? (2·44) 32

15

אֵפוֹא   then (1·15) 66

גרש   41 to drive out, away (5·34·48) 176

מָחֳרָת   42 the morrow, next day; מִמָּחֳרָת = on the morrow (3·32) 564

חָצָה   43 to divide (2·11·15) 345

אָרַב   to lie in wait (5·20·23) 70

פָּשַׁט   44 to put off [one's shelter], i.e., make a dash [from a sheltered place] (4·24·43) 833

נָתַץ   45 to pull down (7·31·42) 683

מֶלַח   salt (1·28) 571

מִגְדָּל   46 tower (9·49) 153

צְרִיחַ   excavation, underground chamber [dub.] (3·4) 863

מִגְדָּל   47 tower (9·49) 153

קַרְדֹּם   48 axe (1·5) 899

שׂוֹכָה   branch, brushwood (1·1) 962

שְׁכֶם   shoulder (1·22) 1014

שׂוֹךְ   49 branch, brushwood (1·1) 962

צְרִיחַ   excavation, underground chamber [dub.] (3·4) 863

הִצִּית   to kindle, set on fire (1·17·27) 428

מִגְדָּל   tower (9·49) 153

מִגְדָּל   51 tower (9·49) 153

גָּג   top, roof (2·29) 150

מִגְדָּל   52 tower (9·49) 153

פֶּלַח   53 millstone (1·6) 812

הרץ   to crush (1·1·19) 954

גֻּלְגֹּלֶת   skull (1·12) 166

שָׁלַף   54 to draw out (10·25·25) 1025

דקר   to pierce (1·7·11) 201

קְלָלָה   57 curse (1·33) 887

Chapter 10

עַיִר   4 male ass (3·9) 747

חוה   tent village (1·7) 295

רעץ   8 to shatter (1·2·2) 950

רוצץ   to grievously oppress (1·1·19) 954

לָחַץ   12 to oppress (3·14·15) 537

נֵכָר   16 that which is foreign (1·36) 648

קָצַר   to be short, impatient (2·11·13) 894

Chapter 11

זוֹנָה   1 harlot (2·33) 275

גרש   2 to drive out, away (5·34·48) 176

הִתְלַקֵּט   3 to collect themselves (1·1·36) 544

רֵק   empty, idle, worthless (3·14) 938

קָצִין   6 chief, commander (2·12) 892

גרש   7 to drive out, away (5·34·48) 176

קָצִין   11 chief, commander (2·12) 892

נָדַר   30 to vow (2·30·30) 623

מַכָּה   33 defeat (2·48) 646

נִכְנַע   to be subdued (3·25·36) 488

תֹּף   34 timbrel, tambourine (1·17) 1074

מחולה   dancing (2·8) 298

יָחִיד   only one (1·12) 402

אֲהָהּ   35 alas! (2·15) 13

הִכְרִיעַ   to cause to bow (2·6·35) 502

עָכַר   to disturb, trouble (1·12·14) 747

פצה   to open (2·15·15) 822

פצה   36 to open (2·15·15) 822

נְקָמָה   vengeance (1·27) 668

הרפה   37 to refrain; ר׳ מִן = to let one alone (1·21·45) 952

בְּתוּלִים   virginity, tokens of virginity (2·10) 144

רעה   companion, attendant (2·3) 946

רעה   38 companion, attendant (2·3) 946

בְּתוּלִים   virginity, tokens of virginity (2·10) 144

נָדַר   39 to vow (2·30·30) 623

תנה   40 to recount, celebrate (2·2·2) 1072

Chapter 12

מוֹשִׁיעַ   3 savior (3·27) 446

פָּלִיט   4 fugitive (2·19) 812

מַעְבָּרָה	5 ford (3·8) 721	
פָּלִיט	fugitive (2·19) 812	
מַעְבָּרָה	6 ford (3·8) 721	
עַיִר	14 male ass (3·9) 747	

Chapter 13

עָקָר	2 barren (2·11) 785
הָרָה	3 to conceive, become pregnant (1·38·40) 247
עָקָר	barren (2·11) 785
שֵׁכָר	4 intoxicating, strong drink (3·23) 1016
הָרָה	5 pregnant (2·16[?]) 248
מוֹרָה	razor (2·3) 559
נוֹרָא	6 fearful, awful (1·44) 431
אֵי	where? = אֵי מִזֶּה (1·39) 32
הָרָה	7 pregnant (2·16[?]) 248
שֵׁכָר	intoxicating, strong drink (3·23) 1016
טֻמְאָה	uncleanness (2·37) 380
עתר	8 to pray, supplicate (1·5·20) 801
בִּי	part. of entreaty, I pray (3·13) 106
הורה	to instruct (1·45[?]·45[?]) 434
שֵׁכָר	14 intoxicating, strong drink (3·23) 1016
טֻמְאָה	uncleanness (2·37) 380
עָצַר	15 to restrain, detain (2·36·46) 783
גְּדִי	kid (5·16) 152
עָצַר	16 to restrain, detain (2·36·46) 783
פֶּלאִי	18 wonderful, incomprehensible (1·2) 811
גְּדִי	19 kid (5·16) 152
הִפְלִיא	to work wonders (1·10·21) 810
לַהַב	20 flame (4·12) 529
לוּ	23 if (2·19) 530
פעם	25 to thrust, impel (1·1·5) 821

Chapter 14

עָרֵל	3 having foreskin, i.e., uncircumcised

	(2·35) 790	
יָשַׁר	to be pleasing (2·13·25) 448	
תֹּאֲנָה	4 opportunity (1·1) 58	
כְּפִיר	5 young lion (1·31) 498	
אֲרִי	lion (2·34) 71	
שָׁאַג	to roar (1·20·20) 980	
שסע	6 to tear in two (1·3·8) 1042	
גְּדִי	kid (5·16) 152	
מְאוּמָה	anything (1·32) 548	
יָשַׁר	7 to be pleasing (1·13·25) 448	
מַפֶּלֶת	8 carcass (1·8) 658	
אַרְיֵה	lion (3·45) 71	
דְּבוֹרָה	bee (1·4) 185	
גְּוִיָּה	carcass, corpse (2·12) 156	
רָדָה	9 to scrape out (2·3·3) 922	
גְּוִיָּה	carcass, corpse (2·12) 156	
אַרְיֵה	lion (3·45) 71	
מִשְׁתֶּה	10 feast (3·45) 1059	
בָּחוּר	young man (1·45) 104	
מרע	11 companion, confidential friend (4·7) 946	
חוד	12 to propound a riddle (3·4·4) 295	
חִידָה	riddle (8·17) 295	
מִשְׁתֶּה	feast (3·45) 1059	
סָדִין	linen wrapper (2·4) 690	
חֲלִיפָה	a change [of raiment] (3·12) 322	
סָדִין	13 linen wrapper (2·4) 690	
חֲלִיפָה	a change [of raiment] (3·12) 322	
חוד	to propound a riddle (3·4·4) 295	
חִידָה	riddle (8·17) 295	
מַאֲכָל	14 food (1·30) 38	
עַז	formidable, fierce (2·22) 738	
מָתוֹק	sweet, a sweet thing (2·12) 608	
חִידָה	riddle (8·17) 295	
פתה	15 to entice (2·17·27) 834	
חִידָה	riddle (8·17) 295	
חִידָה	16 riddle (8·17) 295	
חוד	to propound a riddle (3·4·4) 285	

מִשְׁתֶּה 17 feast (3·45) 1059

הֵצִיק to distress by importunity (2·11·16) 847

חִידָה riddle (8·17) 295

בְּטֶרֶם 18 before (1·39) 382

חֶרֶס sun (1·2) 357

מָתוֹק sweet (2·12) 608

עַז formidable, fierce (2·22) 738

אֲרִי lion (2·35) 71

לוּלֵא unless (1·4) 530

חרשׁ to plough (1·21·24) 360

עֶגְלָה heifer (1·12) 722

חִידה riddle (8·17) 295

חֲלִיצָה 19 what is stripped off a person, as plunder in war (1·2) 322

חֲלִיפה a change [of raiment] (3·12) 322

חִידָה riddle (8·17) 295

מרע 20 companion, confidential friend (4·7) 946

רֵעָה to be a special friend (1·1·6) 946

Chapter 15

קָצִיר 1 time of harvest (1·49) 894

חִטָּה wheat (2·30) 334

גְּדִי kid (5·16) 152

חֶדֶר room, chamber (4·34) 293

מרע 2 companion, confidential friend (4·7) 946

קָטָן small, younger (1·47) 881

נקה 3 to be free from guilt (1·23·37) 667

שׁוּעָל 4 fox, perh. jackal (1·7) 1043

לַפִּיד torch (5·13) 542

זָנָב tail (3·11) 275

לַפִּיד 5 torch (5·13) 542

קָמָה standing grain (2·10) 879

גָּדִישׁ heap, stack (1·4) 155

זַיִת olive, olive tree, olive yards (3·38) 268

חָתָן 6 daughter's husband (2·20) 368

מרע companion, confidential friend (4·7) 946

נקם 7 to avenge oneself (2·12·34) 667

שׁוֹק 8 leg (1·19) 1003

יָרֵךְ thigh (4·34) 437

מַכָּה defeat (2·48) 646

סְעִיף cleft (2·4[?]) 703

נטשׁ 9 to be spread abroad (1·6·40) 643

סְעִיף 11 cleft (2·4[?]) 703

פָּגַע 12 to fall upon (3·40·46) 803

עֲבֹת 13 cord, rope (4·24) 721

הֵרִיעַ 14 to shout a war cry, alarm of battle (2·40·44) 929

עֲבֹת cord, rope (4·24) 721

פֵּשֶׁת flax (1·16) 833

נָמֵס to melt, drop off (1·19·21) 587

אָסוּר band, bond (1·3) 64

לְחִי 15 jawbone (5·21) 534

טרי fresh (1·2) 382

לְחִי 16 jawbone (5·21) 534

חֲמוֹר heap (2·3) 331

לְחִי 17 jawbone (5·21) 534

צמא 18 to be thirsty (2·10·10) 854

תְּשׁוּעָה deliverance, victory (1·34) 448

צָמָא thirst (1·17) 854

עָרֵל having foreskin, i.e., uncircumcised (2·35) 790

מַכְתֵּשׁ 19 hollow, resembling a mortar (1·2) 509

Chapter 16

זוֹנָה 1 harlot (2·33) 275

הֵנָּה 2 hither (2·49) 244

אָרַב to lie in wait (5·20·23) 70

התחרשׁ to keep quiet (1·1·44) 361, 1123

מְזוּזָה 3 gatepost (1·20) 265

בְּרִיחַ bar(s) (1·41) 138

סרן	5 lord (8·21) 710
פתה	to entice (2·17·27) 834
בַּמָּה	wherein? by what means? (8·29) 552
בַּמָּה	6 wherein? by what means? (8·29) 552
יֶתֶר	7 cord (3·6) 452
לַח	new (2·6) 535
חרב	to be dry, dried up (2·2·37[?]) 351
סרן	8 lord (8·21) 710
יֶתֶר	cord (3·6) 452
לַח	new (2·6) 535
חרב	to be dry, dried up (2·2·37[?]) 351
אֹרֵב	liers in wait (8·18[?]) 70
חֶדֶר	room, chamber (4·34) 293
נתק	to tear apart, snap (2·11·27) 683
יֶתֶר	9 cord (3·6) 452
נתק	to be torn apart, snapped (1·10·27) 683
פָּתִיל	cord (1·11) 836
נְעֹרֶת	tow (1·2) 654
הריח	to smell (1·11·14) 926
הֵתֵל	10 to mock, trifle with (3·7·8) 1068
כָּזָב	lie (2·31) 469
בַּמָּה	by what means? (8·29) 552
עֲבֹת	11 rope, cord (4·24) 721
עֲבֹת	12 rope, cord (4·24) 721
אֹרֵב	liers in wait (8·18[?]) 70
חֶדֶר	room, chamber (4·34) 293
נתק	to tear apart, snap (2·11·27) 683
חוּט	thread (1·7) 296
הֵנָּה	13 hitherto (2·49) 244
הֵתֵל	to mock, trifle with (3·7·8) 1068
כָּזָב	lie (2·31) 469
בַּמָּה	by what means? (8·29) 552
ארג	to weave (1·3·3) 70
מחלפה	plait (2·2) 322
מסכת	web (2·2) 651
יָתֵד	14 pin (stick) (6·24) 450
יקץ	to awake (2·11·11) 429
שֵׁנָה	sleep (2·33) 446
אֶרֶג	loom (1·2) 71
מסכת	web (2·2) 651
הֵתֵל	15 to mock, trifle with (3·7·8) 1069
בַּמָּה	wherein? (8·29) 552
הֵצִיק	16 to bring into straits by importunity (2·11·11) 847
אלץ	to urge. (1·1·1) 49
קָצַר	to be short, impatient (2·11·13) 894
מוֹרָה	17 razor (2·3) 559
גֻּלַּח	to be shaven (2·3·23) 164
סרן	18 lord (8·21) 710
ישׁן	19 to make to sleep (1·1·16[?]) 445
בֶּרֶךְ	knee (3·25) 139
גִּלַּח	to shave off (1·18·23) 164
מחלפה	plait (2·2) 322
יקץ	20 to awake (2·11·11) 429
שֵׁנָה	sleep (2·23) 446
ננער	to shake oneself (1·3·10) 654
נָקַר	21 to bore out (1·3·6) 669
טחן	to grind (1·7·7) 377
אָסִיר	prisoner (2·17[?]) 64
שֵׂעָר	22 hair (1·28) 972
צָמַח	to grow abundantly (1·4·33) 855
גֻּלַּח	to be shaven (2·3·23) 164
סרן	23 lord (8·21) 710
צָמַח	to grow abundantly (1·4·33) 855
גֻּלַּח	to be shaven (2·3·23) 164
סרן	lord (8·21) 710
הֶחֱרִיב	24 to make desolate (1·13·37[?]) 351
שׂחק	25 to make sport (1·16·36) 965
אָסִיר	prisoner (2·17[?]) 64
צחק	to make sport (1·7·13) 850
הֵמִישׁ	26 to feel (1·3·4[?]) 559
נִשְׁעָן	to lean (1·22·22) 1043
סרן	27 lord (8·21) 710
גָּג	top, roof (2·29) 150
שָׂחַק	to sport, play (1·18·36) 965

19

נקם 28 to avenge oneself (2·12·34) 667

נָקָם   vengeance (1·17) 668

לפת 29 to grasp (1·1·3) 542

נסמך   to brace oneself (1·6·48) 701

סרן 30 lord (8·21) 710

מֵאֲשֶׁר   from those, than those (1·17) 84

Chapter 17

אַתִּי 2 thou [fem.] (1·7) 61

אָלָה   to curse (1·3·6) 46

פֶּסֶל 3 idol (8·31) 820

מַסֵּכָה   molten image (5·25) 651

צוֹרֵף 4 smelter, refiner, goldsmith (1·10) 864

פֶּסֶל   idol (8·31) 820

מַסֵּכָה   molten image (5·25) 651

אֵפוֹד 5 ephod (6·49) 65

תְּרָפִים   idol (5·15) 1076

בַּאֲשֶׁר 8 in [the place] where (3·20) 84

מֵאַיִן 9 whence? (2·48) 32

בַּאֲשֶׁר   in [the place] where (3·19) 84

עֵרֶךְ 10 order, row, a [complete] suit of clothes (1·33) 789

מִחְיָה   sustenance (2·8) 313

הוֹאִיל 11 to show willingness (4·18·18) 383

Chapter 18

קָצֶה 2 end, whole (1·7) 892

רגל   to go about as explorer, spy (3·14·16) 920

חקר   to search through, explore (2·22·27) 350

הִכִּיר 3 to recognize (1·37·40) 647

הֲלֹם   hither (2·11) 240

פֹּה   here? (3·46) 805

זֶה 4 this; כָּזֶה וְכָזֶה = thus and thus (1·11) 262

שָׂכַר   to hire (2·17·20) 968

נֹכַח 6 before (3·27) 647

בֶּטַח 7 securely (2·43) 105

שָׁקַט   to be quiet, undisturbed, at peace and safety (6·31·41) 1052

עֶצֶר   restraint [dub.] (1·1) 783

הַכְלִים   to restrain [dub.] (1·10·38) 483

הֶחֱשָׁה 9 to show inactivity (1·9·16) 364

נעצל   to be sluggish (1·1·1) 782

מַחְסוֹר 10 lack (3·13) 341

חגר 11 to gird on (4·44·44) 291

רגל 14 to go about as explorer, spy (3·14·16) 920

אֵפוֹד   ephod (6·49) 65

תְּרָפִים   idol (5·15) 1076

פֶּסֶל   idol (8·31) 820

מַסֵּכָה   molten image (5·25) 651

חגר 16 to gird on (4·44·44) 291

רגל 17 to go about as an explorer, spy (3·14·16) 920

פֶּסֶל   idol (8·31) 820

אֵפוֹד   ephod (6·49) 65

תְּרָפִים   idol (5·15) 1076

מַסֵּכָה   molten image (5·25) 651

חגר   to gird on (4·44·44) 291

פֶּסֶל 18 idol (8·31) 820

אֵפוֹד   ephod (6·49) 65

תְּרָפִים   idol (5·15) 1076

מַסֵּכָה   molten image (5·25) 651

הֶחֱרִישׁ 19 to be silent (1·38·46) 361

אֵפוֹד 20 ephod (6·49) 65

תְּרָפִים   idol (5·15) 1076

פֶּסֶל   idol (8·31) 820

טַף 21 children (2·41) 381

כְּבוּדָּה   abundance, riches (1·3[?]) 459

פָּגַע 25 to fall upon (3·40·46) 803

מַר   bitter; מָרֵי נֶפֶשׁ = fierce of temper (1·37) 600

שָׁקַט 27 to be quiet, undisturbed, at peace

and safety (6·31·41) 1052

אוּלָם 29 but, but indeed (1·19) 19

פֶּסֶל 30 idol (8·31) 820

פֶּסֶל 31 idol (8·31) 820

Chapter 19

יַרְכָה 1 extreme parts (2·28) 438

פִּילֶגֶשׁ concubine (12·37) 811

פִּילֶגֶשׁ 2 concubine (12·37) 811

צֶמֶד 3 pair (2·15) 855

חֹתֵן 4 wife's father (5·21) 368

חָתָן 5 daughter's husband (2·20) 368

סָעַד to sustain (2·12·12) 703

פַּת fragment, bit, morsel (1·14) 837

הוֹאִיל 6 to show willingness, accept an invitation (4·18·18) 383

פָּצַר 7 to urge (1·6·7) 823

חֹתֵן wife's father (5·21) 368

סָעַד to sustain (2·12·12) 703

הִתְמַהְמַהּ to tarry (2·9·9) 554

פִּילֶגֶשׁ 9 concubine (12·37) 811

חֹתֵן wife's father (5·21) 368

רָפָה to sink, decline (2·14·44) 951

ערב to become evening (1·2·3) 788

פֹּה here (3·46) 805

נֹכַח 10 in front of; עַד־נ׳ = as far as in front of| (3·27) 647

צֶמֶד pair (2·15) 855

חבש to bind up, equip (1·27·31) 289

פִּילֶגֶשׁ concubine (12·37) 811

נָכְרִי 12 foreigner (1·45) 648

רְחוֹב 15 broad open place, plaza (3·43) 932

אֹרַח 17 journeying, wayfaring (1·4[?]) 72

רְחוֹב broad open place, plaza (3·43) 932

אָנָה whither? (1·39) 33

מֵאַיִן whence? (2·48) 32

יַרְכָה 18 extreme parts (2·28) 438

תֶּבֶן 19 straw (6·17) 1061

מִסְפּוֹא fodder (1·5) 704

מַחְסוֹר lack (3·13) 341

מַחְסוֹר 20 need, thing needed (3·13) 341

רְחוֹב broad open place, plaza (3·43) 932

בלל 21 to give provender (1·1·1) 117

הִתְדַּפֵּק 22 to beat violently (1·1·3) 200

נְבָלָה 23 disgraceful folly (4·13) 615

פִּילֶגֶשׁ 24 concubine (12·37) 811

נְבָלָה disgraceful folly (4·13) 615

פִּילֶגֶשׁ 25 concubine (12·37) 811

הִתְעַלֵּל to deal wantonly, abuse (1·7·17) 759

שַׁחַר dawn (1·23) 1007

פִּילֶגֶשׁ 27 concubine (12·37) 811

סַף threshold (1·25) 706

מַאֲכֶלֶת 29 knife (1·4) 38

פִּילֶגֶשׁ concubine (12·37) 811

נָתַח to cut up (2·9·9) 677

נֵתַח piece of a divided corpse (1·2) 677

עוץ 30 to counsel, plan (1·2·2) 734

Chapter 20

נקהל 1 to assemble (1·19·39) 874

פִּנָּה 2 corner (1·30) 819

רַגְלִי on foot; אִישׁ ר׳ = footmen (1·12) 920

שָׁלַף to draw out (10·25·25) 1025

אֵיכָה 3 in what manner? (1·18) 32

נרצח 4 to be murdered (1·2·43) 953

פִּילֶגֶשׁ concubine (12·37) 811

דָּמָה 5 to think, intend (1·13·27) 197

פִּילֶגֶשׁ concubine (12·37) 811

פִּילֶגֶשׁ concubine (12·37) 811

נָתַח to cut up (2·9·9) 677

זִמָּה wickedness (1·28) 273

נְבָלָה disgraceful folly (4·13) 615

יהב 7 to give, provide (2·27·27) 396

הֲלֹם hither (2·11) 240

רְבָבָה 10 ten thousand (1·6) 914

צֵידָה provision (2·9) 845

21

נְבָלָה disgraceful folly (4·13) 615

חָבֵר 11 united (1·12) 288

שָׁלַף 15 to draw out (10·25·25) 1025

בָּחוּר chosen (3·19) 103

בָּחוּר 16 chosen (3·19) 103

אִטֵּר shut up, bound [of right hand = left handed] (2·2) 32

קָלַע to sling (1·2·4) 887

שַׂעֲרָה a hair (1·3) 972

שָׁלַף 17 to draw out (10·25·25) 1025

תְּחִלָּה 18 beginning; בַּתְּ׳ = first, at first (3·22) 321

שָׁלַף 25 to draw out (10·25·25) 1025

צוּם 26 to fast (1·20·20) 847

אֹרֵב 29 liers in wait (8·18[?]) 70

הנתק 31 to be drawn away from (1·1·27) 683

מְסִלָּה highway (5·27) 700

נָגַף 32 to be smitten (4·23·48) 619

נתק to draw away (1·3·27) 683

מְסִלָּה highway (5·27) 700

אֹרֵב 33 liers in wait (8·18[?]) 70

הגיח to burst forth (1·2·5) 161, 1121

מערה bare space (1·1[?]) 789

מִנֶּגֶד 34 in front of (2·26) 617

בָּחוּר chosen (3·19) 103

נָגַף 35 to smite (1·24·48) 619

שָׁלַף to draw out (10·25·25) 1025

נָגַף 36 to be smitten (4·23·48) 619

אֹרֵב liers in wait (8·18[?]) 70

אֹרֵב 37 liers in wait (8·18[?]) 70

החיש to act quickly (1·6·21) 301

פשט to put off [one's shelter] i.e., make a dash [from a sheltered place] (4·24·43) 833

מָשַׁךְ to proceed (4·30·36) 604

אֹרֵב 38 liers in wait (8·18[?]) 70

מַשְׂאֵת uprising (2·16) 673

עָשָׁן smoke (2·25) 798

נָגַף 39 to be smitten (4·23·48) 619

מַשְׂאֵת 40 uprising (2·16) 673

עָשָׁן smoke (2·25) 798

כָּלִיל whole (1·15) 483

נִבְהַל 41 to be disturbed, dismayed, terrified (1·24·39) 96

כתר 43 to surround (1·3·6) 509

מְנוּחָה rest, quietness [dub.] (1·21) 629

נֹכַח in front of, עַד־נ׳ = as far as in front of (3·27) 647

עוֹלֵל 45 to glean (1·8·17) 760

מְסִלָּה highway (5·27) 700

שָׁלַף 46 to draw out (10·25·25) 1025

מְתֹם 48 soundness, entire (1·4) 1071

Chapter 21

בְּכִי 2 weeping (1·30) 113

מָחֳרָת 4 the morrow, next day מִמָּחֳרָת = on the morrow (3·32) 564

שְׁבוּעָה 5 oath (1·30) 989

לַאֲשֶׁר concerning him who (1·37) 81

נִגְדַּע 6 to be hewn off (1·17·22) 154

טַף 10 children (2·41) 381

מִשְׁכַּב 11 act of lying down (2·46) 1012

הֶחֱרִים to devote to destruction (2·46·49) 355

מִשְׁכַּב 12 act of lying down (2·46) 1012

פֶּרֶץ 15 outburst (1·18) 829

יְרֻשָּׁה 17 possession, inheritance (1·14) 440

פְּלֵיטָה escaped remnant (1·28) 812

נמחה to be blotted out (1·9·33) 562

מְסִלָּה 19 highway (5·27) 700

אָרַב 20 to lie in wait (5·20·23) 70

חוּל 21 to dance (1·6·9) 296

מחולה dancing (2·8) 298

חטף to catch, seize (1·3·3) 310

אָשַׁם 22 to be or become guilty (1·31·33) 79

חוֹלֵל 23 to dance (1·2·9) 296

גָּזַל to tear away, rob (2·29·30) 159

Ruth appears in volume 4, corresponding to its placement in the Hebrew Old Testament.

1 SAMUEL

Chapter 1

מָנָה 4 portion (3·12) 584

מָנָה 5 portion (3·12) 584

רֶחֶם womb (2·33) 933

צָרָה 6 vexer, rival wife (1·1) 865

כַּעַס vexation (2·25?) 495

בַּעֲבוּר in order to (3·45) 721

הַרְעִים to make to fret [dub.] (1·2·2) 947

רֶחֶם womb (2·33) 933

מִדֵּי 7 out of the abundance of, i.e., as often as (3·15) 191

מְזוּזָה 9 doorpost (1·20) 265

מַר 10 bitter; מָרַת נ׳ = the bitterly wretched (3·37) 600

נָדַר 11 to vow (1·30·30) 623

מוֹרָה razor (1·3) 559

נוּעַ 13 to quiver (1·20·36) 631

שִׁכֹּר drunken, drunkard (2·13) 1016

מָתַי 14 when? עַד־מָתַי = how long? (2·40) 607

הִשְׁתַּכֵּר to make oneself drunken (1·1·20) 1016

קָשֶׁה 15 severe (3·36) 904

שֵׁכָר intoxicating drink, strong drink (1·23) 1016

בְּלִיַּעַל 16 worthlessness, good for nothing (6·27) 116

שִׂיחַ anxiety, trouble (1·14) 967

כַּעַס vexation (2·25[?]) 495

הֵנָּה hither (3·49) 244

שלה 17 request (1·1) 982

תקופה 20 circuit (1·4) 880

הָרָה to conceive, become pregnant (2·38·40) 247

נגמל 22 to be weaned (1·3·37) 168

גָּמַל 23 to wean (5·34·37) 168

הֵינִיק to nurse (1·10·18) 413

גָּמַל 24 to wean (5·34·37) 168

אֵיפָה ephah, quantity of wheat, barley, etc. (2·38) 35

קֶמַח flour, meal (2·14) 887

נֵבֶל skin of wine (4·12) 614

בִּי 26 part. of entreaty: I pray (1·13) 10

שְׁאֵלָה 27 thing asked for (2·13) 982

Chapter 2

עלץ 1 to rejoice, exult (1·8·8) 763

רָחַב to be or grow wide (1·3·25) 931

בִּלְתִּי 2 not, except (2·24) 116

גָּבֹהַּ 3 high, haughty (4·41) 147

עָתָק forward, arrogant (1·4) 801

נתכן to be estimated (1·10·18) 1067

עֲלִילָה deed (1·24) 760

חת 4 shattered (1·4) 369

אזר to gird on (1·6·16) 25

שָׂבֵעַ 5 sated (1·10) 960

נשכר to hire oneself out (1·1·20) 968

רָעֵב hungry (1·19) 944

עָקָר barren (1·11) 785

אֻמְלַל to be or grow feeble, languish (1·15·15[?]) 51

העשיר 7 to make rich (2·14·17) 799

הִשְׁפִּיל to lay low, humiliate (1·18·29) 1050

דַּל 8 poor (1·48) 195

אַשְׁפֹּת ash heap [dub.] refuse heap (1·7) 1046

נָדִיב noble (1·27) 622

מצוק support (2·2) 848

תֵּבֵל world (1·36) 385

חָסִיד 9 pious, godly (1·32) 339

נדמם to be made silent (1·5·30) 199

גָּבַר to prevail (1·17·25) 149

הִרְעִים 10 to thunder (2·8·11) 947

דִּין	to execute judgment (1·23·24[?]) 192
אֶפֶס	end, extreme limit (1·27) 67
מָשִׁיחַ	anointed (13·40) 603
בְּלִיַּעַל 12	worthlessness, good for nothing (6·27) 116
בשל 13	to boil (1·20·27) 143
מַזְלֵג	three-pronged fork [dub.] (2·2) 272
כִּיּוֹר 14	pot (1·23) 468
דּוּד	pot, kettle (1·7) 188
קַלַּחַת	caldron (1·2) 886
פָּרוּר	(1·3) 807
מַזְלֵג	three-pronged fork [dub.] (2·2) 272
כָּכָה	thus (2·34) 462
צלה 15	to roast (1·3·3) 852
בְּטֶרֶם	before (2·39) 382
בשל	to be boiled (1·4·27) 143
אָוָה 16	to desire (1·11·27) 16
חָזְקָה	strength, force (1·6) 308
נָאַץ 17	to spurn (1·14·23) 610
חגר 18	to gird (5·44·44) 291
אֵפוֹד	ephod, priestly garment (9·49) 65
בַּד	white linen (2·23) 94
מְעִיל 19	robe (7·28) 591
שְׁאֵלָה 20	thing asked for (2·13) 982
הָרָה 2!	to conceive, become pregnant (2·38·40) 247
זָקֵן 22	to be old, become old (6·25·27) 278
צבא	to serve (1·12·14) 838
שְׁמוּעָה 24	report (2·27) 1035
גָּדֵל 26	becoming great (1·4) 152
אֵפוֹד 28	ephod, priestly garment (9·49) 65
בעט 29	to kick at (1·2·2) 127
מָעוֹן	dwelling (2·18) 732
הבריא	to make oneself fat (1·1·1) 135
חָלִילָה 30	far be it [from] (8·21) 321
בּוֹזֶה	despiser (1·1[?]) 102
גָּדַע 31	to hew off (1·5[?]·22) 154

צָר 32	distress [dub.] (1·29) 865
מָעוֹן	dwelling (2·18) 732
האדיב 33	to cause to grieve (1·1·1) 9
מַרְבִּית	increase (1·5) 916
מָשִׁיחַ 35	anointed (13·40) 603
אֲגוֹרָה 36	payment (1·1) 8
ספח	to attach to (1·1·5) 705
כְּהֻנָּה	priesthood (1·13) 464
פַּת	bit, morsel (2·4) 837

Chapter 3

יָקָר 1	rare (1·35) 429
חָזוֹן	vision (1·35) 302
נפרץ	to spread abroad (1·1·49) 829
כהה 2	dim (1·7) 462
נֵר 3	lamp (1·44) 632
טֶרֶם	not yet (3·16) 382
כבה	to be extinguished (1·14·24) 459
טֶרֶם 7	not yet (3·16) 382
הִתְיַצֵּב 10	to station oneself (6·48·48) 426
צלל 11	to tingle (1·4·4) 852
כהה 13	to rebuke (1·3·8[?]) 462
כָּחֵד 17	to hide (3·15·30) 470
כָּחֵד 18	to hide (3·15·30) 470

Chapter 4

נָטַשׁ 2	to permit [dub.] (7·33·40) 643
נָגַף	to be smitten (3·23·48) 619
מַעֲרָכָה	battle line (15·18) 790
נָגַף 3	to smite (2·24·48) 619
הֵרִיעַ 5	to shout (4·40·44) 929
תְּרוּעָה	shout of joy (3·36) 929
הום	to reecho (1·3·6) 223
תְּרוּעָה 6	shout of joy (3·36) 929
אוֹי 7	woe! alas! (2·22) 17
אֶתְמוֹל	yesterday; אֶ׳ שִׁלְשׁוֹם = formerly (4·8) 1069

שְׁלְשׁוֹם   three days ago (5·25) 1026

אוֹי   8 woe! alas! (2·22) 17

אַדִּיר   majestic (1·27) 12

מַכָּה   plague (7·48) 646

נָגַף   10 to be smitten (3·23·48) 619

מַכָּה   slaughter (7·48) 646

רַגְלִי   footmen, foot soldier (2·12) 920

מַעֲרָכָה   12 battle line (15·18) 790

מַד   garment (4·12) 551

חָרֵד   13 trembling (1·6) 353

צפה   to watch (1·9·18) 859

צְעָקָה   14 cry of distress (2·21) 858

מַעֲרָכָה   16 battle line (15·18) 790

מְבַשֵּׂר   17 bearer of tidings (1·9) 142

מַגֵּפָה   slaughter (2·26) 620

אֲחֹרַנִּית   18 backwards (1·7) 30

מפרקת   neck (1·1) 830

זָקֵן   to be old, become old (6·25·27) 278

כַּלָּה   19 daughter-in-law (1·34) 483

הָרָה   pregnant (1·15?) 248

שְׁמוּעָה   report, news (2·27) 1035

חם   husband's father (2·4) 327

כָּרַע   to bow down (1·29·34) 502

ציר   pang (1·5) 852

חם   21 husband's father (2·4) 327

Chapter 5

הַצִּיג   2 to set, place (1·15·16) 426

מָחֳרָת   3 the morrow, next day; מִמָּחֳרָת = on the morrow (7·32) 564

מָחֳרָת   4 the morrow, next day; מִמָּחֳרָת = on the morrow (7·32) 564

מִפְתָּן   threshold (2·8) 837

מִפְתָּן   5 threshold (2·8) 837

עפל   6 hemorrhoid (5·6) 779

קשה   7 to be hard, severe (1·5·28) 904

סרן   8 lord (11·21) 710

מְהוּמָה   9 confusion (3·12) 223

נשתר   to break out (1·1·1) 979

עפל   hemorrhoid (5·6) 779

סרן   11 lord (11·21) 710

מְהוּמָה   confusion (3·12) 223

עפל   12 hemorrhoid (5·6) 779

שַׁוְעָה   cry for help (1·11) 1003

Chapter 6

קֹסֵם   2 necromancer, diviner (1·9) 890

בַּמֶּה   wherewith? (3·29) 552

רֵיקָם   3 empty (1·16) 938

אָשָׁם   trespass offering (4·46) 79

אָשָׁם   4 trespass offering (4·46) 79

סרן   lord (11·21) 710

עפל   hemorrhoid (5·6) 779

עַכְבָּר   mouse (4·6) 747

מַגֵּפָה   plague (2·26) 620

צֶלֶם   5 image (3·17) 853

עפל   hemorrhoid (5·6) 779

עַכְבָּר   mouse (4·6) 747

אוּלי   perhaps (3·45) 19

הִתְעַלֵּל   6 to deal wantonly, ruthlessly (2·7·17) 759

עֲגָלָה   7 cart (7·25) 722

פָּרָה   cow (5·26) 831

עול   to give suck (2·5·5) 732

על   yoke (1·40) 760

עֲגָלָה   8 cart (7·25) 722

אָשָׁם   trespass offering (4·46) 79

אַרְגַּז   box, chest (3·3) 919

צַד   side; מִצַּד = at the side of (5·31) 841

מִקְרֶה   9 chance, accident (2·9) 894

פָּרָה   10 cow (5·26) 831

עול   to give suck (2·5·5) 732

כלא   to shut up (2·14·17) 476

עֲגָלָה   cart (7·25) 722

עֲגָלָה   11 cart (7·25) 722

אֲרְגַּז   box, chest (3·3) 919

עַכְבָּר   mouse (4·6) 747

צֶלֶם   image (3·17) 853

טְחוֹר   tumor (7·8) 377

יָשַׁר   12 to go straight (3·13·25) 448

פָּרָה   cow (5·26) 831

מְסִלָּה   highway (1·27) 700

גָּעָה   to low (1·2·2) 171

סרן   lord (11·21) 710

קָצַר   13 to reap (2·24·24) 894

קָצִיר   what is harvested, crop (3·49) 894

חִטָּה   wheat (2·30) 334

עֲגָלָה   14 cart (7·25) 722

פָּרָה   cow (5·26) 831

אֲרְגַּז   15 box, chest (3·3) 919

סרן   16 lord (11·21) 710

טְחוֹר   17 tumor (7·8) 377

אָשָׁם   trespass offering (4·46) 79

עַכְבָּר   18 mouse (4·6) 747

סרן   lord (11·21) 710

מִבְצָר   fortification (1·37) 131

כֹּפֶר   a village (1·1) 499

פְּרָזִי   hamlet dweller (1·3) 826

אָבֵל   meadow [dub.] (1·1) 5

הִתְאַבֵּל   19 to mourn (3·19·38) 5

מַכָּה   slaughter (7·48) 646

Chapter 7

ננהה   2 to mourn [dub.] (1·1·1[?]) 624

נֵכָר   3 foreignness (1·36) 648

לְבַדּוֹ   alone (2·35) 94

לְבַדּוֹ   4 alone (2·35) 94

שׁאב   6 to draw (2·14·14) 980

צוֹם   to fast (2·20·20) 847

סרן   7 lord (11·21) 710

הֶחֱרֵשׁ   8 to be deaf (2·38·46) 361

טָלֶה   9 lamb (1·3) 378

חָלָב   milk (2·44) 316

כָּלִיל   whole [offering] (1·15) 483

הִרְעִים   10 to thunder (2·8·11) 947

הָמַם   to confuse, rout (1·13·13) 243

נִגַּף   to be smitten (3·23·48) 619

הֵנָּה   12 hither (3·49) 244

נִכְנַע   13 to be subdued (1·25·36) 488

מִדֵּי   16 out of the abundance of, hence as often as; מִדֵּי שָׁנָה בְּשָׁנָה = yearly (3·15) 191

תְּשׁוּבָה   17 return (1·8) 1000

Chapter 8

זָקֵן   1 to be old, become old (6·25·27) 278

מִשְׁנֶה   2 second [in age] (4·35) 1041

בֶּצַע   3 unjust gain (1·23) 130

שֹׁחַד   bribe (1·23) 1005

זָקֵן   5 to be old, become old (6·25·27) 278

הֵעִיד   9 to affirm solemnly, warn (2·39·44) 729

מֶרְכָּבָה   11 chariot (2·44) 939

חרשׁ   12 to plough (1·21·24) 360

חָרִישׁ   plowing (1·3) 361

קצר   to reap (2·24·24) 894

קָצִיר   what is harvested, crop (3·49) 894

רקה   13 ointment maker, perfumer (1·2) 955

טבחה   female cook (1·1) 371

אֹפֶה   baker (1·12[?]) 66

זַיִת   14 olive, olive tree (1·38) 268

עשׂר   15 to take a tenth of (2·2·9) 797

סָרִיס   eunuch (1·45) 710

בָּחוּר   16 young man (2·45) 104

עשׂר   17 to take a tenth of (2·2·9) 797

מֵאֵן   19 to refuse (2·45·45) 549

Chapter 9

בָּחוּר   2 young man (2·45) 104

שְׁכֶם   shoulder (3·22) 1014

גָּבֹהַּ high, tall (4·41) 147

אָתוֹן 3 she ass (8·35) 87

אָתוֹן 5 she ass (8·35) 87

דָּאַג to be anxious, concerned (2·6·6) 178

אוּלַי 6 perhaps (3·45) 19

אָזַל 7 to be gone, used up (1·6·6) 23

תְּשׂוּרָה gift [dub.] (1·1) 1003

רֶבַע 8 fourth part (1·7) 917

לְפָנִים 9 formerly (2·22) 815

רֹאֶה seer (5·12) 909

מַעֲלֶה 11 ascent (1·19) 751

שָׁאַב to draw (2·14·14) 980

רֹאֶה seer (5·12) 909

בְּטֶרֶם 13 before (2·39) 382

נָגִיד 16 ruler (4·44) 617

צְעָקָה cry of distress (2·21) 858

עָצַר 17 to rule over (2·36·46) 783

אֵי 18 where? אֵי־זֶה = where, then? (4·39) 32

רֹאֶה seer (5·12) 909

רֹאֶה 19 seer (5·12) 909

אָתוֹן 20 she ass (8·35) 87

שִׁלְשׁוֹם three days ago (5·25) 1026

לְמִי to whom? whose? (2·20) 566

חֶמְדָּת desire (1·16) 326

צָעִיר 21 little, insignificant (1·22) 859

לִשְׁכָּה 22 room (1·47) 545

טַבָּח 23 cook (2·32) 371

מָנָה portion (3·12) 584

טַבָּח 24 cook (2·32) 371

שׁוֹק [upper] leg, hind leg (1·19) 1003

גָּג 25 roof (2·29) 150

שַׁחַר 26 dawn (1·23) 1007

גָּג roof (2·29) 150

Chapter 10

פַּךְ 1 flask (1·3) 810

נָשַׁק to kiss (2·26·32) 676

נָגִיד ruler (4·44) 617

קְבוּרָה 2 grave (1·14) 869

אָתוֹן she ass (8·35) 87

נָטַשׁ to abandon (7·33·40) 643

דָּאַג to be anxious, concerned (2·6·6) 178

חָלַף 3 to pass on quickly (1·14·26) 322

הָלְאָה beyond (4·13) 229

אַלּוֹן terebinth, tall tree (1·10) 18

גְּדִי kid (2·16) 152

נֵבֶל skin of wine (4·12) 614

נְצִיב 5 deputy [dub.] (3·11) 662

פָּגַע to meet (4·40·46) 803

חֶבֶל band, company (2·49) 286

נֵבֶל skin of wine (4·12) 614

תֹּף timbrel, tambourine (2·17) 1074

חָלִיל flute, pipe (1·6) 319

כִּנּוֹר lyre (3·41) 490

הוֹחֵל 8 to wait (2·15·42) 403

שְׁכֶם 9 shoulder (3·22) 1014

חֶבֶל 10 band, company (2·49) 286

אֶתְמוֹל 11 yesterday; אֵת׳ שִׁלְשׁוֹם = (from) aforetime (4·8) 1069

שִׁלְשׁוֹם three days ago (5·25) 1026

מָשָׁל 12 proverbial saying (2·39) 605

אָן 14 where? whither? (1·45) 33

אָתוֹן she ass (8·35) 87

אָתוֹן 16 she ass (8·35) 87

מְלוּכָה kingship (5·24) 574

לָחַץ 18 to oppress (1·14·15) 537

מוֹשִׁיעַ 19 savior (1·27) 446

הִתְיַצֵּב to present oneself before (6·48·48) 426

אֶלֶף thousand (2·12[?]) 48

הֲלֹם 22 hither (4·12[?]) 240

נֶחְבָּא to hide oneself (2·16·34) 285

הִתְיַצֵּב 23 to station oneself, stand (6·48·48) 426

גָּבַהּ   to be tall (1·24·34) 146

שְׁכֶם   shoulder (3·22) 1014

הֵרִיעַ   24 to shout in applause (4·40·44) 929

מְלוּכָה   25 kingship (5·24) 574

בְּלִיַּעַל   27 base fellow, worthlessness (6·27) 116

בָּזָה   to despise (2·31·42) 102

הֶחֱרִישׁ   to be silent [dub.] (2·38·46) 361

Chapter 11

נָקַר   2 to bore or pick (1·2·6) 669

הִרְפָּה   3 to refrain, let one alone (2·21·44) 951

צֶמֶד   7 a span [of oxen] (2·15) 855

נִתַּח   to cut up (1·9·9) 677

פַּחַד   dread (1·49) 808

תְּשׁוּעָה   9 deliverance (3·34) 448

חָמַם   to be or grow warm (2·23·26) 328

מָחֳרָת   11 the morrow, next day; מִמָּחֳרָת = on the morrow (7·32) 564

אַשְׁמֹרֶת   watch [div. of time] (1·7) 1038

חֹם   heat (1·4[?]) 328

תְּשׁוּעָה   13 victory (3·34) 448

חִדֵּשׁ   14 to renew (1·9·10) 293

מְלוּכָה   kingship (5·24) 574

Chapter 12

זָקֵן   2 to be old, become old (6·25·27) 288

שִׂיב   to be hoary (1·1·2) 966

נְעוּרִים   youth (2·46) 655

מָשִׁיחַ   3 anointed (13·40) 603

עָשַׁק   to oppress, wrong (2·36·37) 798

רָצַץ   to crush, oppress (2·11·19) 954

כֹּפֶר   ransom (1·13) 497

הֶעְלִים   to hide (1·11·29) 761

עָשַׁק   4 to oppress, wrong (2·36·37) 798

רָצַץ   to crush, oppress (2·11·19) 954

מְאוּמָה   anything (9·32) 548

מָשִׁיחַ   5 anointed (13·40) 603

מְאוּמָה   anything (9·32) 548

הִתְיַצֵּב   7 to take one's stand; to stand (6·48·48) 426

בֶּטַח   11 securely (1·43) 105

הִמְרָה   14 to show rebelliousness (1·22·43) 598

מָרָה   15 to be rebellious (1·21·43) 598

הִתְיַצֵּב   16 to take one's stand; to stand (6·48·48) 426

קָצִיר   17 time of harvest (3·49) 894

חִטָּה   wheat (2·30) 334

מָטָר   rain (2·37) 564

מָטָר   18 rain (2·37) 564

תֹּהוּ   21 [what is] empty, unreal (2·20) 1062

הוֹעִיל   to profit (1·22·22) 418

נָטַשׁ   22 to abandon (7·33·40) 643

בַּעֲבוּר   for the sake of (3·45) 721

הוֹאִיל   to be pleased (1·18·18) 383

חָלִילָה   23 far be it [from] (8·21) 321

הוֹרָה   to instruct (1·45[?]·45[?]) 434

נִסְפָּה   25 to be swept away, destroyed (3·9·18) 705

Chapter 13

נְצִיב   deputy [dub.] (3·11) 662

נְצִיב   deputy [dub.] (3·11) 662

נִבְאַשׁ   to make oneself odious (1·3·16) 92

חוֹל   5 sand (1·22) 297

נִגַּשׁ   6 to be hard pressed (1·3·7) 620

הִתְחַבָּא   to hide oneself (4·10·34) 285

מְעָרָה   cave (8·40) 792

חוֹחַ   briers = thickets as hiding places (1·1[?]) 296

צְרִיחַ   excavation, underground chamber (1·4) 863

חָרַד   7 to go [or come] trembling (5·23·39) 353

הוֹחִל   8 to wait (2·15·42) 403

חִלָּה   12 to entreat the favor of (1·1·1) 318

הִתְאַפֵּק	to compel oneself (1·7·7) 67	
נִסְכַּל	13 to act foolishly (1·4·8) 698	
נָגִיד	14 ruler (4·44) 617	
מַשְׁחִית	17 destroying band (2·19) 1008	
נִשְׁקָף	18 to overhang (1·10·22) 1054	
גַּיְא	valley (3·47) 161	
חָרָשׁ	19 engraver, artificer [worker in metal] (1·38) 360	
חֲנִית	spear (20·46) 333	
לָטֹשׁ	20 to sharpen (1·4·5) 538	
מַחֲרֵשָׁה	ploughshare (3·3) 361	
אֵת	ploughshare [dub.], a cutting instrument of iron (2·5) 88	
קַרְדֹּם	axe (2·5) 899	
פְּצִירָה	21 bluntness [dub.] (1·1) 823	
מַחֲרֵשָׁה	ploughshare (3·3) 361	
אֵת	ploughshare [dub.], a cutting instrument of iron (2·5) 88	
קִלְּשׁוֹן	fine point [dub.] (1·1) 887	
קַרְדֹּם	axe (2·5) 899	
דָּרְבָן	goad (1·2) 201	
חֲנִית	22 spear (20·46) 333	
מַצָּב	23 garrison (6·10) 662	
מַעֲבַר	pass (1·3) 721	

Chapter 14

מַצָּב	1 garrison (6·10) 662	
הַלָּז	this (2·7) 229	
רִמּוֹן	2 pomegranate [tree] (1·32) 941	
אֵפוֹד	3 ephod (9·49) 65	
מַעְבָּרָה	4 pass (1·8) 721	
מַצָּב	garrison (6·10) 662	
מָצוּק	5 pillar [dub.] (2·2) 848	
מוּל	in front of (3·25) 557	
מַצָּב	6 garrison (6·10) 662	
עָרֵל	uncircumcised person (4·35) 790	
אוּלַי	perhaps (3·45) 19	

מַעְצוֹר	hindrance (1·1) 784	
דָּמַם	9 to be still [motionless] (1·3·30) 198	
מַצָּב	11 garrison (6·10) 662	
חֹר	hole (1·7) 359	
הִתְחַבֵּא	to hide oneself (3·10·34) 285	
מַצָּבָה	12 garrison (1·1) 663	
מַכָּה	14 slaughter (7·48) 646	
מַעֲנָה	field for ploughing [dub.] (1·2) 776	
צֶמֶד	a measure of land (2·15) 855	
חֲרָדָה	15 trembling, quaking (2·9) 353	
מַצָּב	garrison (6·10) 662	
מַשְׁחִית	destroying band (2·19) 1008	
חָרַד	to tremble (5·23·39) 353	
רָגַז	to quake (1·30·41) 919	
צֹפֶה	16 watchman (1·19) 859	
נָמוֹג	to melt away (1·8·17) 556	
הֲלֹם	hither (4·12[?]) 240	
מְהוּמָה	20 rout (3·12) 223	
אֶתְמוֹל	21 yesterday; אֶת׳ שִׁלְשׁוֹם = formerly (4·8) 1069	
שִׁלְשׁוֹם	three days ago (5·25) 1026	
הִתְחַבֵּא	22 to hide oneself (3·10·34) 285	
נָקַם	24 to avenge oneself (2·12·34) 667	
טָעַם	to taste (4·11·11) 380	
הֵלֶךְ	26 a going, journey = flowing or dropping of honey (1·2) 237	
הִשִּׂיג	to cause to reach; to put (4·48·48) 673	
שְׁבוּעָה	oath (1·30) 989	
טָבַל	27 to dip (1·15·16) 371	
יַעְרָה	honeycomb (1·1) 421	
עָיֵף	28 to be faint (2·5·5) 746	
עָכַר	29 to disturb, trouble (1·12·14) 747	
אוֹר	to become light, shine (2·6·43) 21	
טָעַם	to taste (4·11·11) 380	
לוּא	30 if (1·3) 530	
מַכָּה	slaughter (7·48) 646	
עָיֵף	31 to be faint (2·5·5) 746	

30

בָּגַד	33 to act or deal faithlessly, deceitfully (1·46·46) 93		נָמֵס	to melt; ptc.= wasted (1·19·21) 587

בָּגַד 33 to act or deal faithlessly, deceitfully (1·46·46) 93

גלל to roll (1·10·18) 164

שֶׂה 34 a sheep [or goat] (4·44) 961

בָּזַז 36 to plunder (1·38·42) 102

הֲלֹם hither (4·12[?]) 240

הֲלֹם 38 hither (4·12[?]) 240

פִּנָּה corner (1·30) 819

בַּמֶּה wherein? (3·29) 552

יהב 41 to give (1·27·27) 396

טָעַם 43 to taste (4·11·11) 380

חָלִילָה 45 far be it [from] (8·21) 321

שַׂעֲרָה a hair (1·7) 972

מְלוּכָה 47 sovereignty (5·24) 574

הִרְשִׁיעַ to act wickedly (1·25·34) 957

שֹׁסֶה 48 plunderer (1·7) 1042

בְּכִירָה 49 first-born (1·6) 114

קָטָן small, younger (4·47) 881

Chapter 15

הֶחֱרִים 3 to devote to destruction (7·46·49) 355

חָמַל to spare, have compassion (4·40·40) 328

עוֹלֵל child (2·11) 760

יוֹנֵק suckling, babe (2·11) 413

שֶׂה a sheep [or goat] (4·44) 961

רַגְלִי 4 footmen, foot soldiers (2·12) 920

הֶחֱרִים 8 to devote to destruction (7·46·49) 355

חָמַל 9 to spare, have compassion (4·40·40) 328

מִיטָב the best (2·6) 406

מִשְׁנֶה second [dub.] (4·35) 1041

כַּר he lamb (1·11) 503

הֶחֱרִים to devote to destruction (7·46·49) 355

נִבְזֶה 9 vile, worthless (1·9) 102

נָמֵס to melt; ptc.= wasted (1·19·21) 587

חָמַל 15 to spare, have compassion (4·40·40) 328

מִיטָב the best (2·6) 406

הֶחֱרִים to devote to destruction (7·46·49) 355

הרפה 16 to let alone (2·21·44) 951

הֶחֱרִים 18 to devote to destruction (7·46·49) 355

חטא sinner (1·19) 308

עיט 19 to dart greedily (1·3·3[?]) 743

הֶחֱרִים to devote to destruction (7·46·49) 355

חֵרֶם 21 devoted thing (1·29) 356

חֵפֶץ 22 delight (2·39) 343

הִקְשִׁיב to give attention (1·45·46) 904

קֶסֶם 23 divination (1·11) 890

מְרִי rebellion (1·22) 598

תְּרָפִים idol (3·15) 1076

הפציר to display pushing, i.e., arrogance, presumption (1·1·7) 823

מְעִיל 27 robe (7·28) 591

ממלכות 28 dominion (1·9) 575

נֵצַח 29 eminence (1·42) 664

שקר to deal falsely (1·5·6) 1055

מַעֲדַנּוֹת 32 bonds (1·2) 772

אָכֵן surely (1·19) 38

מַר bitterness (3·37) 600

שִׁכֵּל 33 to make childless (1·18·24) 1013

שכל to be bereaved (1·4·24) 1013

שִׁסֵּף to hew in pieces (1·1·1) 1043

הִתְאַבֵּל 35 to mourn (3·19·38) 5

Chapter 16

מָתַי 1 when? עַד־מָתַי = how long? (2·42) 607

הִתְאַבֵּל to mourn (3·19·38) 5

עֶגְלָה 2 heifer (1·12) 722

חָרַד 4 to go [or come] trembling (5·23·39) 353

מָשִׁיחַ 6 anointed (13·40) 603

גֹּבַהּ 7 loftiness (4·41) 147

קוֹמָה height (2·45) 879

קָטָן 11 small, youngest (4·47) 881

פֹּה hither (3·44) 806

אַדְמוֹנִי 12 red, ruddy (2·3) 10

יָפֶה beautiful, beauty (3·40) 421

רֳאִי appearance (1·4) 909

בעת 14 to fall upon (2·13·16) 130

בעת 15 to fall upon (2·13·16) 130

נָגֵן 16 to play (7·14·15) 618

כִּנּוֹר lyre (3·41) 490

נָגֵן 17 to play (7·14·15) 618

נָגֵן 18 to play (7·14·15) 618

נָבוֹן [to be] discerning (1·21) 106

תֹּאַר form (3·15) 1061

נֹאד 20 skin (1·6) 609

גְּדִי kid (2·16) 152

כִּנּוֹר 23 lyre (3·41) 490

נָגֵן to play (7·14·15) 618

רָוַח to be spacious, i.e., there was enlargement, relief (1·2·14) 926

Chapter 17

אֵלָה 2 terebinth, tall tree (3·17) 18

גַּיְא 3 valley (3·47) 161

גֹּבַהּ 4 height (1·17) 147

זֶרֶת span (1·7) 284

כּוֹבַע 5 helmet (1·6) 464

שִׁרְיוֹן body armor (3·8) 1056

קַשְׂקֶשֶׂת scale [of fish] (1·8) 903

מִשְׁקָל weight (1·48) 1054

מצחה 6 greave[s] (1·1) 595

כִּידוֹן javelin (2·9) 475

חֲנִית 7 spear (20·46) 333

מְנוֹר beam (1·4) 644

אֹרֵג weaver (1·10[?]) 70

לֶהָבָה point, head (1·19) 529

צִנָּה large shield (2·20) 857

מַעֲרָכָה 8 ranks = army (15·18) 790

ברו scribal error for בחרו (1·1·1) 136

חָרֵף 10 to reproach, taunt (5·34·38) 357

מַעֲרָכָה ranks = army (15·18) 790

זָקֵן 12 to be old, become old (6·25·27) 278

מִשְׁנֶה 13 second in age (4·35) 1041

קָטָן 14 small, youngest (4·47) 881

הַעֲרִיב 16 to do at evening (1·1·3) 788

הִתְיַצֵּב to take one's stand; to stand (6·48·48) 426

אֵיפָה 17 ephah (2·38) 35

קָלִי parched grain (2·6) 885

חָרִיץ 18 thing cut; cut of milk = cheese (1·1[?]) 358

חָלָב milk (2·44) 316

עֲרֻבָּה token (1·2) 786

אֵלָה 19 terebinth, tall tree (3·17) 18

נָטַשׁ 20 to leave, entrust (7·33·40) 643

מַעְגָּל entrenchment (3·3[?]) 722

מַעֲרָכָה battle line (15·18) 790

הֵרִיעַ to shout a war cry, alarm of battle (4·40·44) 929

מַעֲרָכָה 21 battle line (15·18) 790

נָטַשׁ 22 to leave, entrust (7·33·40) 643

מַעֲרָכָה battle line (15·18) 790

מַעֲרָכָה 23 ranks = army (15·18) 790

חָרֵף 25 to reproach, taunt (5·34·38) 357

הֶעֱשִׁיר to make rich (2·14·17) 799

עֹשֶׁר riches (1·37) 799

חָפְשִׁי free (1·17) 344

הַלָּז 26 this (2·7) 229

עָרֵל uncircumcised person (4·35) 790

חָרֵף to reproach, taunt (5·34·38) 357

מַעֲרָכָה ranks = army (15·18) 790

נָטַשׁ 28 to leave, entrust (7·33·40) 643

זָדוֹן insolence (1·12) 268

רֹעַ willfulness (1·19) 947

מֵאֵצֶל 30 from beside (2·6) 69

מוּל in front of; אֶל־מוּל = towards the front of (2·33) 557

נְעוּרִים 33 youth (2·46) 655

אֲרִי 34 lion (3·35) 71

דֹּב bear (3·12) 179

שֶׂה a sheep [or goat] (4·44) 961

עֵדֶר a flock (1·39) 727

זָקָן 35 chin [lower jaw] (2·18) 278

אֲרִי 36 lion (3·35) 71

דֹּב bear (3·12) 179

עָרֵל uncircumcised person (4·35) 790

חֵרֵף to reproach, taunt (5·34·38) 357

מַעֲרָכָה ranks = army (15·18) 790

אֲרִי 37 lion (3·35) 71

דֹּב bear (3·12) 179

מַד 38 garment (4·12) 551

קוֹבַע helmet (1·2) 875

שִׁרְיוֹן body armor (3·8) 1056

חָגַר 39 to gird on (5·44·44) 291

מַד garment (4·12) 551

הוֹאִיל to voluntarily undertake to do (1·18·18) 383

נִסָּה to test, try (2·36·36) 650

מַקֵּל 40 staff (2·18) 596

חָלָק smooth (1·1) 325

יַלְקוּט wallet [dub.] (1·1) 545

קֶלַע sling (3·6) 887

קָרֵב 41 approaching (1·11) 898

צִנָּה large shield (2·20) 857

בָּזָה 42 to despise (3·31·42) 102

אַדְמוֹנִי red, ruddy (2·3) 10

יָפֶה beautiful, beauty (3·40) 421

כֶּלֶב 43 dog (2·32) 476

מַקֵּל staff (2·18) 596

חֲנִית 45 spear (20·46) 333

כִּידוֹן javelin (2·9) 475

מַעֲרָכָה ranks = army (15·18) 790

חֵרֵף to reproach, taunt (5·34·38) 357

פֶּגֶר 46 corpse (1·22) 803

חֲנִית 47 spear (20·46) 333

מַעֲרָכָה 48 battle line (15·18) 790

קָלַע 49 to sling (2·2·4) 887

מֵצַח forehead (2·13) 594

טָבַע to sink (1·6·10) 371

קֶלַע 50 sling (3·6) 887

שָׁלַף 51 to draw out (2·24·24) 1025

תַּעַר sheath (1·13) 789

הֵרִיעַ 52 to shout a war cry, alarm of battle (4·40·44) 929

גַּיְא valley (3·47) 161

דָּלַק 53 to pursue hotly (1·7·9) 196

שָׁסַס to plunder (1·3·5) 1042

עֶלֶם 56 young man (2·2) 761

Chapter 18

נִקְשַׁר 1 to be bound up (1·2·44) 905

הִתְפַּשֵּׁט 4 to strip oneself (1·1·43) 832

מְעִיל robe (7·28) 591

מַד garment (4·12) 551

חֲגוֹר belt, girdle (1·3) 292

מְחוֹלָה 6 dancing (3·8) 298

תֹּף timbrel, tambourine (2·17) 1074

שָׁלִישׁ a [three-stringed(?) three-barred(?) three-cornered(?)] musical instrument, perh, sistrum or triangle (1·1) 1026

עָנָה 7 to sing (3·13·16) 777

שָׂחַק to play (1·17·36) 965

רְבָבָה ten thousand (4·6) 914

רְבָבָה 8 ten thousand (4·6) 914

מְלוּכָה kingship (5·24) 574

עַיִן 9 to eye, look at (1·1·1) 745

הָלְאָה onward (4·13) 229

מָחֳרָת 10 the morrow, next day; מִמָּחֳרָת = on the morrow (7·32) 564

נַגֵּן to play (7·14·15) 618

חֲנִית spear (20·46) 333

הֵטִיל 11 to cast (2·9·14) 376

חֲנִית spear (20·46) 333

גוּר 15 to be afraid of (1·10·10) 158

חָתָן 18 daughter's husband (2·20) 368

יָשַׁר 20 to be pleasing (3·13·25) 448

מוֹקֵשׁ 21 lure (1·27) 430

התחתן to make oneself a daughter's husband (5·11·11) 368

לָט 22 secrecy; בַּלָּט = secretly (2·7) 532

התחתן to make oneself a daughter's husband (5·11·11) 368

נָקְלָה 23 to be lightly esteemed (1·5·6) 885

התחתן to make oneself a daughter's husband (5·11·11) 368

רָשׁ poor man (1·21) 930

חֵפֶץ 25 delight (2·39) 343

מֹהַר purchase price (1·3) 555

עָרְלָה foreskin (2·16) 790

נקם to avenge oneself (2·12·34) 667

יָשַׁר 26 to be pleasing (3·13·25) 448

התחתן to make oneself a daughter's husband (5·11·11) 368

עָרְלָה 27 foreskin (2·16) 790

התחתן to make oneself a daughter's husband (5·11·11) 368

מִדֵּי 30 out of the abundance of, hence as often as (3·15) 191

יקר to be precious, esteemed (2·9·11) 429

Chapter 19

סֵתֶר 2 hiding place (2·35) 712

נֶחְבָּא to hide oneself (2·16·34) 285

תְּשׁוּעָה 5 victory (3·34) 448

נָקִי innocent (1·43) 667

חִנָּם without cause (2·32) 336

אֶתְמוֹל 7 yesterday; אֶת׳ שִׁלְשׁוֹם = formerly (4·8) 1069

שִׁלְשׁוֹם three days ago (5·25) 1026

מַכָּה 8 slaughter (7·48) 646

חֲנִית 9 spear (20·46) 333

נַגֵּן to play (7·14·15) 618

חֲנִית 10 spear (20·46) 333

פָּטַר to remove [oneself], escape (1·7·8) 809

חַלּוֹן 12 window (1·30) 319

תְּרָפִים 13 idol (3·15) 1076

מִטָּה bed (= bier) (4·29) 641

כביר perh. quilt (2·2) 460

מראשות bed [= bier] (4·29) 641

מִטָּה 15 head place (6·10) 912

תְּרָפִים 16 idol (3·15) 1076

מִטָּה bed [= bier] (4·29) 641

כביר perh. quilt (2·2) 460

מראשות head place (6·10) 912

כָּכָה 17 thus (2·34) 462

רָמָה to deal treacherously with, betray (2·8·8) 941

להקה 20 band, company [dub.] (1·1) 530

אֵיפֹה 22 where? (1·10) 33

פָּשַׁט 24 to strip off (6·24·43) 832

עָרֹם naked (1·16) 736

Chapter 20

חָלִילָה 2 far be it [from] (8·21) 321

נֶעֱצַב 3 to be pained (2·7·15) 780

אוּלָם but, but indeed (2·19) 19

פֶּשַׂע step (1·1) 832

חָלִילָה 9 far be it [from] (8·21) 321

קָשָׁה 10 severe (3·36) 904

חָקַר 12 to search [find out one's sentiments] (1·22·27) 350

מוֹשָׁב 18 seat (3·43) 444

שִׁלֵּשׁ 19 to stay three days (1·4·9) 1026

אזל   read הַלָּאז = this (1·1) 23

צַד 20 side (5·31) 841

הוֹרָה   to shoot [2·11(?)·25(?)] 434

מַטָּרָה   target (1·16) 643

הֵנָּה 21 hitherwards, i.e., on this side (3·49) 244

עֶלֶם 22 young man (2·2) 761

הָלְאָה   onward (4·13) 229

מוֹשָׁב 25 seat (3·43) 444

צַד   side; מִצַּד = at the side of (5·31) 841

מְאוּמָה 26 anything (9·32) 548

מִקְרֶה   accident, chance (2·9) 889

בִּלְתִּי   not (2·24) 116

מָחֳרָת 27 the morrow, next day; מִמָּחֳרָת = on the morrow (7·32) 564

תְּמוֹל   yesterday (4·8) 1069

נָעֲוָה 30 to be bent, twisted (1·4·17?) 730

מַרְדּוּת   rebelliousness (1·1) 397

בֹּשֶׁת   shame (2·30) 102

הֵטִיל 33 to cast (2·9·14) 376

חֲנִית   spear (20·46) 333

חֳרִי 34 burning (1·6) 354

נֶעֱצַב   to be pained (2·7·15) 780

הכלים   to put to shame (2·10·38) 483

הוֹרָה 36 to shoot (2·11[?]·25[?]) 434

יָרָה   to shoot (2·13·25[?]) 434

יָרָה 37 to shoot (2·13·25[?]) 434

הָלְאָה   onwards (4·13) 229

חוּשׁ 38 to make haste (1·15·22) 301

לָקַט   to gather up (1·21·36) 544

מְאוּמָה 39 anything (9·32) 548

מֵאֵצֶל 41 from beside (2·6) 69

נָשַׁק   to kiss (2·26·32) 676

Chapter 21

חָרַד 2 to go [or come] trembling (5·23·39) 353

מְאוּמָה 3 in anything at all (9·32) 548

פְּלֹנִי   a certain one, such a one; פְּלֹנִי אַלְמֹנִי ... מָלִים = such and such a place (1·6) 811

אַלְמֹנִי   some one, a certain [one] (1·3) 48

חֹל 5 profaneness, commonness (2·7) 320

עָצַר 6 to keep away (2·36·46) 783

תְּמוֹל   yesterday; כְּתְ׳ שִׁלְשׁוֹם = as formerly (4·8) 1069

שִׁלְשׁוֹם   three days ago (5·25) 1026

חֹל   profaneness, commonness (2·7) 320

חֹם 7 heat (1·4) 328

נעצר 8 to be under restraint or detention (1·10·46) 783

אַבִּיר   mighty (1·17) 7

פֹּה 9 here (3·44) 805

חֲנִית   spear (20·46) 333

נחץ   to urge [dub.] (1·1·1) 637

אֵלָה 10 terebinth, tall tree (3·17) 18

לוט   to wrap (1·4·5) 532

שִׂמְלָה   covering (1·29) 971

אֵפוֹד   ephod, priestly garment (9·49) 65

זוּלָה   except besides (1·16) 265

לָזֶה 12 of, about this one (2·4) 260

מחולה   dancing (3·8) 298

עָנָה   to sing (3·13·16) 777

רְבָבָה   ten thousand (4·6) 914

שָׁנָה 14 to change, alter (1·9·26[?]) 1039

טַעַם   judgment (2·13) 381

תוה   to make a mark (1·1·2) 1063

רִיר   spittle (1·2) 938

זָקָן   chin (2·18) 287

השתגע 15 to show madness (2·2·7) 993

חָסֵר 16 in want of (1·17) 341

שׁגע   to be mad (1·5·7) 993

השתגע   to show madness (2·2·7) 993

Chapter 22

מְעָרָה	1	cave (8·40) 792
מָצוֹק	2	straits (1·6) 848
נֹשֶׁא		creditor (1·4) 674
מַר		bitter; מַר נֶפֶשׁ = discontented (3·37) 600
מְצוּדָה	4	fastness (5·18) 845
מְצוּדָה	5	fastness (5·18) 845
אֶשֶׁל	6	tamarisk tree (2·3) 79
רָמָה		perh. high place (1·5) 928
חֲנִית		spear (20·46) 333
קָשַׁר	8	to conspire (2·36·44) 905
אֹרֵב		lier in wait (2·18[?]) 70
צֵידָה	10	provision (1·9) 845
קָשַׁר	13	to conspire (2·36·44) 905
אֹרֵב		lier in wait (2·18[?]) 70
חָתָן	14	daughter's husband (2·20) 368
משמעת		prob. body guard (1·4) 1036
חָלִילָה	15	far be it [from] (8·21) 321
פָּגַע	17	to fall upon (4·40·46) 803
פָּגַע	18	to fall upon (4·40·46) 803
אֵפוֹד		ephod, priestly garment (9·49) 65
בַּד		white linen (2·13) 94
עוֹלֵל	19	child (2·11) 760
יוֹנֵק		suckling (2·11) 413
שֶׂה		a sheep [or goat] (4·44) 961

Chapter 23

שסה	1	to plunder (1·4·5) 1042
גֹּרֶן		threshing floor (1·34) 175
פֹּה	3	here (3·44) 805
מַעֲרָכָה		ranks = army (15·18) 790
נָהַג	5	to drive away (1·20·30) 624
מַכָּה		slaughter (7·48) 646
אֵפוֹד	6	ephod used in consulting (9·49) 65
נָכַּר	7	to alienate [dub.] (1·4·8) 649
בְּרִיחַ		bar[s] (1·41) 138
צוּר	8	to besiege (1·31·31) 848

החריש	9	to fabricate mischief (1·1·9) 360
אֵפוֹד		ephod used in consulting (9·49) 65
בַּעֲבוּר	10	on account of (3·45) 721
בַּאֲשֶׁר	13	in [the place] where (1·20) 84
מְצַד	14	mountain fastness (3·11) 844
מִשְׁנֶה	17	second rank (4·35) 1041
מְצַד	19	mountain fastness (3·11) 844
אַוּת	20	desire [good pleasure] (1·7) 16
חָמַל	21	to have compassion (4·40·40) 328
ערם	22	to be crafty (1·1·5) 791
הערים		to be crafty (1·4·5) 791
מחבא	23	hiding place (1·1) 285
התחבא		to hide oneself (4·10·34) 285
חפש		to search for (1·8·23) 344
אֶלֶף		thousand (2·12[?]) 48
צַד	26	side; מִצַּד = on the side of (5·31) 841
נחפז		to become hurried (1·4·10) 342
עטר		to surround (1·2·7) 742
פָּשַׁט	27	to put off [one's shelter] i.e., make a dash [from a sheltered place] (6·24·4) 832
מַחְלְקוֹת	28	smoothness (1·1) 325

Chapter 24

מְצַד	1	mountain fastness (3·11) 844
בָּחוּר	3	chosen (2·19[?]) 103
יעל		mountain goat (1·3) 418
גְּדֵרָה	4	wall: גְדרת צֹאן = shepfolds (1·8) 155
מְעָרָה		cave (8·40) 792
הסך		to cover (1·5·18[?]) 696
ירכה		recesses (1·28) 438
מְעִיל	5	robe (7·28) 591
לָט		secrecy: בַּלָּט = secretly (2·7) 532
חָלִילָה	7	far be it [from] (8·21) 321
מָשִׁיחַ		anointed (13·40) 603
שסע	8	to tear in two [dub.]: perh. = restrain (1·3·8) 1042
מְעָרָה		cave (8·40) 792

מְעָרָה 9 cave (8·40) 792

קדד to bow down (2·15·15) 869

מְעָרָה 11 cave (8·40) 792

חום to look on with compassion (1·24·24) 299

מָשִׁיחַ anointed (13·40) 603

מְעִיל 12 robe (7·28) 591

צָדָה to lie in wait (1·2·2) 841

נקם 13 to avenge (1·13·34) 667

מָשָׁל 14 proverb (2·39) 605

קַדְמֹנִי ancients (1·10) 870

כֶּלֶב 15 dog (2·32) 476

פַּרְעֹשׁ flea (2·2) 829

דַּיָּן 16 judge (1·2) 193

גָּמַל 18 to deal out to; to do to (5·34·37)

מְצוּדָה 23 fastness (5·18) 845

Chapter 25

ספד 1 to lament (2·27·29) 704

גזז 2 to shear (4·14·15) 159

שֶׂכֶל 3 prudence, good sense (1·16) 968

יָפֶה beautiful (3·40) 421

תֹּאַר form (3·15) 1061

קָשֶׁה rough, rude (3·36) 904

מעלל practice (1·41) 760

גזז 4 to shear (4·14·15) 159

גזז 7 to shear (4·14·15) 159

הכלים to put to shame (2·10·38) 483

מְאוּמָה anything (9·32) 548

התפרץ 10 to break away (1·1·49) 829

טִבְחָה 11 slaughtered meat (1·4) 370

טבח to slaughter (1·11·11) 370

גזז to shear (4·14·15) 159

אֵי where? אֵי־מִזֶּה = whence? (3·49) 32

חגר 13 to gird on (5·44·44) 291

עיט 14 to scream (3·3·3) 743

הכלם 15 to be insulted (1·2·38) 483

מְאוּמָה anything (9·32) 548

בְּלִיַּעַל 17 base fellow, worthlessness (6·27) 116

נֵבֶל 18 skin of wine (4·12) 614

סְאָה measure of grain (1·9) 684

קָלִי parched grain (2·6) 885

צמוק bunch of raisins (2·4) 856

דְּבֵלָה lump of pressed figs (2·5) 179

סֵתֶר 20 cover (2·35) 712

פגש to meet (1·10·14) 803

לָזֶה 21 to this one (2·4) 260

מְאוּמָה anything (9·32) 548

הַשְׁתִּין 23 to urinate (2·6·6) 1010

בְּלִיַּעַל 25 base fellow, worthlessness (6·27) 116

נְבָלָה senselessness, inhospitable churlishness (1·13) 615

מָנַע 26 to withhold (2·25·29) 586

צְרוֹר 29 bundle (1·7) 865

קלע to sling (2·2·4) 887

קֶלַע sling (3·6) 887

נָגִיד 30 ruler (4·44) 617

פּוּקָה 31 tottering, staggering (1·1) 807

מִכְשׁוֹל stumbling block (1·14) 506

חִנָּם without cause (2·32) 336

טַעַם 33 judgment (2·13) 381

כלא to restrain (2·14·17) 476

אוּלָם 34 but, but indeed (2·19) 19

מָנַע to withhold (2·25·29) 586

לוּלֵי unless (1·10) 530

הַשְׁתִּין to urinate (2·6·6) 1010

מִשְׁתֶּה 36 feast (2·45) 1059

שִׁכֹּר drunken (2·13) 1016

נָגַף 38 to strike (3·24·48) 619

חָשַׂךְ 39 to keep [one from evil] (1·26·28) 362

Chapter 26

בָּחוּר 2 chosen (2·19[?]) 103

מרגל 4 spy (1·10) 920

מַעְגָּל 5 entrenchment (3·3[?]) 722

יָשֵׁן 7 sleeping (2·9) 445

מַעְגָּל entrenchment (3·3[?]) 722

חֲנִית spear (20·46) 333

מעך to press (1·2·3) 590

מראשות head place (6·10) 912

חֲנִית 8 spear (20·46) 333

שָׁנָה to do again (1·13·26[?]) 1040

מָשִׁיחַ 9 anointed (13·40) 603

נָקָה to be exempt from punishment (1·23·27) 667

נָגַף 10 to strike (3·24·48) 619

נִסְפָּה to be swept away (3·9·18) 705

חָלִילָה 11 far be it [from] (8·21) 321

מָשִׁיחַ anointed (13·40) 333

חֲנִית spear (20·46) 333

מראשות head place (6·10) 912

צַפַּחַת jar or jug (3·7) 860

חֲנִית 12 spear (20·46) 333

צַפַּחַת jar or jug (3·7) 860

מראשות head place (6·10) 912

הֵקִיץ to awake (1·22·23) 884

יָשֵׁן sleeping (2·9) 445

תַּרְדֵּמָה deep sleep (1·7) 922

מָשִׁיחַ 16 anointed (13·40) 603

אֵי where? (4·39) 32

חֲנִית spear (20·46) 333

צַפַּחַת jar or jug (3·7) 860

מראשות head place (6·10) 912

הִכִּיר 17 to recognize (1·37·40) 647

הֵסִית 19 to instigate (1·18·18) 694

הֵרִיחַ to smell (1·11·14) 926

גרש to drive out, away (1·37·48) 176

הִסְתַּפֵּחַ to join oneself [with] (1·1·5) 705

פַּרְעֹשׁ 20 flea (2·2) 829

קֹרֵא partridge (1·2) 896

יקר 21 to be precious (2·9·11) 429

הִסְכִּיל to play the fool (1·2·8) 698

שגה to go astray (1·17·21) 993

חֲנִית 22 spear (20·46) 333

מָשִׁיחַ 23 anointed (13·40) 603

Chapter 27

נִסְפָּה 1 to be swept away (3·9·18) 705

נוֹאַשׁ to despair (1·5·6) 384

פָּשַׁט 8 to put off [one's shelter], i.e., make a dash [from a sheltered place] (6·24·43) 832

פָּשַׁט 10 to put off [one's shelter] i.e., make a dash [from a sheltered place] (6·24·43) 832

הִבְאִישׁ 12 to stink, become abhorred (1·7·16) 93

Chapter 28

ספד 3 to lament (3·27·29) 704

אוֹב necromancer (5·16) 15

יִדְּעֹנִי familiar spirit (2·11) 396

חָרַד 5 to be terrified (5·23·39) 353

אוּרִים Urim (1·7) 22

בעלה 7 mistress (2·4) 128

אוֹב necromancy (5·16) 15

הִתְחַפֵּשׂ 8 to disguise oneself (1·8·23) 344

קסם to practice divination (1·11·11) 890

אוֹב necromancy (5·16) 15

אוֹב 9 necromancer (5·16) 15

יִדְּעֹנִי familiar spirit (2·11) 396

התנקש to strike at (1·1·5) 669

קרה 10 to befall (1·13·27) 899

רָמָה 12 to deceive (2·8·8) 941

תֹּאַר 14 form (3·15) 1061

עָטָה to wrap [oneself] with (1·11·14) 741

מְעִיל robe (7·28) 591

קדד to bow down (2·15·15) 869

הִרְגִּיז 15 to cause disquiet = disturb (1·7·41) 919

עָר 16 adversary [dub.] (1·2) 786

חָרוֹן 18 [burning of] anger (1·41) 354

קוֹמָה 20 height, length (2·45) 879

נִבְהַל 21 to be dismayed, terrified (1·24·39) 96

פַּת 22 bit, morsel (2·14) 837

מֵאֵן 23 to refuse (2·45·45) 549

פָּרַץ perh. read פצר = to urge (1·46·49) 829, 823

מִטָּה couch, bed (4·29) 641

עֵגֶל 24 calf (1·35) 722

מַרְבֵּק stall (1·4) 918

קֶמַח flour, meal (2·14) 887

לוּשׁ to knead (1·5·5) 534

אָפָה to bake (1·9·12) 66

Chapter 29

סֶרֶן 2 lord (11·21) 710

מְאוּמָה 3 anything (9·32) 548

קָצַף 4 to be angry (1·28·34) 893

שָׂטָן adversary (1·27) 966

בַּמֶּה by what means? (3·29) 552

הִתְרַצָּה to make oneself acceptable (1·1·50[?]) 953

עָנָה 5 to sing (3·13·16) 777

רְבָבָה ten thousand (4·6) 914

מחולה dancing (3·8) 298

סֶרֶן 6 lord (11·21) 710

סֶרֶן 7 lord (11·21) 710

אוֹר 10 to become light, shine (2·6·43) 21

Chapter 30

פָּשַׁט 1 to put off [one's shelter], i.e., make a dash [from a sheltered place] (6·24·43) 832

שָׁבָה 2 to take captive (1·29·37) 985

נָהַג to drive [away, off] (4·20·30) 624

נִשְׁבָּה 3 to be taken captive (2·8·37) 985

נִשְׁבָּה 5 to be taken captive (2·8·37) 985

סָקַל 6 to stone to death (1·12·22) 709

מָרַר to be bitter (1·6·14) 600

אֵפוֹד 7 ephod used in consulting (9·49) 65

גְּדוּד 8 marauding band (4·33) 151

הִשִּׂיג to overtake (4·48·48) 673

פגר 10 to be faint (2·2·2) 803

פֶּלַח 12 split, slice (1·6) 812

דְּבֵלָה lump of pressed figs (2·5) 179

צמוק bunch of raisins (2·4) 856

לְמִי 13 to whom? whose? (2·20) 566

אֵי where? אֵי־מִזֶּה = whence? (4·39) 32

פָּשַׁט 14 to put off [one's shelter], i.e., make a dash [from a sheltered place] (6·24·43) 832

גְּדוּד 15 marauding band (4·33) 151

נָטַשׁ 16 to leave, let alone (7·33·40) 643

חגג to enjoy oneself merrily (1·6·16) 290

נֶשֶׁף 17 twilight (1·12) 676

מָחֳרָת the following day (7·32) 564

נֶעְדָּר 19 to be lacking (1·6·7) 727

נָהַג 20 to drive [away, off] (4·20·30) 624

פגר 21 to be faint (2·2·2) 803

בְּלִיַּעַל 22 worthlessness, good for nothing (6·27) 116

נָהַג to drive [away, off] (4·20·30) 624

גְּדוּד 23 marauding band (4·33) 151

לַאֲשֶׁר 27 to those who (13·38) 81

לַאֲשֶׁר 28 to those who (13·38) 81

לַאֲשֶׁר 29 to those who (13·38) 81

לַאֲשֶׁר 30 to those who (13·38) 81

לַאֲשֶׁר 31 to those who (13·38) 81

Chapter 31

מוֹרֶה 3 archer (2·4[?]) 435

39

שָׁלַף	4 to draw out (2 · 24 · 24) 1025		הִפְשִׁיט	9 to strip off (1 · 15 · 43) 833
דקר	to pierce (2 · 7 · 11) 201		בשׂר	to gladden with good tidings
עָרֵל	uncircumcised person (4 · 35) 790			(1 · 14 · 15) 142
הִתְעַלֵּל	to deal wantonly, ruthlessly		עצב	idol (1 · 17) 781
	(2 · 7 · 17) 759		גְּוִיָּה	10 corpse (3 · 12) 156
מָחֳרָת	8 the morrow; מחרת = on the morrow		גְּוִיָּה	12 corpse (3 · 12) 156
	(7 · 32) 564		אֵשֶׁל	13 tamarisk tree (2 · 3) 79
פשׁט	to strip the slain (1 · 3 · 43) 832		צום	to fast (2 · 20 · 20) 847

2 SAMUEL

Chapter 1

אֵי — 3 where? (3·39) 32

נִקְרָה — 6 to chance to be present (1·6·27) 899

נִשְׁעָן — to lean, support oneself (1·22·22) 1043

חֲנִית — spear (9·46) 333

שָׁבָץ — 9 cramp [dub.] (1·1) 990

נֵזֶר — 10 crown (1·23) 634

אֶצְעָדָה — armlet, band clasping upper arm (1·2) 858

הֵנָּה — here, hither (5·49) 244

ספד — 12 to lament (3·27·29) 704

צום — to fast (5·20·20) 847

אֵי — 13 where? (3·39) 32

מִזֶּה, אֵי מִזֶּ — idiom; whence? i.e., from where? [?] 262

פָּגַע — 15 to fall upon (1·10·46) 803

קוֹנֵן — 17 to chant (2·8·8) 884

קִינָה — elegy, dirge (1·17) 884

צְבִי — 19 beauty, decoration (1·18) 840

בִּשַּׂר — 20 to gladden with good tidings (4·14·15) 142

עלז — to exult, triumph (1·16·16) 759

עָרֵל — uncircumcised (1·35) 790

טַל — 21 dew (2·31) 378

מָטָר — rain (2·37) 564

נִגְעַל — to be defiled (1·1·10) 171

בְּלִי — not, negation (1·23) 115

נָשׁוֹג, נסוג — 22 to turn oneself away, turn back (1·14·25) 690

אָחוֹר — backwards, back (2·41) 30

רֵיקָם — in vain, without effect (1·16) 938

נָעִים — 23 delightful (2·13) 653

נפרד — to be divided (1·12·26) 825

נֶשֶׁר — eagle (1·26) 676

אֲרִי — lion (2·35) 71

גָּבַר — to be strong, prevail (2·17·25) 149

שָׁנִי — 24 scarlet (1·42) 1040

עֶדֶן — luxuries (1·3) 726

עֲדִי — ornaments (1·13) 725

לְבוּשׁ — clothing (2·39) 528

נעם — 26 to be pleasant (1·8·8) 653

נפלא — to be extraordinary, wonderful (2·13·24) 810

Chapter 2

אָנָה — 1 whence? whither? (2·37) 33

פגש — 13 to meet, encounter (1·14) 803

בְּרֵכָה — pool, pond (4·17) 140

מִזֶּה . . . וּמִזֶּה — on one side . . . on the other side, para. 6e. זֶה 262

שָׂחַק — 14 to make sport (3·17·36) 965

צַד — 16 side (2·31) 841

חֶלְקָה — portion of ground (6·24) 324

קָשֶׁה — 17 severe (2·36) 904

נִגַּף — to be smitten (4·23·48) 619

קַל — 18 light, swift, fleet (1·13) 886

צְבִי — gazelle (1·11) 840

חֲלִיצָה — 21 what is stripped off a person [as plunder] (1·2) 322

מֵאֵן — 23 to refuse (2·46·46) 549

בְּאַחֲרֵי — hinder part [under plural substantive definition] (1·1) 29

חֲנִית — spear (9·46) 333

חֹמֶשׁ — belly (4·4) 332

אֲגֻדָּה — 25 band [of men] (1·4) 8

נֶצַח — 26 everlastingness (1·42) 664

מַר — bitter (2·37) 600

מָתַי — when? (1·42) 607

לוּלֵא — 27 if not, unless (1·4) 530

בִּתְרוֹן — 29 cleft, ravine, could be the proper name of a territory (1·1[?]) 144

אוֹר — 32 to be or become light (1·5·40) 21

Chapter 3

אָרֹךְ 1 long (1·3) 74

חָזֵק firm, strong; BDB lists as verb (1·2[?]) 304

דַּל weak, low, poor (2·48) 195

הֹלֵךְ getting ever [weaker et al.] para.4. 232

מִשְׁנֶה 3 second (1·35) 1041

פִּלֶגֶשׁ 7 concubine (9·37) 811

כֶּלֶב 8 dog (3·32) 476

מֵרֵעַ friend (1·7) 946

יִרְאָה 11 fear; specific entry does not occur in BDB (2·45) 432

לְמִי 12 to whom, whose (2·20) 566

אָרַשׂ 14 to betroth (1·6·11) 76

עָרְלָה foreskin (1·16) 790

תְּמוֹל 17 yesterday; תמול שלשום means "formerly" (2·23) 1069

שִׁלְשֹׁם three days ago (2·25) 1026

מִשְׁתֶּה 20 feast (1·45) 1059

אָוָה 21 to desire (1·11·27) 16

גְּדוּד 22 raid, troop (3·33) 151

פתה 25 to deceive (1·17·27) 834

מוֹצָא a going forth (1·27) 425

מוֹבָא incoming (1·2) 100

שֶׁלִי 27 quietness (1·1) 1017

חֹמֶשׁ belly (4·4) 332

נָקִי 28 innocent 667

חיל 29 to whirl about (1·6·9) 296

זָב flow (1·13[?]) 264

מְצֹרָע leprous (1·15) 863

פֶּלֶךְ whirl of spindle (1·10) 813

חָסֵר needy, lacking (1·17) 341

חגר 31 to gird, gird on (5·44·44) 291

שַׂק sackcloth (2·48) 974

ספד to lament (3·27·29) 704

מִטָּה bed, bier (2·29) 641

קונן 33 to chant (2·8·8) 884

נָבָל foolish (2·18) 614

עַוְלָה 34 injustice, unrighteousness (2·32) 732

הברה 35 to cause to eat (2·2·5) 136

בְּעוֹד while yet, so long as (2·20) 728

טָעַם to taste (2·11·11) 380

מְאוּמָה anything (2·32) 548

הִכִּיר 36 to recognize (1·37·40) 647

רַךְ 39 tender, delicate, soft (1·16) 940

קָשֶׁה severe (2·36) 904

Chapter 4

רָפָה 1 to sink, drop (1·14·44) 951

נִבְהַל to be disturbed, dismayed, terrified (1·24·39) 96

גְּדוּד 2 marauding band, troop (3·33) 151

נָכֶה 4 stricken (2·3) 647

שְׁמוּעָה report (2·27) 1035

אֹמֵן foster [mother] (1·7) 52

חפז to be in a hurry or alarm (1·6·9) 342

נפסח to make to limp (1·1·7) 820

חמם 5 to be[come] warm (1·23·26) 328

מִשְׁכָּב lying down (7·46) 1012

צָהֳרַיִם midday, noon (1·23) 843

חִטָּה 6 wheat (2·30) 334

חֹמֶשׁ belly (4·4) 332

מִטָּה 7 bed (2·29) 641

חֶדֶר room, chamber (3·34) 293

מִשְׁכָּב lying down (7·46) 1012

נְקָמָה 8 vengeance (2·27) 668

מְבַשֵּׂר 10 bearer of good tidings (2·9) 142

בְּשֹׂרָה reward for good news, good news (5·6) 142

מִשְׁכָּב 11 bed (7·46) 1012

בָּעֵר to consume, burn (1·26·28[?]) 129

קָצַץ 12 to cut, hew off (1·9·14) 893

תָּלָה to hang up (2·23·27) 1067

בְּרֵכָה pool, pond (4·17) 140

Chapter 5

אֶתְמוֹל 2 yesterday, recently (1·8) 1069

שִׁלְשֹׁם three days ago; אתמול שלשום
formerly, previously, hitherto
(2·25) 1026

מֵבִי = מביא

נָגִיד ruler (3·44) 617

הֵנָּה 6 here, hither (5·49) 244

עִוֵּר blind (3·25) 734

פִּסֵּחַ lame (5·14) 820

מְצוּדָה 7 stronghold (5·18) 845

צִנּוֹר 8 pipe, spout, conduit [dub.] (1·2) 857

פִּסֵּחַ lame (5·14) 820

עִוֵּר blind (3·25) 734

מְצוּדָה 9 stronghold (5·18) 845

הָלוֹךְ וְגָדוֹל 10 growing greater and greater,
para. 4. 232

חָרָשׁ 11 graver, artificer (2·36[?]) 360

בַּעֲבוּר 12 on account of, for the sake of
(10·45) 721

פִּלֶגֶשׁ 13 concubine (9·37) 811

יִלּוֹד 14 born (2·5) 407

מְצוּדָה 17 stronghold (5·18) 845

נטשׁ 18 to be spread abroad (2·6·40) 643

פָּרַץ 20 to break out on (4·46·49) 829

פֶּרֶץ bursting forth (2·18) 829

עָצָב 21 idol (1·17) 781

נטשׁ 22 to be spread abroad (2·6·40) 643

מִמּוּל 23 from the front of (1·9) 557

בָּכָא balsam tree (2·5) 113

צְעָדָה 24 marching (1·3) 857

בָּכָא balsam tree (2·5) 113

חרץ to act with decision (1·1·1[?]) 358

Chapter 6

בָּחוּר 1 chosen (2·19[?]) 103

עֲגָלָה 3 cart (2·25) 722

נהג to drive (1·20·30) 624

שׂחק 5 to play (3·17·36) 965

בְּרוֹשׁ cypress, fir (1·20) 141

כִּנּוֹר lyre (1·41) 490

נֶבֶל harp (1·27) 614

תֹּף timbrel, tambourine (1·17) 1074

מְנַעַנְעִים a kind of rattle [dub.] (1·1) 631

צֶלְצְלִים cymbals (1·3) 852

גֹּרֶן 6 threshing floor (5·34) 175

שׁמט to let drop, let fall (1·6·8) 1030

שַׁל 7 hastiness, error, irreverence [dub.]
(1·1) 1016

פָּרַץ 8 to break out on (4·46·49) 829

פֶּרֶץ bursting forth (2·18) 811

בַּעֲבוּר 12 on account of, for the sake of
(10·46) 721

צָעַד 13 to step, march (1·7·8) 857

צַעַד step, pace (2·14) 857

מְרִיא fatling (1·8) 597

כרכר 14 to dance (2·2·2) 502

חגר to gird on (5·44·44) 291

אֵפוֹד priestly garment (1·49) 65

בַּד white linen (1·23) 94

תְּרוּעָה 15 shout or blast of war, alarm, or joy
(1·36) 929

נשׁקף 16 to lean over, look down (1·10·22)
1054

חַלּוֹן window (1·30) 319

פזז to show agility, leap (1·1·2) 802

כרכר to dance (2·2·2) 502

בָּזָה to despise (3·31·42) 102

הִצִּיג 17 to place (1·5·16) 426

חַלָּה 19 a kind of cake (1·14) 319

אֶשְׁפָּר cake, roll [dub.] (1·2) 80

אֲשִׁישָׁה [pressed-]raisin cake (1·5) 84

רֵיק 20 empty, worthless (1·14) 938

נָגִיד 21 ruler (3·44) 617

שׂחק to play (3·17·36) 965

43

שָׁפָל 22 humiliated (1·18) 1050

Chapter 7

מִסָּבִיב 1 from round about, from every side (1·42) 686

נָוֶה 8 abode [of sheep] (2·45) 627

נָגִיד ruler (3·44) 617

רָגַז 10 to be disquieted (3·30·41) 919

עַוְלָה injustice, unrighteousness (2·32) 732

לְמִן 11 from (2·14) 583

מֵעֶה 12 inward parts (3·31) 588

הֶעֱוָה 14 to commit iniquity (3·9·17) 731

חִזָּיוֹן 17 vision (1·9) 303

הֲלֹם 18 hither, here (1·11 [?]) 240

קטן 19 to be insignificant (1·3·4) 881

לְמֵרָחוֹק from afar = long before (1·6[?]) 583 (para. 9b. of מִן)

בַּעֲבוּר 21 on account of, for the sake of (10·45) 721

גְּדוּלָה greatness (2·12) 153

זוּלָה 22 except, only, save that (1·16) 265

גְּדוּלָּה 23 greatness (2·12) 153

נוֹרָא dreadful, wonderful thing (1·44) 431

הוֹאִיל 29 to be pleased (1·18·18) 383

Chapter 8

הִכְנִיעַ 1 to subdue (1·11·36) 488

מֶתֶג bridle, control (1·5) 607

אַמָּה mother city, metropolis (1·1) 52

חֶבֶל 2 measuring cord, line (5·49) 286

רַגְלִי 4 on foot (2·12) 920

עִקֵּר to hamstring (1·5·7) 785

נְצִיב 6 deputy (3·11) 662

שֶׁלֶט 7 shield [dub.] (1·7) 1020

כִּבֵּשׁ 11 to subdue (1·1·14) 461

גֵּיְא 13 valley (1·47) 161

מֶלַח salt (1·28) 571

נְצִיב 14 deputy (3·11) 662

מַזְכִּיר 16 recorder (2·9) 271

Chapter 9

בַּעֲבוּר 1 on account of, for the sake of (10·45) 721

אָפֶס 3 cessation of…!, a particle of negation (2·43) 67

נָכֵה stricken (2·3) 647

אֵיפֹה 4 where? (1·10) 33

בַּעֲבוּר 7 on account of, for the sake of (10·45) 721

כֶּלֶב 8 dog (3·32) 476

קָטֹן 12 young (2·47) 881

מוֹשָׁב those dwelling [collective of dweller] (1·43) 444

פִּסֵּחַ 13 lame (5·14) 820

Chapter 10

בַּעֲבוּר 3 in order to (10·45) 721

חָקֹר to search through, explore (1·22·27) 350

רִגֵּל to go about as a spy, explorer (2·14·16) 920

גִּלַּח 4 to shave [off] (4·18·23) 164

זָקָן beard (3·18) 278

מַדְוֶה garment (1·2) 551

שֵׁת seat of body, buttocks (1·4) 1059

נכלם 5 to be humiliated (2·26·38) 483

צָמַח to grow abundantly (1·4·33) 855

זָקָן beard (3·18) 278

נִבְאַשׁ 6 to make oneself odious, become odious (2·3·16) 92

שָׂכַר to hire (1·17·20) 968

רַגְלִי on foot (2·12) 920

אָחוֹר 9 the hinder side, back part; with מִן = behind (2·41) 30

בָּחוּר chosen (2·19[?]) 103

נִגַּף 15 to be smitten (4·23·48) 619

יַחַד together, altogether (3·44) 403

נִגַּף 19 to be smitten (4·23·48) 619

Chapter 11

תְּשׁוּבָה 1 return (1·8) 1000

צוּר to shut in, besiege (2·31·31) 848

מִשְׁכָּב 2 bed (7·46) 1012

גָּג roof, top (4·29) 150

טֻמְאָה 4 uncleanness (1·37) 380

הָרָה 5 to conceive, become pregnant (1·38·40) 247

הָרֶה pregnant (1·15[?]) 247

מַשְׂאָה 8 portion (1·16) 673

סֻכָּה 11 booth (2·31) 697

מָחֳרָת 12 the morrow (1·32) 564

שׁכר 13 to make drunk (1·4·20) 1016

מִשְׁכָּב bed (7·46) 1012

יהב 15 set; elsewhere: give, ascribe, come now (2·33) 396

מוּל the forefront of (1·25) 557

הורה 20 to shoot (2·11[?]·25[?]) 434

פֶּלַח 21 millstone (1·6) 812

גָּבַר 23 to be strong, prevail (2·17·25) 149

הורה 24 to shoot (2·11[?]·25[?]) 434

מוֹרֶה archer (1·4[?]) 435

זֹה 25 this; כָּזֹה וְכָזֶה thus and thus (1·11) 262

הָרַס to throw down, tear down (1·30·43) 248

ספד 26 to lament (3·27·29) 704

אֵבֶל 27 mourning (3·24) 5

Chapter 12

עָשִׁיר 1 rich (3·23) 799

רָאשׁ poor man [men] (3·21) 930

עָשִׁיר 2 rich (3·23) 799

רָשׁ 3 poor man [men] (3·21) 930

כִּבְשָׂה ewe lamb (3·8) 461

קָטָן small (2·47) 881

פַּת fragment, bit, morsel (1·14) 837

כּוֹס cup (1·31) 468

חֵיק bosom, fold of garment at breast (2·38) 300

הֵלֶךְ 4 traveler (1·2) 237

עָשִׁיר rich (3·23) 799

חָמַל to spare, have compassion on (3·40·40) 328

אֹרַח wanderer, wayfarer (1·4) 72

כִּבְשָׂה ewe lamb (3·8) 461

רָאשׁ poor man [men] (3·21) 930

כִּבְשָׂה 6 ewe lamb (3·8) 461

עֵקֶב because (2·15) 784

חָמַל to spare, have compassion on (3·40·40) 328

חֵיק 8 bosom, fold of garment at breast (2·38) 300

כָּהֵנָּה וְכָהֵנָּה again as much, para. 8c.* 241

בָּזָה 9 to despise (3·31·42) 102

עֵקֶב 10 because (2·15) 784

בָּזָה to despise (3·31·42) 102

רֵעֶה 11 friend (3·5) 946

סֵתֶר 12 secrecy (1·35) 712

אֶפֶס 14 save that; howbeit, but, when followed by כי (2·43) 67

נָאֵץ to cause to scorn (1·15·24) 610

יִלּוֹד born (2·5) 409

נָגַף 15 to smite (1·24·48) 619

נאשׁ to be sick (1·1·1[?]) 60

צוֹם 16 to fast (5·20·20) 847

צוֹם fast, fasting (1·25) 847

בָּרָה 17 to eat (3·3·5) 136

התלחש 19 to whisper together (1·2·3) 538

סוּךְ 20 to anoint oneself (1[?]·1[?]·9[?]) 691

חלף to change (1·2·26) 322

שִׂמְלָה wrapper, mantle (1·29) 971

בַּעֲבוּר 21 for the sake of, because of (10·46) 721

צוֹם to fast (5·20·20) 847

בְּעוֹד 22 while yet, so long as (2·20) 728

* based on definition given, specific entry not listed

45

צוֹם		to fast (5·20·20) 847
צוֹם	23	to fast (5·20·20) 847
בַּעֲבוּר	25	on account of, in order that, for the sake of (10·46) 721
מְלוּכָה	26	kingship (2·24) 574
עֲטָרָה	30	crown (1·23) 742
מִשְׁקָל		weight (3·48) 1054
יָקָר		precious (1·35) 429
מְגֵרָה	31	saw (1·3) 176
חָרִיץ		sharp instrument (1·2) 358
מַגְזֵרָה		axe (1·1) 160
מַלְבֵּן		brick mold (1·3) 527

Chapter 13

יָפֶה	1	beautiful (3·40) 421
בַּעֲבוּר	2	on account of, for the sake of, in order that (10·46) 721
בְּתוּלָה		virgin (2·50) 143
נפלא		to be beyond one's power (2·13·24) 810
מְאוּמָה		anything (2·32) 548
כָּכָה	4	thus (2·33) 462
דַּל		weak, thin, poor, low (2·48) 195
מִשְׁכָּב	5	bed (7·46) 1012
הברה		to cause to eat (2·2·5) 136
בִּרְיָה		food (3·3) 136
לבב	6	to make cakes (2·2·2) 525
לְבִבָה		cakes (3·3) 525
בָּרָה		to eat (3·3·5) 136
בִּרְיָה	7	food (3·3[?]) 136
בָּצֵק	8	dough (1·5) 130
לוש		to knead (1·5·5) 534
לבב		to make cakes (2·2·2) 525
בשל		to cook, boil (1·20·27) 143
לְבִבָה		cakes (3·3) 525
מַשְׂרֵת	9	pan [dub.] (1·1) 602
מֵאֵן		to refuse (2·45·45) 549
בִּרְיָה	10	food (3·3[?]) 136
חֶדֶר		room, chamber (3·34) 293

בָּרָה		to eat (3·3·5) 136
לְבִבָה		cakes (3·3) 525
נְבָלָה	12	disgraceful folly (1·13) 615
אָנָה	13	where? (2·37) 33
נָבָל		foolish (2·18) 614
מָנַע		to withhold (1·25·29) 586
שִׂנְאָה	15	hating, hatred (2·17) 971
אוֹדוֹת	16	cause, because; here BDB reconstructs the text to read אל אחי כי 15
מְשָׁרֵת	17	servant (2·20) 1058
נָעַל		to lock (2·7[?]·8[?]) 653
כְּתֹנֶת	18	tunic (3·30) 509
פַּס*		flat of hand or foot (2·5) 821
בְּתוּלָה		virgin (2·50) 143
מְעִיל		robe (1·28) 591
מְשָׁרֵת		servant (2·20) 1058
נָעַל		to lock (2·7[?]·8[?]) 653
אֵפֶר	19	ashes (1·22) 68
כְּתֹנֶת		tunic (3·30) 509
פַּס*		flat of hand or foot (2·5) 821
הֶחֱרִישׁ	20	to be silent (2·36·44) 361
לְמִן	22	the expression למן ...ועד an idiomatic expression to deno[te] comprehensively an entire class, par[.] 9b.(1) מן 583
גזז	23	to shear (2·14·15) 159
גזז	24	to shear (2·14·15) 159
פָּרַץ	25	to spread [become known] (4·46·49) 829
פָּרַץ	27	to spread [become known] (4·46·49) 829
פֶּרֶד	29	mule (4·14) 825
שְׁמוּעָה	30	report (2·27) 1035
שׁוּמָה	32	not in Lis.; BDB "perhaps n.f., token of unluckiness, scowl" (0·0[?]) 965
צֹפֶה	34	watchman (6·19) 859
צַד		side (2·31) 841
בְּכִי	36	weeping (1·30) 113

הִתְאַבֵּל 37 to mourn (4·19·38) 5

Chapter 14

הִתְאַבֵּל 2 to mourn (4·19·38) 5

אָבֵל mourning (3·24) 5

סוּךְ to anoint oneself (1[?]·1[?]·9[?]) 691

אֲבָל 5 verily, truly, indeed (1·11) 6

נצה 6 to struggle with each other (1·5·8) 663

כְּתֹנֶת פַּסִּים tunic reaching to palms and soles 821

יוֹרֵשׁ 7 heir (1·5) 439

כבה to extinguish (2·10·24) 459

גַּחֶלֶת coal (3·18) 160

נָקִי 9 free from punishment (2·43) 667

גָּאַל 11 kinsman, redeemer (1·44[?]) 145

שַׂעֲרָה a [single] hair (1·7) 972

אָשֵׁם 13 guilty (1·3) 79

נִדָּח banished one (2·11) 623

נגר 14 to be poured (1·4·5) 620

נדח to be thrust down; this specific entr not in BDB (1·2·2[?]) 191

נִדָּח banished one (2·11) 623

אוּלַי 15 perhaps (2·45) 19

יַחַד 16 together, altogether (3·44) 403

מִנְחָה 17 security, assurance (1·21) 629

כָּחַד 18 to hide (1·15·30) 470

אִישׁ 19 there is, was, will be = יֵשׁ (1·3) 441

הֵמִין to turn to the right (1·5) 412

הִשְׂמִיל to turn to the left (1·5·5) 970

לְבַעֲבוּר 20 in order to (2·3) 721

יָפֶה 25 fair (3·40) 421

קָדְקֹד head, crown of head (1·11) 869

מוּם blemish (1·21[?]) 548

גָּלַח 26 to shave [off] (4·18·23) 164

שָׁקַל to weigh out (2·19·22) 1053

שֵׂעָר hair (1·28) 972

יָפֶה 27 beautiful (3·40) 421

חֶלְקָה 30 portion of ground (6·24) 324

שְׂעֹרָה barley (3·34) 972

הִצִּית to kindle, set on fire (3·17·27) 428

הִצִּית 31 to kindle, set on fire (3·17·27) 428

חֶלְקָה portion of ground (6·24) 324

הֵנָּה 32 here, hither (5·49) 244

נָשַׁק 33 to kiss (4·26·32) 676

Chapter 15

מֶרְכָּבָה 1 chariot (1·44) 939

אֵי 2 where? (3·39) 32

נָכֹחַ 3 right (1·8) 647

הַצַּדִּיק 4 to do justice (1·12·41) 842

נָשַׁק 5 to kiss (4·26·32) 676

גָּנַב 6 to steal away (1·2·39) 170

נָדַר 7 to vow (2·31·31) 623

נָדַר 8 to vow (2·31·31) 623

מְרַגֵּל 10 spy (1·10) 920

תֹּם 11 innocence, simplicity (1·23) 1070

יוֹעֵץ 12 counselor (1·22) 419

קֶשֶׁר conspiracy (1·14) 905

אַמִּיץ mighty (1·6) 55

פְּלֵיטָה 14 escaped remnant (1·28) 812

הִשִּׂיג to overtake (1·48·48) 673

הִדִּיחַ to thrust (1·27·43) 623

פִּלֶגֶשׁ 16 concubine (9·37) 811

מֶרְחָק 17 distance (1·18) 935

נָכְרִי 19 foreigner (1·45) 648

תְּמוֹל 20 yesterday (2·23) 1069

הֵנִיעַ to cause to wander (2·14·38) 631

טַף 22 children (1·41) 381

נָוֶה 25 habitation (2·45) 627

הִתְמַהְמֵהַּ 28 to tarry (1·9) 554

עֲבָרָה ford (2·2) 720

מַעֲלֶה 30 ascent (1·19) 751

זַיִת olive tree (1·38) 268

חפה to cover (2·6·12) 341

יָחֵף barefoot (1·5) 405

חפה to cover (2·6·12) 341

קָשַׁר 31 to league together, conspire (1·36·44) 905

סכל to turn into foolishness (1·2·8) 698

כְּתֹנֶת 32 tunic (3·30) 509

מַשָּׂא 33 burden (2·43) 672

מֵאָז 34 idiom: from that time = time past [old] (1·17) 23

הֵפֵר to break, frustrate (2·41·44) 830

רֵעֶה 37 friend (3·5) 946

Chapter 16

צֶמֶד 1 couple, pair (1·15) 855

חבש to bind, bind on, bind up (3·27·31) 289

צִמּוּקָה bunch of raisins (1·4) 856

קַיִץ summer fruit (2·20) 884

נֵבֶל skin (1·11) 614

קַיִץ 2 summer fruit (2·20) 884

יָעֵף weary (1·4) 419

אַיֵּה 3 where? (2·44) 32

מַמְלְכוּת dominion (1·9) 575

סקל 6 to stone (2·4·22) 709

בְּלִיַּעַל 7 worthless, good-for-nothing, base fellow (4·27) 116

מְלוּכָה 8 kingship (2·24) 574

כֶּלֶב 9 dog (3·32) 476

מַה לִּי וָלָכֶם 10 idiomatic formula of repudiation, or emphatic denial: what is there (common) to me and to you? what have I to do with you? para. 1d. (c). BDB (1·6) 553

מֵעֶה 11 inward parts (3·31) 588

אוּלַי 12 perhaps (2·45) 19

קְלָלָה curse (1·33) 887

צֵלָע 13 rib [ridge] of hill (1·39) 854

לְעֻמָּה close by, side by side, with (2·32) 769

סקל to stone (2·4·22) 709

עֵפָר to keep dusting (1·1·1) 780

עָיֵף 14 faint, weary (2·17) 746

נפש to refresh oneself (1·3·3) 661

רֵעֶה 16 friend (3·5) 946

לְמִי 19 to whom, whose (2·20) 566

יהב 20 with reflex לְ = provide; give (2·33·33) 396

פִּלֶגֶשׁ 21 concubine (9·37) 811

נִבְאַשׁ to make oneself odious, become odious (2·3·16) 92

גַּג 22 roof, top (4·29) 150

פִּלֶגֶשׁ concubine (9·37) 811

Chapter 17

יָגֵעַ 2 weary (1·3) 388

רָפֶה slack (1·4) 952

הֶחֱרִיד to drive in terror, rout (1·16·39) 353

ישר 4 to be pleasing, agreeable, right (1·13·25) 448

מַר 8 bitter (2·37) 600

דֹּב bear (1·12) 179

שַׁכּוּל bereaved, robbed of offspring (1·6) 1014

נֶחְבָּא 9 to hide oneself, be hidden (1·16·34) 285

פַּחַת pit (2·10) 809

תְּחִלָּה beginning (3·22) 321

מַגֵּפָה slaughter (4·26) 620

אַרְיֵה 10 lion (1·45) 71

נָמֵס to melt (2·19·21) 587

חוֹל 11 sand (1·22) 297

קְרָב battle, war (1·8) 898

טַל 12 dew (2·31) 378

חֶבֶל 13 cord, rope (5·49) 286

סחב to drag (1·5·5) 694

צְרוֹר pebble (1·2) 866

הֵפֵר 14 to break, frustrate (2·41·44) 830

לְבַעֲבוּר in order to [+infin.] (2·3) 721

כָּזֹאת וְ	15	thus and thus (2·5) para. 6d. זֶה 262
בָּלַע	16	to be swallowed up, destroyed (1·2·2) 118
בְּאֵר	18	well (3·36) 91
מָסָךְ	19	covering (1·25) 697
בְּאֵר		well (3·36) 91
שטח		to spread, spread abroad (1·4·5) 1008
רִפֻאוֹת		some grain or fruit (1·2) 937
אַיֵּה	20	where? (2·44) 32
מִיכָל		stream (1·1) 568
בְּאֵר	21	well (3·36) 91
כָּכָה		thus (2·33) 462
נֶעְדָּר	22	to be lacking (1·6·7) 727
חבש	23	to equip [a beast] for riding, to bind on (3·27·31) 289
נחנק		to strangle oneself (1·1·2) 338
מִשְׁכָּב	28	bed, lying down [?] (7·46) 1012
סַף		basin (1·6) 706
יוֹצֵר		potter (1·17) 427
חִטָּה		wheat (2·30) 334
שְׂעֹרָה		barley (3·34) 972
קֶמַח		flow, meal (1·14) 887
קָלִי		parched grain (2·6) 885
פּוֹל		beans [collective] (1·2) 806
עֲדָשָׁה		lentil (2·4) 727
חֶמְאָה	29	curd, curdled milk (1·10) 326
שְׁפוֹת		cream [dub.] (1·1) 1045
רָעֵב		hungry (1·19) 944
עָיֵף		faint, weary (2·17) 746
צָמֵא		thirsty (1·9) 854

Chapter 18

אַט	5	gentleness, with לְ = gently (1·5) 31
נגף	7	to be smitten (4·23·48) 619
מַגֵּפָה		slaughter (4·26) 620
מֵאֲשֶׁר	8	than those (1·17) 84
פֶּרֶד	9	mule (4·14) 825
שׂוֹבֶךְ		network of boughs (1·1) 959
אֵלָה		terebinth [tree] (4·17) 18
תָּלָה	10	to hang up, hang (2·23·27) 1067
אֵלָה		terebinth [tree] (4·17) 18
חֲגֹרָה	11	girdle, loin covering, belt (1·5) 292
לֻא	12	though, if (2·17) 530
שָׁקַל		to weigh out (2·19·22) 1053
נֶחְבָּא	13	to be hidden (1·9·30) 470
הִתְיַצֵּב		to take one's stand (4·48·48) 426
מִנֶּגֶד		aloof (1·26) 617
הוֹחִיל	14	to wait, tarry (1·15·42) 403
אֵלָה		terebinth [tree] (4·17) 18
חָשַׂךְ	16	to withhold, refrain (1·26·28) 362
פַּחַת	17	pit (2·10) 809
גַּל		heap [of stones] (1·20) 164
מַצֶּבֶת	18	pillar (2·35) 663
בַּעֲבוּר		in order to [+infin.] (10·45) 721
בִּשֵּׂר	19	to bear tidings (4·14·15) 142
בְּשֹׂרָה	20	news, tidings (5·6) 142
בִּשֵּׂר		to bear tidings (4·14·15) 142
בְּשֹׂרָה	22	reward for good news, good news (5·6) 142
צֹפֶה	24	watchman (6·19) 859
גַּג		roof, top (4·29) 150
צֹפֶה	25	watchman (6·19) 859
בְּשׂוֹרָה		news, tidings (5·6) 142
קָרֵב		approaching (1·11) 898
הָלוֹךְ וְקָרֵב		nearer and nearer, para. 4c. (3) 233
צֹפֶה	26	watchman (6·19) 859
שֹׁעֵר		porter (1·37) 1045
מְבַשֵּׂר		one bearing tidings (2·9[?]) 142
צֹפֶה	27	watchman (6·19) 859
מְרוּצָה		running (2·4) 930
בְּשׂוֹרָה		news, tidings (5·6) 142
הִתְיַצֵּב	30	to take one's stand (4·48·48) 426
הִתְבַּשֵּׂר	31	to receive good tidings (1·1·15) 142

Chapter 19

רָגַז	1 to be excited, perturbed (3·30·41) 919
עֲלִיָּה	roof chamber (1·20) 751
הִתְאַבֵּל	2 to mourn (4·19·38) 5
תְּשׁוּעָה	3 deliverance (3·34) 448
אֵבֶל	mourning (3·24) 5
נֶעֱצַב	to be pained [for] (1·7·15) 780
הִתְגַּנֵּב	4 to go by stealth, steal away (2·2·39) 170
נכלם	to be put to shame (2·26·28) 483
לוֹט	5 to wrap tightly (1·4·5) 532
פִּלֶגֶשׁ	6 concubine (9·37) 811
שֹׂנֵא	7 enemy (2·41) 971
אֹהֵב	friend (1·36[?]) 12
לוּ, לֹא	if (2·17) 530
נְעוּרִים	8 youth (1·46) 655
נדון	10 to be at strife (1·1·23) 192
הֶחֱרִישׁ	11 to be silent (2·36·44) 361
עֲבָרָה	ford (2·2) 720
הֶעֱוָה	20 to commit iniquity (3·9·17) 731
שָׂטָן	23 adversary (1·27) 966
שָׂפָם	25 moustache (1·5) 974
לְמִן	from (2·14) 583
רִמָּה	27 to deceive, mislead (1·8·8) 941
חבש	to equip [a beast] for riding, bind up (3·27·31) 289
פִּסֵּחַ	lame (5·14) 820
רגל	28 to slander (2·14·16) 920
זָקֵן	33 to be old, become old (1·25·27) 278
כִּלְכֵּל	to sustain (3·23·36) 465
שִׂיבָה	sojourn (1·1) 444
כִּלְכֵּל	34 to sustain (3·23·36) 465
כַּמָּה	35 how much? how many? (1·13) 552
טָעַם	36 to taste (2·11·11) 380
שָׁר	singer (2·9) 1010
מַשָּׂא	burden (2·43) 672

גמל	37 to recompense, repay, deal fully with (2·34·37) 169
גְּמוּלָה	dealing, recompense (1·3) 168
נָשַׁק	40 to kiss (4·26·32) 676
גנב	42 to steal, take by stealth (2·30·39) 170
קשה	44 to be hard, severe (1·5·28) 904

Chapter 20

בְּלִיַּעַל	1 worthless, good-for-nothing, base fellow (4·27) 116
פִּלֶגֶשׁ	3 concubine (9·37) 811
כִּלְכֵּל	to sustain (3·23·36) 465
אַלְמָנוּת	widowhood (1·4) 48
חַיּוּת	life, lifetime (1·1) 313
פֹּה	4 here, hither (1·44) 805
הֶאֱחִיר	5 to show delay, delay (1·1·17) 29
יָעַד	to appoint (1·5·28) 416
בָּצוּר	6 fortified (1·25[?]) 130
חגר	8 to gird (5·44·44) 291
חֲגוֹר	belt, girdle (1·3) 292
מַד	garment (1·12) 551
לְבוּשׁ	garment (2·31) 528
צמד	to be bound (1·1·5) 855
מָתְנַיִם	loins (1·50) 608
תַּעַר	sheath (1·13) 789
זָקָן	9 beard (3·18) 278
נָשַׁק	to kiss (4·26·32) 676
חֹמֶשׁ	10 belly (4·4) 332
מֵעֶה	inward parts, internal organs (3·32) 588
שָׁנָה	to repeat (1·13·25) 1040
הִתְגַּלְגֵּל	12 to roll oneself (1·2·17) 164
מְסִלָּה	highway (3·27) 700
הִגָּה	13 to thrust away (1·1·1) 387
מְסִלָּה	highway (3·27) 700
נקהל	14 to assemble (1·19·39) 874
צור	15 to shut in, besiege (2·31·31) 848

סֹלְלָה mound (1·11) 700

חֵל rampart, fortress [i.e., a little wall] (1·9) 298

הֵנָּה 16 here, hither (5·49) 244

שָׁלֵם 19 peaceable psv. ptc. (1·1[?]) 1023

אָמוּן faithful one (1·3[?]) 52

בִּלַּע to swallow up, destroy (2·20·41) 118

חָלִיל 20 far be it [from me, you, etc.] (2·20[?]) 321

בִּלַּע to swallow up, destroy (2·20·41) 118

מַס 24 labor band (1·23) 586

מַזְכִּיר recorder (2·9) 271

Chapter 21

שִׁירָה 1 song (1·13) 1010

קִנֵּא 2 to be zealous [for] (1·28·32) 888

בַּמֶּה 3 wherewith? (1·29) 552

דָּמָה 5 to imagine, devise (1·13·27) 197

הִתְיַצֵּב to take one's stand (4·48·48) 426

הוֹקִיעַ 6 of some solemn form of execution; meaning uncertain (2·3·8) 429

בָּחִיר chosen (1·13) 104

חָמַל 7 to spare, have compassion on (3·40·40) 328

שְׁבוּעָה oath (1·30) 989

הוֹקִיעַ 9 of some solemn form of execution; meaning uncertain (2·3·8) 429

יַחַד together, altogether (3·44) 403

קָצִיר harvest (4·49) 894

תְּחִלָּה beginning (3·22) 321

שְׂעֹרָה barley (3·34) 972

שַׂק 10 sackcloth (2·48) 974

תְּחִלָּה beginning (3·22) 321

נִתַּךְ to be poured out (1·8·21) 677

קָצִיר harvest (4·49) 894

פִּלֶגֶשׁ 11 concubine (9·37) 811

גָּנַב 12 to steal, take by stealth (2·30·39) 39

רְחֹב broad open place, plaza (1·43) 932

תָּלָה to hang (1·3·3) 1067

הוֹקַע 13 passive of Hiph. form, of some solemn form of execution; meaning uncertain (1·1·8) Qal. form means "dislocated, alienated" 429

נֶעְתַּר 14 to be entreated (2·8·20) 801

עָיֵף 15 to be faint, weary (1·5·5) 746

יָלִיד 16 children, sons (2·13) 409

מִשְׁקָל weight (3·48) 1054

קַיִן spear (1·1) 883

חָגַר to gird on (5·44·44) 291

כָּבָה 17 to extinguish (2·10·24) 459

נֵר lamp (2·44) 632

יָלִיד 18 children, sons (2·13) 409

חֲנִית 19 spear (9·46) 333

מָנוֹר beam (1·4) 644

אֹרֵג weaver (1·10[?]) 70

מָדוֹן 20 stature (1·1) 551

אֶצְבַּע finger, toe (2·31) 840

חֵרֵף 21 to reproach, say sharp things against (2·34·38) 357

Chapter 22

שִׁירָה 1 song (1·13) 1010

מְצוּדָה 2 stronghold (5·18) 845

פִּלֵּט to bring into security (2·24·27) 812

חָסָה 3 to seek refuge (2·37·37) 340

יֶשַׁע salvation (4·36) 447

מִשְׂגָּב secure height (1·17) 960

מָנוֹס place of refuge (1·8) 631

מוֹשִׁיעַ savior (2·27) 446

אָפַף 5 to surround, encompass (1·5·5) 67

מִשְׁבָּר breaker (1·5) 991

בְּלִיַּעַל ruin, destruction, worthlessness (4·27) 116

בִּעֵת to assail, fall upon (1·13·16) 129

חֶבֶל 6 cord (5·49) 286

קִדֵּם to meet, confront (2·24·26) 869

51

מוֹקֵשׁ	lure (1·27) 430	

מוֹקֵשׁ lure (1·27) 430

שַׁוְעָה 7 cry for help (1·11) 1003

גָּעַשׁ 8 to quake (1·2·10) 172

רָעַשׁ to quake, shake (1·21·29) 950

מוֹסָד foundation (2·13) 414

רָגַז to quake (3·30·41) 919

הִתְגָּעַשׁ to shake back and forth, toss or reel to and fro, (2·5·10) 172

עָשָׁן 9 smoke (1·25) 798

גַּחֶלֶת coal (3·18) 160

עֲרָפֶל 10 cloud, heavy cloud (1·15) 791

עוּף 11 to fly, fly away (1·18·25) 733

סֻכָּה 12 booth (2·31) 697

חַשְׁרָה collection, mass (1·1) 366

עָב cloud mass (2·30) 728

שַׁחַק cloud (1·21) 1007

נֹגַהּ 13 brightness (2·19) 618

גַּחֶלֶת coal (3·18) 160

הִרְעִים 14 to cause to thunder (1·11·11) 947

בָּרָק 15 lightning (1·20) 140

הָמַם to confuse, rout (1·13·13) 243

אָפִיק 16 channel, stream bed, ravine (1·18) 67

מוֹסָד foundation (2·13) 414

תֵּבֵל world (1·36) 385

גְּעָרָה rebuke (1·15) 172

נְשָׁמָה breath (1·24) 675

הַמְשָׁה 17 to draw out (1·2·3) 602

עַז 18 strong, mighty (1·22) 738

שֹׂנֵא enemy (2·41) 971

אָמֵץ to be strong, stout (1·16·41) 54

קִדֵּם 19 to meet, confront (2·24·26) 869

אֵיד distress, calamity (1·24) 15

מִשְׁעָן support (1·3) 1044

מֶרְחָב 20 broad place (1·6) 932

חִלֵּץ to rescue, deliver, pull out (1·14·27) 322

גָּמַל 21 to deal fully with, repay (2·34·37) 168

בֹּר cleanness, pureness (2·7[?]) 141

רָשַׁע 22 to be wicked, act wickedly (1·9·34) 957

לְנֶגֶד 23 in front of, before (2·32) 617

בֹּר 25 cleanness, pureness (2·7[?]) 141

לְנֶגֶד in the sight of, before (2·32) 617

חָסִיד 26 kind, pious (1·32) 339

הִתְחַסֵּד to be kind, good (1·2·2) 338

נָבְרַר 27 to purify oneself (1·3·15) 140

הִתְבָּרַר to show oneself pure, just, kind; t purify oneself (1·3·15) 140

עִקֵּשׁ twisted, perverted (1·11) 786

הִתְפַּתַּל to deal tortuously (1·2·5[?]) 83 [BDB's suggested correction]

רָם 28 high (1·31[?]) 926

הִשְׁפִּיל to lay low, humiliate (1·18·29) 1050

נֵיר 29 lamp (2·44) 632

הִגִּיהַּ to enlighten (!·3·6) 618

גְּדוּד 30 marauding band, troop (3·33) 151

דִּגֵּל to carry up, set up (1·4·5) 186

שׁוּר wall (1·3) 1004

אִמְרָה 31 utterance, speech, word (1·30) 57

צָרַף to smelt, refine (1·18·21) 864

חָסָה to seek refuge (2·37·37) 340

מִבַּלְעֲדֵי 32 apart from, without (2·12) 116

מָעוֹז 33 refuge (1·36) 731

הִתִּיר to set free, unbind (1·3·22[?]) BDB amends to יתן from נתן, "to set" 684

שִׁוָּה 34 to please, set (1·5·16) 1001

אַיָּלָה hind, doe (1·11) 19

נָחַת 35 to press down (1·3·8) 639

יֵשַׁע 36 salvation (4·36) 447

הִרְחִיב 37 to enlarge (1·21·25) 931

צַעַד step, pace (2·14) 857

מָעַד to slip (1·5·7) 588

קַרְסֹל ankle (1·2) 902

סֹלְלָה mound (1·11) 700

חֵל rampart, fortress [i.e., a little wall] (1·9) 298

הֵנָּה 16 here, hither (5·49) 244

שָׁלֵם 19 peaceable psv. ptc. (1·1[?]) 1023

אָמוּן faithful one (1·3[?]) 52

בִּלַּע to swallow up, destroy (2·20·41) 118

חָלִיל 20 far be it [from me, you, etc.] (2·20[?]) 321

בִּלַּע to swallow up, destroy (2·20·41) 118

מַס 24 labor band (1·23) 586

מַזְכִּיר recorder (2·9) 271

Chapter 21

שִׁירָה 1 song (1·13) 1010

קִנֵּא 2 to be zealous [for] (1·28·32) 888

בַּמֶּה 3 wherewith? (1·29) 552

דִּמָּה 5 to imagine, devise (1·13·27) 197

הִתְיַצֵּב to take one's stand (4·48·48) 426

הוֹקִיעַ 6 of some solemn form of execution; meaning uncertain (2·3·8) 429

בָּחִיר chosen (1·13) 104

חָמַל 7 to spare, have compassion on (3·40·40) 328

שְׁבוּעָה oath (1·30) 989

הוֹקִיעַ 9 of some solemn form of execution; meaning uncertain (2·3·8) 429

יַחַד together, altogether (3·44) 403

קָצִיר harvest (4·49) 894

תְּחִלָּה beginning (3·22) 321

שְׂעֹרָה barley (3·34) 972

שַׂק 10 sackcloth (2·48) 974

תְּחִלָּה beginning (3·22) 321

נִתַּךְ to be poured out (1·8·21) 677

קָצִיר harvest (4·49) 894

פִּלֶגֶשׁ 11 concubine (9·37) 811

גָּנַב 12 to steal, take by stealth (2·30·39) 39

רְחֹב broad open place, plaza (1·43) 932

תָּלָה to hang (1·3·3) 1067

הוֹקַע 13 passive of Hiph. form, of some solemn form of execution; meaning uncertain (1·1·8) Qal. form means "dislocated, alienated" 429

נֶעְתַּר 14 to be entreated (2·8·20) 801

עָיֵף 15 to be faint, weary (1·5·5) 746

יָלִיד 16 children, sons (2·13) 409

מִשְׁקָל weight (3·48) 1054

קַיִן spear (1·1) 883

חָגַר to gird on (5·44·44) 291

כָּבָה 17 to extinguish (2·10·24) 459

נֵר lamp (2·44) 632

יָלִיד 18 children, sons (2·13) 409

חֲנִית 19 spear (9·46) 333

מָנוֹר beam (1·4) 644

אֹרֵג weaver (1·10[?]) 70

מָדוֹן 20 stature (1·1) 551

אֶצְבַּע finger, toe (2·31) 840

חֵרֵף 21 to reproach, say sharp things against (2·34·38) 357

Chapter 22

שִׁירָה 1 song (1·13) 1010

מְצוּדָה 2 stronghold (5·18) 845

פִּלֵּט to bring into security (2·24·27) 812

חָסָה 3 to seek refuge (2·37·37) 340

יֶשַׁע salvation (4·36) 447

מִשְׂגָּב secure height (1·17) 960

מָנוֹס place of refuge (1·8) 631

מוֹשִׁיעַ savior (2·27) 446

אָפַף 5 to surround, encompass (1·5·5) 67

מִשְׁבָּר breaker (1·5) 991

בְּלִיַּעַל ruin, destruction, worthlessness (4·27) 116

בָּעַת to assail, fall upon (1·13·16) 129

חֶבֶל 6 cord (5·49) 286

קִדֵּם to meet, confront (2·24·26) 869

מוֹקֵשׁ lure (1·27) 430

שַׁוְעָה 7 cry for help (1·11) 1003

גָּעַשׁ 8 to quake (1·2·10) 172

רעשׁ to quake, shake (1·21·29) 950

מוֹסָד foundation (2·13) 414

רָגַז to quake (3·30·41) 919

התגעשׁ to shake back and forth, toss or reel to and fro, (2·5·10) 172

עָשָׁן 9 smoke (1·25) 798

גַּחֶלֶת coal (3·18) 160

עֲרָפֶל 10 cloud, heavy cloud (1·15) 791

עוּף 11 to fly, fly away (1·18·25) 733

סֻכָּה 12 booth (2·31) 697

חַשְׁרָה collection, mass (1·1) 366

עָב cloud mass (2·30) 728

שַׁחַק cloud (1·21) 1007

נֹגַהּ 13 brightness (2·19) 618

גַּחֶלֶת coal (3·18) 160

הִרְעִים 14 to cause to thunder (1·11·11) 947

בָּרָק 15 lightning (1·20) 140

הָמַם to confuse, rout (1·13·13) 243

אָפִיק 16 channel, stream bed, ravine (1·18) 67

מוֹסָד foundation (2·13) 414

תֵּבֵל world (1·36) 385

גְּעָרָה rebuke (1·15) 172

נְשָׁמָה breath (1·24) 675

המשׁה 17 to draw out (1·2·3) 602

עַז 18 strong, mighty (1·22) 738

שֹׂנֵא enemy (2·41) 971

אמץ to be strong, stout (1·16·41) 54

קדם 19 to meet, confront (2·24·26) 869

אֵיד distress, calamity (1·24) 15

מִשְׁעָן support (1·3) 1044

מֶרְחָב 20 broad place (1·6) 932

חלץ to rescue, deliver, pull out (1·14·27) 322

גמל 21 to deal fully with, repay (2·34·37) 168

בֹּר cleanness, pureness (2·7[?]) 141

רשׁע 22 to be wicked, act wickedly (1·9·34) 957

לְנֶגֶד 23 in front of, before (2·32) 617

בֹּר 25 cleanness, pureness (2·7[?]) 141

לְנֶגֶד in the sight of, before (2·32) 617

חָסִיד 26 kind, pious (1·32) 339

התחסד to be kind, good (1·2·2) 338

נברר 27 to purify oneself (1·3·15) 140

התברר to show oneself pure, just, kind; to purify oneself (1·3·15) 140

עִקֵּשׁ twisted, perverted (1·11) 786

התפתל to deal tortuously (1·2·5[?]) 83 [BDB's suggested correction]

רָם 28 high (1·31[?]) 926

הִשְׁפִּיל to lay low, humiliate (1·18·29) 1050

נֵיר 29 lamp (2·44) 632

הִגִּיהַּ to enlighten (!·3·6) 618

גְּדוּד 30 marauding band, troop (3·33) 151

דגל to carry up, set up (1·4·5) 186

שׁוּר wall (1·3) 1004

אִמְרָה 31 utterance, speech, word (1·30) 57

צָרַף to smelt, refine (1·18·21) 864

חסה to seek refuge (2·37·37) 340

מִבַּלְעֲדֵי 32 apart from, without (2·12) 116

מָעוֹז 33 refuge (1·36) 731

הִתִּיר to set free, unbind (1·3·22[?]) BDB amends to יתן from נתן, "to set" 684

שִׁוָּה 34 to please, set (1·5·16) 1001

אַיָּלָה hind, doe (1·11) 19

נָחַת 35 to press down (1·3·8) 639

יֶשַׁע 36 salvation (4·36) 447

הִרְחִיב 37 to enlarge (1·21·25) 931

צַעַד step, pace (2·14) 857

מעד to slip (1·5·7) 588

קַרְסֹל ankle (1·2) 902

מָחַץ 39 to shatter (1·14·14) 563

אזר 40 to gird [on] (1·6·16) 25

הִכְרִיעַ to cause to bow down (1·6·35) 502

קָם adversary (2·12) 878

תַּתָּה 41 = נָתַתָּה 678; G.K. para. 19.i.

עֹרֶף back of neck (1·33) 791

הצמית to exterminate, annihilate (1·10·15) 856

שָׁעָה 42 to gaze [at], regard (1·12·15) 1043

מוֹשִׁיעַ savior (2·27) 446

שחק 43 to rub away, beat fine, pulverize (1·4·4) 1007

טִיט mire (1·13) 376

הֲדַק to make dust of, pulverize (1·8·13) 200

רקע to stamp down (1·6·11) 955

פלט 44 to bring into security (2·24·27) 812

נֵכָר 45 that which is foreign (2·36) 648

התכחש to come cringing (1·1·22) 471

נֵכָר 46 that which is foreign (2·36) 648

נבל to sink down (1·20·25[?]) 615

חגר to gird on (5·44·44) 291

מִסְגֶּרֶת fastness (1·17) 689

יֵשַׁע 47 salvation (4·36) 447

נְקָמָה 48 vengeance (2·27) 668

קָם 49 adversary (2·12) 878

זמר 50 to sing [in praise of] (1·43·43) 274

מִגְדּוֹל 51 tower (1·1) 154

Chapter 23

עַל 1 on high (1·7) 752

נָעִים lovely (2·13) 653

זָמִיר song (1·6) 274

מִלָּה 2 word (1·38) 576

יִרְאָה 3 fear, reverence (2·45) 432

זָרַח 4 to rise (1·18·18) 280

עָב dark cloud (2·30) 728

נֹגַהּ brightness (2·19) 618

מָטָר rain (2·37) 564

דֶּשֶׁא grass (1·14) 206

יֵשַׁע 5 welfare, prosperity, salvation (4·36) 447

חֵפֶץ desire, longing, delight (1·39) 343

הצמיח to cause to sprout, grow (1·14·33) 855

בְּלִיַּעַל 6 worthlessness (4·27) 116

קוֹץ thorn (1·1) 881

הדד to be thrust away, chased away (1·2·24) 622

חֲנִית 7 spear (9·46) 333

שֶׁבֶת place (1·7) 443

שָׁלִישׁ 8 adjutant, officer (1·16) 1026

עָדִין voluptuous (1·2) 726

עֶצֶן listed in BDB under עדין only, but not explained (1·1) 726

חֵרֵף 9 to reproach, say sharp things against (2·34·38) 357

יָגַע to grow weary (1·20·26) 388

תְּשׁוּעָה 10 deliverance (3·34) 448

פשט to strip (1·3·43) 833

חַיָּה 11 troop [dub.] (2·3) 312

חֶלְקָה portion of ground (6·24) 324

עֲדָשָׁה lentile (2·4) 727

התיצב 12 to station oneself (4·48·48) 426

חֶלְקָה portion of ground (6·24) 324

תְּשׁוּעָה deliverance (3·34) 448

קָצִיר 13 harvest (4·49) 894

מְעָרָה cave (1·40) 792

חַיָּה troop, community (2·3) 312

מְצוּדָה 14 stronghold (5·18) 845

מַצָּב garrison (1·10) 662

הִתְאַוָּה 15 to desire, long for, lust after (1·16·27) 16

שאב 16 to draw [water] (1·14·14) 980

הֵסִיךְ to pour out (1·13·24[?]) 650

חָלִילָה 17 far be it [from me, you, etc.] (2·20[?]) 321

חֲנִית 18 spear (9·46) 333

פֹּעַל 20 deed, thing done (1·37) 821

אֲרִי lion (2·35) 71

שֶׁלֶג snow (1·20) 1017

חֲנִית 21 spear (9·46) 333

גָּזַל to tear away, seize, rob (1·29·30) 159

מִשְׁמַעַת 23 bodyguard (1·4) 1036

Chapter 24

הֵסִית 1 to instigate (1·18·18) 694

מָנָה to number (1·12·28) 584

שׁוּט 2 to go, rove about (2·7·13) 1001

מִבְצָר 7 fortification (1·37) 131

שׁוּט 8 to go, rove about (2·7·13) 1001

מִפְקָד 9 muster, appointed place (1·5) 824

שָׁלַף to draw out (1·24·24) 1025

נסכל 10 to act foolishly (1·4·8) 698

חֹזֶה 11 seer (1·17) 302

נָטַל 12 to lift (1·3·4) 642

דֶּבֶר 13 plague, pestilence (2·46) 184

רַחֲמִים 14 compassion (1·38) 933

דֶּבֶר 15 plague, pestilence (2·46) 184

הרפה 16 to let drop (1·21·44) 951

גֹּרֶן threshing floor (5·34) 175

הֶעֱוָה 17 to commit iniquity (3·9·17) 731

גֹּרֶן 18 threshing floor (5·34) 175

הִשְׁקִיף 20 to look down (1·12·12) 1054

גֹּרֶן 21 threshing floor (5·34) 175

נעצר to be restrained (2·10·46) 783

מַגֵּפָה plague (4·26) 620

מוֹרַג 22 threshing sledge (1·3) 558

רצה 23 to accept, be pleased with (1·42·50) 958

מְחִיר 24 price (1·15) 564

חִנָּם without cost, out of favor, gratis (1·32) 336

גֹּרֶן threshing floor (5·34) 175

נֶעְתַּר 25 to be entreated (2·8·20) 801

נעצר to be restrained (2·10·46) 783

מַגֵּפָה plague (4·26) 620

1 KINGS

Chapter 1

זָקֵן	1	to be old, become old (2·25·27) 278
חמם		to be warm, grow warm (2·23·26) 328
בְּתוּלָה	2	virgin (1·50) 143
סֹכֶנֶת		servant [female] (2·3) 698
חֵיק		bosom (5·38) 300
חמם		to be warm, grow warm (2·23·26) 328
יָפֶה	3	beautiful (2·40) 421
יָפֶה	4	beautiful (2·40) 421
סֹכֶנֶת		servant [female] (2·3) 698
עצב	6	to pain (1·3·15) 780
כָּכָה		thus (3·33) 462
תֹּאַר		outline, form (1·15) 1061
מְרִיא	9	fatlings (3·8) 597
זֹחֶלֶת		crawling thing, serpent [meaning dub.] (1·1) 267
חֶדֶר	15	chamber, room (3·37) 293
זָקֵן		to be old, become old (2·25·27) 278
קדד	16	to bow down (2·15·15) 869
מְרִיא	19	fatlings (3·8) 597
חַטָּא	21	sinner (1·19) 308
מְרִיא	25	fatlings (3·8) 597
קדד	31	to bow down (2·15·15) 869
פִּרְדָּה	33	she-mule (3·3) 825
נָגִיד	35	ruler (3·44) 617
אָמֵן	36	verily, truly (1·26) 53
פִּרְדָּה	38	she-mule (3·3) 825
חלל	40	to play the pipe (1·1·1) 320
חָלִיל		flute, pipe (1·6) 319
שָׂמֵחַ		glad, joyful, merry (4·21) 970
קִרְיָה	41	town, city (2·30) 900
חמה		to be in a commotion, stir, (1·33·33) 242

בִּשֵּׂר	42	to bear tidings, bear glad tidings (1·14·15) 142
אֲבָל	43	verily, truly, indeed (1·11) 6
פִּרְדָּה	44	she-mule (3·3) 825
שָׂמֵחַ	45	glad, joyful, merry (4·21) 970
הום		to be in a stir (1·3·6) 223
קִרְיָה		town, city (2·30) 900
מְלוּכָה	46	kingship (7·24) 574
מִשְׁכָּב	47	bed (1·46) 1012
כָּכָה	48	thus (3·33) 462
חָרַד	49	to tremble (1·23·39) 353
שַׂעֲרָה	52	a hair (1·7) 972

Chapter 2

עֵדָה	3	testimony (1·32) 730
חֲגוֹרָה	5	girdle, loin covering, belt (1·5) 292
מָתְנַיִם		loins (5·50) 608
נַעַל		sandal (1·22) 653
שֵׂיבָה	6	grey hair, hoary head (3·20[?]) 966
קְלָלָה	8	curse (1·33) 887
נמרץ		to be grievous (1·3·4) 599
נקה	9	to leave unpunished (1·13·37) 667
שֵׂיבָה		grey hair, hoary head (3·20[?]) 966
מְלוּכָה	15	kingship (7·24) 574
שְׁאֵלָה	16	request, petition (2·13) 982
שְׁאֵלָה	20	request, petition (2·13) 982
קָטָן		small (4·47) 881
מְלוּכָה	22	kingship (7·24) 574
פָּגַע	25	to fall upon (6·40·46) 803
גרש	27	to drive out, away (1·34·48) 176
שְׁמוּעָה	28	report (2·27) 1035
פָּגַע	29	to fall upon (6·40·46) 803
פֹּה	30	here, hither (4·44) 805
פָּגַע	31	to fall upon (6·40·46) 803
חִנָּם		without cause (1·32) 336
פָּגַע	32	to fall upon (6·40·46) 803
פָּגַע	34	to fall upon (6·40·46) 803
אָנֶה וְאָנָה	36	where, anywhere (4·37) 33

חֲבֹשׁ 40 to bind up, equip [a beast] for riding (6·28·32) 289

הֵעִיד 42 to testify (3·39·44) 729

אָנֶה וָאָנָה where, anywhere (4·37) 33

שְׁבוּעָה 43 oath (1·30) 989

פָּגַע 46 to fall upon (6·40·46) 803

Chapter 3

הִתְחַתֵּן 1 to make oneself a daughter's husband, form a marriage alliance with (1·11·11) 368

יְשָׁרָה 6 uprightness (1·1) 449

נִמְנָה 8 to be able to be numbered (2·6·28) 584

כָּבֵד 9 massive, abundant (4·39) 458

עֹשֶׁר 11 riches (3·37) 799

נָבוֹן 12 Niph. ptc.: intelligent, discreet; discerning (1·21[?]) 106

עֹשֶׁר 13 riches (3·37) 799

הֶאֱרִיךְ 14 to prolong (2·31·34) 73

יִקָץ 15 to awake (2·11·11) 429

מִשְׁתֶּה feast (1·45) 1059

זוֹנָה 16 ptc.: harlot (2·33[?]) 275

בִּי 17 particle of entreaty craving permission to address a superior, "excuse me" (2·12) 106

זוּלָה 18 except only, save that (2·16) 265

מֵאֵצֶל 19 from beside (2·6) 69

יָשֵׁן 20 to sleep (1·15·16[?]) 445

חֵיק bosom (5·38) 300

הֵינִיק 21 to give suck to (1·10·18) 413

גָּזַר 25 to divide, cut in two (2·6·12) 160

נִכְמַר 26 to grow warm and tender (1·4·4) 485

רֶחֶם womb (1·33) 933

בִּי craving permission to address a superior (2·12) 106

גַּם ... גַּם idiom; with a negative = neither...nor, גַּם, para. 1. 169

גָּזַר to divide, cut in two (2·6·12) 160

Chapter 4

מַזְכִּיר 3 recorder (1·9) 271

נִצָּב 5 deputy (6·7) 662

רֵעֶה friend (1·5) 946

מַס 6 labor band (7·23) 586

נִצָּב 7 deputy (6·7) 662

כִּלְכֵּל to sustain (8·24·38) 465

נֹפָה 11 height (1·4) 632

חַוָּה 13 tent village (1·7) 295

חֶבֶל region, measured portion (3·49) 286

בְּרִיחַ bar (1·41) 138

נְצִיב 19 prefect (1·11) 662

חוֹל 20 sand (2·22) 297

שָׂמֵחַ glad, joyful, merry (4·21) 970

Chapter 5

כֹּר* 2 a measure (4·8) 499

קֶמַח flour, meal (4·14) 887

בָּרִיא 3 fat (1·14) 135

רְעִי pasture (1·1) 945

אַיָּל hart, stag, deer (1·11) 19

צְבִי gazelle (1·11) 840

יַחְמוּר roebuck (1·2) 331

בַּרְבֻּר bird, fowl (1·1) 141

אבס to feed, fatten (1·2·2) 7

רדה 4 to have dominion, to rule (3·22·23) 921

בֶּטַח 5 securely, security (1·43) 105

תְּאֵנָה fig tree, fig (1·39) 1061

אֻרְוָה 6 manger, crib (1·3) 71

כֹּר חֹמֶר* [dry measure] = approx. 394 liters. 331

מֶרְכָּב chariot (1·3) 939

כִּלְכֵּל 7 to sustain (8·24·38) 465

56

נִצָּב   deputy (6·7) 662

קָרֵב   approaching (1·11) 898

עָדַר   to leave lacking (1·1·7) 727

שְׂעֹר   8 barley (1·34) 972

תֶּבֶן   straw (1·17) 1061

רֶכֶשׁ   (coll.) steeds (1·3) 940

תְּבוּנָה   9 the object of knowledge, understanding (2·42) 108

חוֹל   sand (2·22) 297

חכם   11 to be wise, become wise (1·18·26) 314

מָשָׁל   12 poem (2·39) 605

אֵזוֹב   13 hyssop (1·10) 23

רֶמֶשׂ   creeping things (1·16) 943

דָּג   fish (1·19) 185

אֹהֵב   15 friend, lover (1·36[?]) 12

שָׂטָן   18 adversary (4·27) 966

פֶּגַע   occurrence, chance (1·2) 803

שָׂכָר   20 wages (1·29) 969

חֵפֶץ   22 desire, longing (5·39) 343

בְּרוֹשׁ   cypress of fir tree (5·20) 141

דֹּבְרוֹת   23 floats, rafts (1·1) 184

נָפֵץ   to dash to pieces, to break up (1·15·21[?]) 1125

חֵפֶץ   desire, longing (5·39) 343

בְּרוֹשׁ   24 cypress, fir (5·20) 141

חֵפֶץ   desire, longing (5·39) 343

כֹּר •   25 a measure (4·8) 499

חִטָּה   wheat (1·30) 334

מַכֹּלֶת   foodstuff (1·1) 38

כָּתִית   beaten (1·5) 510

מַס   27 labor band (7·23) 586

חֲלִיפָה   28 relay, change (1·12) 322

מַס   labor band (7·23) 586

סַבָּל   29 burden-bearer (1·5) 688

חֹצֵב   ptc.: hewer of stone (1·8[?]) 345

רדה   to have dominion, to rule (3·22·23) 921

יָקָר   31 precious, costly (7·35) 429

יְסַד   to establish (2·10·42) 413

גָּזִית   a cutting, hewing (5·11) 159

פסל   32 to hew out (1·6·6) 820

Chapter 6

קוֹמָה   2 height (13·45) 879

אוּלָם   3 porch (10·49) 17

חַלּוֹן   4 window (1·30) 319

שְׁקוּף   frame, window casing (2·2) 1054

אטם   to shut, stop [up], (1·8·8[?]) 31

יָצִיעַ   5 flat surface (3·3) 427

דְּבִיר   innermost room (11·16) 184

צֵלָע   side chamber, cells (7·39) 854

יָצִיעַ   6 flat surface (3·3) 427

תַּחְתּוֹן   lower, lowest (2·13) 1066

תִּיכוֹן   middle (4·12) 1064

מִגְרָעָה   recess, ledge (1·1) 175

שָׁלֵם   7 finished (5·28) 1023

מַסָּע   quarry (1·1) 652

מַקֶּבֶת   hammer (1·4) 666

גַּרְזֶן   axe (1·4) 173

צֵלָע   8 side chamber, cell (7·39) 854

תִּיכוֹן   middle (4·12) 1064

יְמָנִי   right hand, right (3·33) 412

לוּל   shaft or enclosed space with steps or ladder (1·1) 533

ספן   9 to cover (3·6·6) 706

גֵּב   beam? rafter? (1·3[?]) 155

שְׂדֵרָה   technical terminology of architecture, meaning unknown (1·4) 690

יָצִיעַ   10 flat surface (3·3) 427

קוֹמָה   height (13·45) 879

מִבַּיִת   15 on the inside of (3·9) בַּיִת, para. 8a. 110

צֵלָע   planks, boards (7·39) 854

קַרְקַע   floor (6·8) 903

סִפֻּן   ceiling (1·1) 706

57

צִפָּה — to overlay, plate (13·44·46) 860

בְּרוֹשׁ — cypress, fir (5·20) 141

יַרְכָה 16 extreme parts (1·28) 438

צֶלָע — planks, boards (7·39) 854

קַרְקַע — floor (6·8) 903

מִבַּיִת — on the inside of (3·9) בַּיִת para. 8a. 110

דְּבִיר — innermost room (11·16) 184

לִפְנַי 17 anterior (1·1) 819

פְּנִימָה 18 within (1·5) 819

מִקְלַעַת — carving (4·4) 887

פְּקָעִים — ball or knob-shaped wood or metal ornaments (3·3) 825

פֶּטֶר — to set free (4·8·9) 809

צִיץ — blossom, flower (4·15) 847

דְּבִיר 19 innermost room (11·16) 184

מִפְּנִימָה — within (2·3) 819

דְּבִיר 20 innermost room (11·16) 184

קוֹמָה — height (13·45) 879

צִפָּה — to overlay, plate (13·44·46) 860

סָגוּר — closed up, closely joined (5·8) 688

צִפָּה 21 to overlay, plate (13·44·46) 860

מִפְּנִימָה — within (2·3) 819

סָגוּר — closed up, closely joined (5·8) 688

רַתּוֹק — chain (1·2) 958

דְּבִיר — innermost room (11·16) 184

צִפָּה 22 to overlay, plate (13·44·46) 860

דְּבִיר — innermost room (11·16) 184

דְּבִיר 23 innermost room (11·16) 184

קוֹמָה — height (13·45) 879

קְצוֹת 24 tips (4·7) 892

קֶצֶב 25 shape (2·3) 891

קוֹמָה 26 height (13·45) 879

פְּנִימִי 27 inner (4·33) 819

צִפָּה 28 to overlay, plate (13·44·46) 860

מֵסַב 29 round about (1·5) 687

קָלַע — to carve (3·3·3) 887

פִּתּוּחַ — engraving (1·11) 836

מִקְלַעַת — carving (4·4) 887

תִּמֹרָה — palm [tree] figure (5·19) 1071

פֶּטֶר — to set free (4·8·9) 809

צִצִּים — blossom, flower (4·15) 847

מִלְפָנִים — within (1·1) 819

חִיצוֹן — outer, external (2·25) 300

קַרְקַע 30 floor (6·8) 903

צִפָּה — to overlay, plate (13·44·46) 860

לִפְנִימָה — within (1·5) 819

חִיצוֹן — outer, external (2·25) 300

דְּבִיר 31 innermost room (11·16) 184

אַיִל — projecting pillar or pilaster (1·22) 18

מְזוּזָה — doorpost (3·20) 265

חֲמִשִׁית — fifth part; [Lis. p. 508 "five-cornered"] (1·1[?]) 332

קָלַע 32 to carve (3·3·3) 887

מִקְלַעַת — carving (4·4) 887

תִּמֹרָה — palm [tree] figure (5·19) 1071

פֶּטֶר — to set free (4·8·9) 809

צִיץ — blossom, flower (4·15) 847

צִפָּה — to overlay, plate (13·44·46) 860

הָרַד — to beat out (1·1·3) 921

מְזוּזָה 33 doorpost (3·20) 265

בְּרוֹשׁ 34 cypress, fir (5·20) 141

צֶלָע — leaves of door (7·39) 854

גָּלִיל — turning, folding = revolving (2·4[?]) 165

קֶלַע — curtain, hanging (1·16) 887

קָלַע 35 to carve (3·3·3) 887

תִּמֹרָה — palm [tree] figure (5·19) 1071

פֶּטֶר — to set free (4·8·9) 809

צִיץ — blossom, floor (4·15) 847

צִפָּה — to overlay, plate (13·44·46) 860

יָשַׁר — to be made level (1·1·25) 448

חִקָּה — to cut in, carve; ptc. = carved work (1·3·4) 348

פְּנִימִי 36 inner (4·33) 819

טוּר — row (11·26) 377

גָּזִית — a cutting, hewing (5·11) 159

כְּרֻתֹת — hewn beams (3·3) 503

יֻסַּד 37 — to be founded (2·7·42) 413

יֶרַח — calendar month (3·12) 437

יֶרַח 38 — calendar month (3·12) 437

Chapter 7

קוֹמָה 2 — height (13·45) 879

טוּר — row (11·26) 377

כְּרֻתוֹת — hewn beams (3·3) 503

סִפֻּן 3 — to cover (3·6·6) 706

מִמַּעַל — above, on top of (4·29) 751

צֵלָע — side chambers, cells (7·39) 854

טוּר — row (11·26) 377

שָׁקוּף 4 — frame, window casing (2·2) 1054

טוּר — row (11·26) 377

מֶחֱזָה — light (4·4) 303

מְזוּזָה 5 — doorpost (3·20) 265

רבע — Qal. psv. ptc. = square, squared (1·9·12) 917

שֶׁקֶף — framework, door casing (1·1) 1054

מוּל — front (1·25) 557

מֶחֱזָה — light (4·4) 303

אוּלָם 6 — porch (10·49) 17

עָב — a structure of wood, perhaps projecting roof, beam (1·3) 712

אוּלָם 7 — porch (10·49) 17

סִפֻּן — to cover (3·6·6) 706

קַרְקַע — floor (6·8) 903

מִבֵּית לְ 8 — within (2·9) בַּיִת, para. 8b. 110

אוּלָם — porch (10·49) 17

יָקָר 9 — precious, costly (7·35) 429

גָּזִית — a cutting, hewing (5·11) 159

גרר — ptc. = sawn; to drag, chew (1·1·4) 176

מְגֵרָה — saw (1·3) 176

מִבַּיִת — on the inside; see בַּיִת, para. 8a. 110

מֻסָּד — foundation (1·1) 414

טְפַח — coping [architectural term] (2·9) 381

יֻסַּד 10 — to be founded (2·7·42) 413

יָקָר — precious, costly (7·35) 429

מִלְמַעְלָה 11 — above (3·24) 751

יָקָר — costly, precious (7·35) 429

גָּזִית — a cutting, hewing (5·11) 159

טוּר 12 — row (11·26) 377

גָּזִית — a cutting, hewing (5·11) 159

כְּרֻתֹת — hewn beams (3·3) 503

פְּנִימִי — inner (4·33) 819

אוּלָם — porch (10·49) 17

חרשׁ 14 — to cut in, engrave (2·23·26) 360

תְּבוּנָה — the object of knowledge (2·42) 108

צוּר 15 — to fashion (1·2·2) 849

קוֹמָה — height (13·45) 879

חוּט — line [as a measure of length] (1·7) 296

כֹּתֶרֶת 16 — capital of pillar (14·23) 509

מוּצָק — a casting (1·2) 427

קוֹמָה — height (13·45) 879

שְׂבָכָה 17 — latticework, network (7·16) 959

גְּדִל — festoons on capitals of columns (1·2) 153

שַׁרְשְׁרָה — chain (1·8) 1057

כֹּתֶרֶת — capital of pillar (14·23) 509

טוּר 18 — row (11·26) 377

שְׂבָכָה — latticework, network (7·16) 959

כֹּתֶרֶת — capital of pillar (14·23) 509

רִמּוֹן — pomegranate (4·32) 941

כֹּתֶרֶת 19 — capital of pillar (14·23) 509

שׁוּשַׁן — lily (3·17) 1004

אוּלָם — porch (10·49) 17

כֹּתֶרֶת 20 — capital of pillar (14·23) 509

מִמַּעַל — above, on top of (4·29) 751

מִלְעֻמַּת — close beside (1·1) 769

בֶּטֶן — architectural word = rounded projection, bell, cushion (1·1) para. 4. 106

שְׂבָכָה   latticework, network (7·16) 959

רִמּוֹן   pomegranate (4·32) 941

טוּר   row (11·26) 377

אוּלָם 21   porch (10·49) 17

יְמָנִי   right hand, right (3·33) 412

שְׂמָאלִי   left, on the left (1·9) 970

שׁוּשַׁן 22   lily (3·17) 1004

עָגֹל 23   round (5·6) 722

קוֹמָה   height (13·45) 879

קָו   line (1·17) 876

פְּקָעִים 24   ball or knob-shaped ornaments of carved wood or metal (3·3) 825

הִקִּיף   to encompass (1·16·17) 668

קוֹף   ape (1·2) 880

טוּר   row (11·26) 377

יְצֻקָה   casting (2·2) 427

מִלְמַעְלָה 25   above (3·24) 751

אָחוֹר   hinder part, back part (1·41) 30

בַּיְתָה   inwards (1·6) בית para. 7. 110

עֳבִי 26   thickness (1·5) 716

טֶפַח   span, handbreadth (2·9) 381

כּוֹס   cup (1·31) 468

פֶּרַח   bud, sprout (2·17) 827

שׁוּשָׁן   lily (3·17) 1004

בַּת   measure = 40 litres (2·13) 144

הֵכִיל   to contain (3·12·38) 465

מְכוֹנָה 27   base (15·25) 467

קוֹמה   height (13·45) 879

מְכוֹנָה 28   base (15·25) 467

מִסְגֶּרֶת   border (7·17) 689

שְׁלַבִּים   joining [of bases] (3·3) 1016

מִסְגֶּרֶת 29   border (7·17) 689

שְׁלַבִּים   joining [of bases] (3·3) 1016

אֲרִי   lion (5·36) 71

כֵּן   pedestal (2·17) 487

מִמַּעַל   above, on top of (4·29) 751

לֹיָה   wreath [dub.] (3·3) 531

מוֹרָד   descent (1·5) 434

אוֹפַן 30   wheel (5·34) 66

מְכוֹנָה   base (15·25) 467

סֶרֶן   axle (1·1) 710

כִּיּוֹר   basin (7·23) 468

לֹיָה   wreath [dub.] (3·3) 531

מִבֵּית לְ 31   inside, para. 8b. בית 110

כֹּתֶרֶת   capital of pillar (14·23) 509

עָגֹל   round (5·6) 722

כֵּן   pedestal (2·17) 487

מִקְלַעַת   carving (4·4) 887

מִסְגֶּרֶת   border (7·17) 689

רבע   pual ptc. = square (1·3·12) 917

אוֹפַן 32   wheel (5·34) 66

לְמִתַּחַת   under, beneath (1·1) 1066

מִסְגֶּרֶת   border (7·17) 689

יָד   axletree, idiom inder יָד, para. 4 d. (2·2) 390

מְכוֹנָה   base (15·25) 467

קוֹמָה   height (13·45) 879

אוֹפַן 33   wheel (5·34) 66

מֶרְכָּבָה   chariot (5·44) 939

יָד   axletree, idiom inder יָד, para. 4d. (2·2) 390

גַּב   rim of wheel, anything convex (1·13) 146

חִשֻּׁקִים   spokes of a wheel (1·1) 366

חִשֻּׁרִים   hubs of wheels (1·1) 366

פִּנָּה 34   corner (1·30) 819

מְכוֹנָה   base (15·25) 467

מְכוֹנָה 35   base (15·25) 467

קוֹמָה   height (13·45) 879

עָגֹל   round (5·6) 722

יָד   stays, idiom under יָד, para. 4e. "hand" (4·6) 390

מִסְגֶּרֶת   border (7·17) 689

פתח 36   to engrave (1·8·9) 836

לוּחַ   plate (2·40) 531

יָד — stays, idiom under יָד, para. 4e. "hand" (4·6) 390

מִסְגֶּרֶת — border (7·17) 689

אֲרִי — lion (5·35) 71

תִּמֹרָה — palm [tree] figure (5·19) 1071

מַעַר — bare place (1·2[?]) 789

לֹיָה — wreath [dub.] (3·3) 531

מְכוֹנָה — 37 base (15·25) 467

מוּצָק — a casting (1·2) 427

קֶצֶב — shape (2·3) 891

כִּיּוֹר — 38 basin (7·23) 468

בַּת — measure = 40 litres (2·13) 144

הֵכִיל — to contain (3·12·38) 465

מְכוֹנָה — base (15·25) 467

מְכוֹנָה — 39 base (15·25) 467

יְמָנִי — right hand, right (3·33) 412

קֶדֶם — eastward (2·26) 870

מִמּוּל — from the front of (1·9) 557

כִּיּוֹר — 40 basin (7·23) 468

יָע — shovel (2·9) 418

מִזְרָק — basin (3·32) 284

גֻּלָּה — 41 bowl or globe shape, bowl, basin (3·15) 165

כֹּתֶרֶת — capital of pillar (14·23) 509

שְׂבָכָה — latticework, network (7·16) 959

גֻּלָּה — bowl or globe shape, bowl, basin (3·15) 165

רִמּוֹן — 42 pomegranate (4·32) 941

שְׂבָכָה — latticework, network (7·16) 959

טוּר — row (11·26) 377

גֻּלָּה — bowl or globe shape, bowl, basin (3·15) 165

כֹּתֶרֶת — capital of pillar (14·23) 509

מְכוֹנָה — 43 base (15·25) 467

כִּיּוֹר — basin (7·23) 468

סִיר — 45 pot (1·29) 696

יָע — shovel (2·9) 418

מִזְרָק — basin (3·32) 284

מרט — to be polished (1·5·14) 598

מַעֲבֶה — 46 compactness (1·1[?]) 716

נֶחְקַר — 47 to be searched out, found out (1·4·27) 350

מִשְׁקָל — wieght (2·48) 1054

מְנוֹרָה — 49 lampstand (1·39) 633

דְּבִיר — innermost room (11·16) 184

סָגוּר — closely joined (5·8) 688

פֶּרַח — bud, sprout (2·17) 827

נֵר — lamp (1·44) 632

מֶלְקָחַיִם — snuffers (1·6) 544

סַף — 50 basin (1·6) 706

מְזַמֶּרֶת — snuffers (1·5) 275

מִזְרָק — basin (3·32) 284

כַּף — pan, vessel [hollow] para. 4b. 497

מַחְתָּה — firepan (1·21) 367

סָגוּר — closely joined (5·8) 688

פֹּת — sockets [for door pivots, (dub.)] (1·2) 834

פְּנִימִי — inner (4·33) 819

Chapter 8

הִקְהִיל — 1 to summon an assembly (2·20·39) 874

נִקְהַל — 2 to assemble (1·19·39) 874

יֶרַח — month (3·12) 437

אֵיתָן — 4 steady flowing, month of steady flowing = 7th month [Oct–Nov] (1·14) 450

נוֹעַד — 5 to assemble by appointment (1·18·28) 416

נִמְנָה — to be numbered (2·6·28) 584

דְּבִיר — 6 innermost room (11·16) 184

סָכַךְ — 7 to cover (1·12·18[?]) 696

בַּד — pole, stave (3·41) 94

מִלְמַעְלָה — above (3·24) 751

הֶאֱרִיךְ — 8 to be long (2·31·34) 73

בַּד — pole, stave (3·41) 94

דְּבִיר innermost room (11·16) 184

לוּחַ 9 tablet (2·40) 531

עֲרָפֶל 12 cloud, heavy cloud (1·15) 791

זְבֻל 13 elevation, height, lofty abode (1·5) 259

מָכוֹן fixed or established place (4·17) 467

הטיב to do well (1·3·20) 373

חָלָץ 19 only in dual form = loins (1·10) 323

מִמַּעַל 23 above, on top of (4·29) 751

אָמְנָם 27 verily, truly, indeed (1·5) 53

כִּלְכֵּל to contain (8·24·38) 465

תְּחִנָּה 28 supplication for favor (9·25) 337

רִנָּה ringing cry (2·33) 943

תְּחִנָּה 30 supplication for favor (9·25) 337

סלח to forgive (5·33·46) 699

אָלָה 31 oath (2·36) 46

האלה to put under oath (1·3·6) 46

הִרְשִׁיעַ 32 to condemn as guilty (1·25·34) 957

הִצְדִּיק to declare righteous, justify (1·12·41) 842

נָגַף 33 to be smitten (1·23·48) 619

סלח 34 to forgive (5·33·46) 699

נעצר 35 to be shut up, restrained (1·10·46) 783

מָטָר rain (4·37) 564

סלח 36 to forgive (5·33·46) 699

הורה to teach (1·45·45) 434

מָטָר rain (4·37) 564

דֶּבֶר 37 plague, pestilence (1·46) 184

שִׁדָּפוֹן smut (1·5) 995

יֵרָקוֹן rust (1·6) 439

אַרְבֶּה a kind of locust (1·24) 916

חָסִיל a kind of locust (1·6) 340

מַחֲלָה sickness, disease (1·4) 318

תְּחִנָּה 38 supplication for favor (9·25) 337

מָכוֹן 39 fixed or established place (4·17) 467

סלח to forgive (5·33·46) 699

נָכְרִי 41 foreigner (4·45) 648

מָכוֹן 43 fixed or established place (4·17) 467

נָכְרִי foreigner (4·45) 648

תְּחִנָּה 45 supplication for favor (9·25) 337

אנף 46 to be angry (1·8·14) 60

שָׁבָה to take captive (2·29·37) 985

שֹׁבֶה captives (3·9) 985

נִשְׁבָּה 47 to be taken captive (1·8·37) 985

שֹׁבֶה captives (3·9) 985

הֶעֱוָה to commit iniquity (1·9·17[?]) 731

רשע to be wicked, act wickedly (1·9·34) 957

שָׁבָה 48 to take captive (2·29·37) 985

מָכוֹן 49 fixed or established placed (4·17) 467

תְּחִנָּה supplication for favor (9·25) 337

סלח 50 to forgive (5·33·46) 699

פָּשַׁע to transgress (2·40·41) 833

רַחֲמִים compassion (1·38) 933

שֹׁבֶה captives (3·9) 985

רִחַם to have compassion (1·41·46) 933

כּוּר 51 furnace (1·8) 468

תְּחִנָּה 52 supplication for favor (9·25) 337

הִבְדִּיל 53 to separate (1·32·42) 95

תְּחִנָּה 54 supplication for favor (9·25) 337

כָּרַע to bow (2·29·35) 502

בֶּרֶךְ knee (3·25) 139

מְנוּחָה 56 rest (1·21) 629

נָטַשׁ 57 to forsake (1·33·40) 643

שָׁלֵם 61 complete, perfect (5·28) 1023

חָנַךְ 63 to dedicate (1·5·5) 335

הכיל to contain (3·12·38) 465

שָׂמֵחַ 66 glad, rejoicing, merry (4·21) 970

Chapter 9

חֵשֶׁק 1 desire = thing desired (2·4) 366

תְּחִנָּה 3 supplication for favor (9·25) 337

תָּם 4 integrity (2·23) 1070

יֹשֶׁר uprightness (1·14) 449

מָשָׁל 7 byword (2·39) 605

שְׁנִינָה sharp word, taunt (1·4) 1042

שָׁרַק to hiss (1·12·12) 1056

כָּכָה thus (3·33) 462

בְּרוֹשׁ 11 cypress, fir (5·20) 141

חֵפֶץ desire, longing (5·39) 343

יָשַׁר 12 to be pleasing (1·13·25) 448

מַס 15 labor band (7·23) 586

שִׁלּוּחִים 16 parting gift (1·3) 1019

תַּחְתּוֹן 17 lower, lowest (2·13) 1066

מִסְכְּנוֹת 19 storage (1·7) 698

חֵשֶׁק desire = thing desired (2·4) 366

חָשַׁק to love (1·8·11) 365

מֶמְשָׁלָה dominion (1·17) 606

הֶחֱרִים 21 to ban, devote to destruction (1·46·49) 355

מַס labor band (7·23) 586

שָׁלִישׁ 22 adjutant, officer (1·16) 1026

נִצָּב 23 deputy (6·7) 662

רדה to have dominion, to rule (3·22·23) 921

אֳנִי 26 ships, fleet (6·7) 58

אֳנִי 27 ships, fleet (6·7) 58

אֳנִיָּה ship (4·31) 58

Chapter 10

מַלְכָּה 1 queen (4·35) 573

שֵׁמַע hearing, report (1·17) 1034

נִסָּה to test (1·36·36) 650

חִידָה perplexing question, riddle (1·17) 295

כָּבֵד 2 numerous (4·39) 458

בֹּשֶׂם spice, balsam (4·30) 141

יָקָר precious (7·35) 429

נֶעְלַם 3 to be concealed (1·11·29) 761

מַלְכָּה 4 queen (4·35) 573

מַאֲכָל 5 food (1·30) 38

מוֹשָׁב sitting company, assembly (1·43) 444

מַעֲמָד service (1·5) 765

מְשָׁרֵת servant (1·20) 1058

מַלְבּוּשׁ raiment (1·8) 528

מַשְׁקֶה cupbearer (2[?]·19[?]) 1052

שְׁמוּעָה 7 report (2·27) 1035

אֶשֶׁר 8 happiness, blessedness (2·44) 80–81

בֹּשֶׂם 10 spice, balsam (4·30) 141

יָקָר precious (7·35) 429

מַלְכָּה queen (1·35) 573

אֳנִי 11 ships, fleet (6·7) 58

אַלְמֻגִּים trees; Lis. sandalwood (3·6) 38

יָקָר precious (7·35) 429

אַלְמֻגִּים 12 trees (3·6) 38

מִסְעָד support (1·1) 703

כִּנּוֹר lyre (1·41) 490

נֶבֶל harp (1·27) 614

שָׁר singer (1·9) 1010

מַלְכָּה 13 queen (4·35) 573

חֵפֶץ desire, longing (5·39) 343

מִלְּבַד besides (1·33) 94

מִשְׁקָל 14 weight (2·48) 1054

תָּר 15 merchants (1·2) 1064

מִסְחָר merchandise [dub.] (1·1) 695

רֹכֵל trader (1·17) 940

עֶרֶב mixed company, i.e., foreigners (1·2) 786

פֶּחָה governor (2·28) 808

צִנָּה 16 large shield [covering whole body] (2·20) 857

שחט Qal. pass. ptc. = beaten, hammered (2·6·6) 1006

שחט 17 Qal pass. ptc. = beaten, hammered (2·6·6) 1006

מָנֶה mina (1·5) 584

צִפָּה 18 to overlay, plate (13·44·46) 860

הפז to be refined [dub.] (1·1) 808

מַעֲלָה 19 stair (2·47) 752

עָגֹל round (5·6) 722

63

יָד	stays, idiom under "hand," para. 4e. יַד (4·6) 390
מִזֶּה וּמִזֶּה	on the one side . . . on the other, para. 6e. זֶה 262
אֲרִי	lion (5·36) 71
אֲרִי	20 lion (5·36) 71
מַעֲלָה	stair (2·47[?]) 752
מִזֶּה וּמִזֶּה	on the one side . . . on the other, para. 6e. זֶה 262
מַשְׁקֶה	21 drink (2·19[?]) 1052
סָגוּר	closely joined (5·8) 688
לִמְאוּמָה	anything (1·2) 548
אֳנִי	22 ships, fleet (6·7) 58
שֶׁנְהַבִּים	ivory (1·2) 1042
קוֹף	ape (1·2) 880
תֻּכִּיִּים	peacocks (1·2) 1067
עֹשֶׁר	23 riches (3·37) 799
שַׂלְמָה	25 clothes (3·16) 971
נֶשֶׁק	equipment, weapons (1·10) 676
בֹּשֶׂם	spice, balsam (4·30) 141
פֶּרֶד	mule (2·14) 825
הנחה	26 to lead (1·26·40) 634
נתן כ ...	27 to make [to be] like, para. 3c. נתן 681
שִׁקְמָה	sycamore tree (1·7) 1054
שְׁפֵלָה	lowland (1·20) 1050
מוֹצָא	28 that which goes forth, export (1·27) 425
מִקְוֵה	collection, company (2·7) 876
סֹחֵר	trader (1·16) 695
מְחִיר	price (2·15) 564
מֶרְכָּבָה	29 chariot (5·44) 939

Chapter 11

נָכְרִי	1 foreign (4·45) 648
אָכֵן	2 surely, truly (1·19) 38
שָׂרָה	3 princess, noble lady (1·5) 979
פִּלֶגֶשׁ	concubine (1·37) 811
זִקְנָה	4 old age (2·6) 279

שָׁלֵם	complete, perfect (5·28) 1023
שִׁקֵּץ	5 detested thing (3·28) 1055
שִׁקֵּץ	7 detested thing (3·28) 1055
נָכְרִי	8 foreign (4·45) 648
הִתְאַנַּף	9 to be angry (1·6·14) 60
שָׂטָן	14 adversary (4·27) 966
קָטָן	17 young (4·47) 881
גְּבִירָה	19 queen (2·15) 150
גָּמַל	20 to wean (1·34·37) 168
חָסֵר	22 lacking (1·17) 341
שָׂטָן	23 adversary (4·27) 966
גְּדוּד	24 band, troop (1·33) 151
שָׂטָן	25 adversary (4·27) 966
קוּץ	to feel a loathing, to abhor (1·8·8) 880
פֶּרֶץ	27 breach (1·18) 829
סֵבֶל	28 burden, burdensome labor (1·3) 687
שַׂלְמָה	29 outer garment (3·16) 971
שַׂלְמָה	30 outer garment (3·16) 971
קְרָעִים	torn piece [of garment], rag (2·4) 902
קְרָעִים	31 torn piece [of garment], rag (2·4) 902
מְלוּכָה	35 kingship (7·27) 574
נִיר	36 lamp (2·5) 633
אִוָּה	37 to desire (1·16·27) 16

Chapter 12

הִקְשָׁה	4 to make severe (1·21·28) 904
עֹל	yoke (8·40) 760
כָּבֵד	heavy (4·39) 458
קָשָׁה	severe (3·36) 904
עֹל	9 yoke (8·40) 760
עֹל	10 yoke (8·40) 760
קֹטֶן	little [finger] (1·2) 882
עבה	to be thick (1·3·3) 716
מָתְנַיִם	loins (5·50) 608
הֶעְמִיס	11 to load (1·2·9) 1126/770
עֹל	yoke (8·40) 760
כָּבֵד	heavy (4·39) 458

יִסֵּר to chasten (4·30·41) 415

שׁוֹט whip, scourge (2·8) 1002

עַקְרָב scorpion (2·9) 785

קָשָׁה 13 severe (3·36) 904

עֹל 14 yoke (8·40) 760

יִסֵּר to chasten (4·30·41) 415

שׁוֹט whip, scourge (2·8) 1002

עַקְרָב scorpion (2·9) 785

סִבָּה 15 turn [of affairs] (1·1) 686

מַס 18 labor band (7·23) 586

רגם to kill by stoning, to stone (1·15·15) 920

הִתְאַמֵּץ to make oneself alert, make haste (1·4·41) 54

מֶרְכָּבָה chariot (5·44) 939

פָּשַׁע 19 to rebel, revolt (2·41) 833

זוּלָה 20 except, besides (2·16) 265

הִקְהִיל 21 to summon an assembly (2·20·39) 874

בָּחוּר chosen (1·19[?]) 103

מְלוּכָה kingship (7·24) 574

עֵגֶל 28 calf (2·35) 722

קְצוֹת 31 whole (4·7) 892

עֵגֶל 32 calf (2·35) 722

בָּדָא 33 to devise (1·2·2) 94

Chapter 13

מוֹפֵת 3 sign (3·36) 68

דֶּשֶׁן fat ashes (2·15) 206

דֶּשֶׁן 5 fat ashes (2·15) 206

מוֹפֵת sign (3·36) 68

סָעַד 7 to sustain (1·12·12) 703

מַתָּת gift (1·6) 682

אֵי 12 where? (2·39) 32

חבשׁ 13 to bind up, equip [a beast] for riding (6·28·32) 289

אֵלָה 14 terebinth, a deciduous tree with pinnate leaves and red berries; grows

to great age (1·17) 18

כָּחַשׁ 18 to deceive (1·19·22) 471

מָרָה 21 to be rebellious (2·21·43) 598

נְבֵלָה 22 corpse (10·48) 615

חבשׁ 23 to bind up, equip [a beast] for riding (6·28·32) 289

אַרְיֵה 24 lion (8·45) 71

נְבֵלָה corpse (10·48) 615

נְבֵלָה 25 corpse (10·48) 615

אַרְיֵה lion (8·45) 71

מָרָה 26 to be rebellious (2·21·43) 598

אַרְיֵה lion (8·45) 71

חבשׁ 27 to bind up, equip [a beast] for riding (6·28·32) 289

נְבֵלָה 28 corpse (10·48) 615

אַרְיֵה lion (8·45) 71

נְבֵלָה 29 corpse (10·48) 615

ספד to lament (4·27·29) 704

נְבֵלָה 30 corpse (10·48) 615

ספד to lament (4·27·29) 704

קְצוֹת 33 whole (4·7) 892

חָפֵץ delight in, have pleasure in (2·12) 343

הִכְחִיד 34 to annihilate (1·6·30) 470

Chapter 14

הִשְׁתַּנָּה 2 to disguise oneself (1·1·26[?]) 1039

אַתִּי you [fem.; old form] (1·7) 61

נָקֻד 3 a kind of [hard] biscuit or cake [?] (1·3) 666

בַּקְבֻּק flask (1·3) 132

קום 4 idiomatic use of קום here meaning to be set, fixed, without vision. Qal. para. 7j. 878

שִׂיב old [hoary] age (3·20[?]) 966

זֹה 5 this; this and thus כָּזֹה כָזֶה (1·11) 272

הִתְנַכֵּר to feign to be a stranger (2·3·8) 649

הִתְנַכֵּר 6 to feign to be a stranger (2·3·8) 649

65

קָשֶׁה severe, with a severe message (3·36) 904

נָגִיד 7 ruler (3·44) 617

מַסֵּכָה 9 molten image (1·25) 651

גּו back (1·3); הִשְׁלִיךְ אַחֲרֵי גַו = to put out of mind, ignore, reject 156

הִשְׁתִּין 10 to urinate, מַשְׁתִּין בְּקִיר = a male person (3·6·6) 1010

עָצַר to restrain, retain (3·36·46) 783

בָּעַר to burn, consume (4·26·28) 129

גָּלָל dung (1·2) 165

כֶּלֶב 11 dog (7·32) 476

ספד 13 to lament (4·27·29) 704

נוד 15 to waver (1·19·26) 626

נָתַשׁ to pull up (1·17·22) 684

זרה to scatter, disperse (1·25·38) 279

אֲשֵׁרָה Canaanite goddess of fortune and happiness; sacred pole representing her (5·40) 81

בִּגְלַל 16 on account of (1·10) 164

סַף 17 threshold (1·25) 706

ספד 18 to lament (4·27·29) 704

קִנֵּא 22 to excite to jealous anger (5·30·34) 888

מַצֵּבָה 23 stump (1·35) 663

אֲשֵׁרָה Canaanite goddess of fortune and happiness (5·40) 81

גָּבֹהַּ high, exalted (1·41) 147

רַעֲנָן luxuriant, fresh (1·19) 947

קָדֵשׁ 24 temple prostitute [male] (3·11) 873

רָץ 27 runner (3·25) 930

מִדֵּי 28 out of the abundance of, i.e., as often as (1·15) 191

רָץ runner (3·25) 930

תָּא chamber (1·13) 1060

Chapter 15

שָׁלֵם 3 complete, perfect (5·28) 1023

נִיר 4 lamp (2·5) 633

קָדֵשׁ 12 temple prostitute [male] (3·11) 873

גִּלּוּל idol (2·48) 165

גְּבִרָה 13 queen mother (2·15) 150

מִפְלֶצֶת horrid thing (2·4) 814

אֲשֵׁרָה Canaanite goddess of fortune and happiness (5·40) 81

שָׁלֵם 14 complete, perfect (5·28) 1023

שֹׁחַד 19 present, bribe (1·23) 1005

הֵפֵר to break, frustrate (1·41·43) 830

נָקִי 22 exempt from obligations (1·43) 667

זִקְנָה 23 old age (2·6) 279

קָשַׁר 27 to conspire (4·36·44) 905

צוּר to shut in, besiege (3·31·31) 848

נְשָׁמָה 29 every breathing thing (2·24) 675

כַּעַס 30 vexation, anger (2·25[?]) 495

Chapter 16

נָגִיד 2 ruler (3·44) 617

הִבְעִיר 3 to consume, destroy (1·2·28) 129

כֶּלֶב 4 dog (7·32) 476

קָשַׁר 9 to conspire (4·36·44) 905

מַחֲצִית half (1·16) 345

שִׁכּוֹר drunken (2·13) 1016

הִשְׁתִּין 11 to urinate, מַשְׁתִּין בְּקִיר = a male person (3·6·6) 1010

גֹּאֵל [redeemer-] kinsman (1·44[?]) 145

קָשַׁר 16 to conspire (4·36·44) 905

צוּר 17 to shut in, beseige (3·31·31) 848

אַרְמוֹן 18 citadel, stronghold, palace (1·33) 74

קֶשֶׁר 20 conspiracy (1·14) 905

קָשַׁר to conspire (4·36·44) 905

אֲשֵׁרָה 33 sacred tree or pole representing Canaanite goddess of fortune and happiness (5·40) 81

יָסַד 34 to found (2·10·42) 413

צָעִיר little, young (1·22) 859

Chapter 17

תּוֹשָׁב	1 sojourner (1·14) 444
טַל	dew (1·31) 378
מָטָר	rain (4·37) 564
קֶדֶם	3 eastward (2·26) 870
עֹרֵב	4 raven (2·12) 788
כִּלְכֵּל	to sustain (8·24·38) 465
עֹרֵב	6 raven (2·12) 788
גֶּשֶׁם	7 rain, shower (5·35) 177
כִּלְכֵּל	9 to sustain (8·24·38) 465
קוֹשֵׁשׁ	10 to gather stubble (2·6·8) 905
פַּת	11 fragment, bit, morsel (1·14) 837
מָעוֹג	12 cake (1·2) 728
מְלֹא	fullness (1·38) 571
קֶמַח	flour, meal (4·14) 887
כַּד	jar (4·18) 461
צַפַּחַת	jar, jug (4·7) 860
קוֹשֵׁשׁ	to gather stubble (2·6·8) 905
עֻגָה	13 cake of bread (2·7) 728
קָטֹן	small (4·47) 881
כַּד	14 jar (4·18) 461
קֶמַח	flour, meal (4·14) 887
צַפַּחַת	jar, jug (4·7) 860
חָסֵר	to be lacking, to need (2·20·24) 341
גֶּשֶׁם	rain (5·35) 177
כַּד	16 jar (4·18) 461
קֶמַח	flour, meal (4·14) 887
צַפַּחַת	jar, jug (4·7) 860
חָסֵר	to be lacking, to need (2·20·24) 341
בַּעֲלָה	17 mistress (1·4) 128
חֳלִי	sickness (1·24) 318
נְשָׁמָה	breath (2·24) 675
מַה לִּי וָלָךְ, מַה	18 what have I to do with you? para. 1d. 553
חֵיק	bosom (5·38) 300
עֲלִיָּה	roof chamber (2·20) 751
מִטָּה	bed (2·29) 641
עֲלִיָּה	23 roof chamber (2·20) 751

Chapter 18

מָטָר	1 rain (4·37) 564
הֶחְבִּיא	4 to hide (2·6·34) 285
מְעָרָה	cave (4·40) 792
כִּלְכֵּל	to sustain (8·24·38) 465
מַעְיָן	5 spring (1·23) 745
אוּלַי	perhaps (3·45) 19
חָצִיר	green grass, herbage (1·18[?]) 348
פֶּרֶד	mule (2·14) 825
הִכִּיר	7 to recognize (2·37·40) 647
נְעוּרִים	12 youth (1·46) 655
הֶחְבִּיא	13 to hide (2·6·34) 285
מְעָרָה	cave (4·40) 792
כִּלְכֵּל	to sustain (8·24·38) 465
עָכַר	17 to disturb, trouble (2·12·14) 747
עָכַר	18 to disturb, trouble (2·12·14) 747
אֲשֵׁרָה	19 Canaanite goddess of fortune and happiness (5·40) 81
מָתַי	21 when? with עַד before = until when? how long? (1·42) 607
פסח	to limp (1·5·7) 820
סְעִיפָּה	division, divided opinion (1·1) 704
נִתַּח	23 to cut up into pieces (2·9·9) 677
צָהֳרַיִם	26 midday, noon (4·23) 843
פסח	to go limping (1·1·7) 820
צָהֳרַיִם	27 midday, noon (4·23) 843
הִתֵּל	to deceive, mock (1·1·1) 251
שִׂיחַ	musing (1·14) 967
שִׂיג	a moving back, away (1·1) 691
אוּלַי	perhaps (3·45) 19
יָשֵׁן	sleeping (2·9) 445
יקץ	to awake (2·11·11) 429
הִתְגּדַד	28 to cut oneself (1·7·8) 151
רֹמַח	spear, lance (1·15) 942
צָהֳרַיִם	29 midday, noon (4·23) 843
קֶשֶׁב	attention, one who pays attention, attentiveness (1·4) 904
הָרַס	30 to throw down (3·30·43) 248

67

תְּעָלָה 32 trench (3·9) 752

סְאָה   a measure of grain (1·9)

בְּבֵית סָאתַיִם   like a receptacle holding 2 seahs. בַּיִת, para. 3. 109

נָתַח 33 to cut up into pieces (2·9·9) 677

כַּד 34 jar (4·18) 461

שָׁנָה   to repeat (2·13·26[?]) 1040

שִׁלֵּשׁ   to do a third time (2·4·9) 1026

תְּעָלָה 35 trench (3·9) 752

אֲחֹרַנִּית 37 backwards (1·7) 30

תְּעָלָה 38 trench (3·9) 752

לָחַךְ   to lick up (1·5·6) 535

גֶּשֶׁם 41 rain, shower (5·35) 177

גָּהַר 42 to bend, crouch (1·3·3) 155

בֶּרֶךְ   knee (3·25) 139

מְאוּמָה 43 anything (2·32) 548

עָב 44 dark cloud (2·30) 728

קָטֹן   small (4·47) 881

עָצַר   to restrain, retain (3·36·46) 783

גֶּשֶׁם   rain, shower (5·35) 177

עַד כֹּה וְעַד כֹּה 45 till now and till then, i.e., meanwhile (1·1) כֹּה, para. 3. 462

הִתְקַדֵּר   to grow dark (1·1·17) 871

עָב   dark cloud (2·30) 728

גֶּשֶׁם   rain, shower (5·35) 177

שִׁנֵּס 46 to gird up (1·1·1) 1042

מָתְנַיִם   loins (5·50) 608

Chapter 19

רֹתֶם 4 broom plant, retem (2·4) 958

יָשַׁן 5 to sleep (1·15·16[?]) 445

רֹתֶם   broom plant, retem (2·4) 958

מְרַאֲשׁוֹת 6 place at the head (1·10) 912

עֻגָה   cake of bread (2·7) 728

רֶצֶף   glowing stone, coal (1·2) 954

צַפַּחַת   jar, jug (4·7) 860

אֲכִילָה 8 a meal (1·1) 38

מְעָרָה 9 cave (4·40) 792

פֹּה   here, hither (4·44) 805

קִנֵּא 10 to be zealous (5·30·34) 888

הָרַס   to tear down, throw down (3·30·43) 248

פָּרַק 11 to tear off (1·3·10) 830

רַעַשׁ   earthquake (3·17) 950

רַעַשׁ 12 earthquake (3·17) 950

דְּמָמָה   whisper, silence (1·3) 199

דַּק   small, thin (1·14) 201

הֶלִיט 13 to wrap (1·1·5) 532

אַדֶּרֶת   cloak, mantle (2·12) 12

מְעָרָה   cave (4·40) 792

פֹּה   here, hither (4·44) 805

קִנֵּא 14 to be zealous, to tear down (5·30·43) 888

הָרַס   to tear down, throw down (3·30·43) 248

בֶּרֶךְ 18 knee (3·25) 139

כָּרַע   to bow (2·29·35) 502

נָשַׁק   to kiss (2·26·32) 676

חָרַשׁ 19 to plough (2·23·26) 360

צֶמֶד   couple, pair; span [of oxen] (2·15) 855

אַדֶּרֶת   cloak, mantle (2·12) 12

נָשַׁק 20 to kiss (2·26·32) 676

צֶמֶד 21 couple, pair, span [of oxen] (2·15) 855

בִּשֵּׁל   to cook (1·20·27) 143

Chapter 20

צוּר 1 to shut in, besiege (3·31·31) 848

חִפֵּשׂ 6 to search through, search (1·8·23) 344

מַחְמָד   desire (1·13) 326

מָנַע 7 to withhold (1·25·29) 586

שָׂפַק 10 to suffice (1·1·1[?]) 974

שֹׁעַל   handful (1·3) 1043

חָגַר 11 to gird on (2·44·44) 291

סֻכָּה	12 booth (2·31) 697		אֲפֵר	covering, bandage (2·2) 68

סֻכָּה 12 booth (2·31) 697

בְּמִי 14 by whom? (1·1) 566

אָסַר הַמִּלְ to begin the battle [?·?] 536

צָהֳרַיִם 16 midday, noon (4·23) 843

שִׁכּוֹר drunken (2·13) 1016

סֻכָּה booth (2·31) 697

מַכָּה 21 slaughter (2·48) 646

תְּשׁוּבָה 22 return (2·8) 1000

אוּלָם 23 but, but indeed (1·19) 19

מִישׁוֹר plain (2·23) 449

פֶּחָה 24 governor (2·28) 808

מָנָה 25 to number (1·12·28) 584

מִישׁוֹר plain (2·23) 449

תְּשׁוּבָה 26 return (2·8) 1000

כִּלְכֵּל 27 to be supplied (1·1·36) 465

חָשִׂיף little flock [dub.] (1·1) [based on versions] 362

נֹכַח 29 opposite to, in front of (2·22) 647

רַגְלִי on foot; as substantive = foot soldiery, infantry (1·12) 920

חֶדֶר 30 room, chamber (3·37) 293

שַׂק 31 sack cloth (4·48) 974

מָתְנַיִם loins (5·50) 608

חֶבֶל cord (3·49) 286

אוּלַי perhaps (3·45) 19

חגר 32 to gird on (2·44·44) 291

שַׂק sack cloth (4·48) 974

מָתְנַיִם loins (5·50) 608

חֶבֶל cord (3·49) 286

נָחַשׁ 33 to observe signs (1·9·9) 638

חלט to snatch, catch (1·1·1) 319

מֶרְכָּבָה chariot (5·44) 939

מֵאֵן 35 to refuse (2·45·45) 549

אַרְיֵה 36 lion (8·45) 71

מֵאֵצֶל from beside (2·6) 69

פצע 37 to wound [by bruising] (1·3·3) 822

הִתְחַפֵּשׂ 38 to disguise oneself [let one be searched for] (3·8·23) 344

אֲפֵר covering, bandage (2·2) 68

שָׁקַל 39 to weigh out (1·19·22) 1053

הֵנָּה וְהֵנָּה 40 hitherwards and thitherwards = in different directions (2·49) 244

חָרַץ to decide, cut, sharpen (1·5·10) 358

אֲפֵר 41 covering, bandage (2·2) 68

הִכִּיר to recognize (2·37·40) 647

חֵרֶם 42 devotion, ban involving destruction (1·29) 356

סַר 43 sullen, stubborn, resentful (3·3) 711

זָעֵף out of humor, vexed (2·2) 277

Chapter 21

גַּן 2 garden (1·41) 171

יָרָק herbs (1·3) 438

מְחִיר price (2·15) 564

חָלִילָה 3 far be it [from me, you etc.] (1·21) 321

סַר 4 sullen, stubborn, resentful (3·3) 711

זָעֵף out of humor, vexed (2·2) 277

מִטָּה bed (2·29) 641

סַר 5 sullen, stubborn, resentful (3·3) 711

חָפֵץ 6 delighting in, having pleasure in (2·12) 343

מְלוּכָה 7 kingship (7·24) 574

חתם 8 to seal, affix one's seal (1·23·27) 367

חֹתָם seal, signet ring (1·13) 368

חֹר noble (2·13) 359

צוֹם 9 fast, fasting (2·25) 847

בְּלִיַּעַל 10 good for nothing, worthless (3·27) 116

הֵעִיד to testify (3·39·44) 729

סקל to stone (2·12·22) 709

ברך* see note on p. 70

חֹר 11 noble (2·13) 359

צוֹם 12 fast, fasting (2·25) 847

בְּלִיַּעַל 13 good for nothing, worthless (3·27) 116

הֵעִיד to testify (3·39·44) 729

69

סָקַל to stone (2·12·22) 709

בֵּרֵךְ* see note below

סָקַל 14 to be stoned (2·2·22) 709

סָקַל 15 to be stoned (2·2·22) 709

מֵאֵן to refuse (2·45·45) 549

רָצַח 19 to murder, slay (1·38·43) 953

לקק to lick (3·5·7) 545

כֶּלֶב dog (7·32) 476

בָּעַר 21 to burn, consume (4·26·28) 129

הִשְׁתִּין to urinate, מַשְׁתִּין בְּקִיר = a male person (3·6·6) 1010

עָצַר to restrain, retain (3·36·46) 783

כַּעַס 22 vexation, anger (2·25[?]) 495

כֶּלֶב 23 dog (7·32) 476

חֵיל rampart [dub.] (1·9) 298

כֶּלֶב 24 dog (7·32) 476

הֵסִית 25 to instigate (1·18·18) 694

הִתְעִיב 26 to do abominably (1·4·21) 1073

גִּלּוּל idol (2·48) 165

שַׂק 27 sackcloth (4·48) 974

צוֹם to abstain from food, fast (1·1·20) 847

אַט softly, gentleness (1·5) 31

נִכְנַע 28 to humble oneself (2·25·36) 488

Chapter 22

הֶחֱשָׁה 3 to show inactivity (1·9·16) 364

פֹּה 7 here, hither (4·44) 805

סָרִיס 9 eunuch (1·45) 710

גֹּרֶן 10 threshing floor (1·34) 175

נגח 11 to push (1·6·11) 618

כַּמֶּה (עַד) 16 how many? (1·13) 552

נפץ 17 BDB lists under פוץ niphal — "to be scattered" (1·15·21) 806

פָּתָה 20 to deceive (3·17·27) 834

בְּ כֹה . . . בְּ כֹה in this way . . . in that way (2·2) 462

פָּתָה 21 to deceive (3·17·27) 834

בַּמֶּה by what means? (1·29) 552

פָּתָה 22 to deceive (3·17·27) 834

לְחִי 24 cheek (1·21) 534

אֵי where? (2·39) 32

חֶדֶר 25 chamber, room (5·37) 293

נֶחְבָּה to withdraw, hide oneself (1·3·4) 285

כֶּלֶא 27 imprisonment (1·10) 476

לַחַץ oppression (2·11) 537

הִתְחַפֵּשׂ 30 to disguise oneself [let one be searched for] (3·8·23) 344

מָשַׁךְ 34 to draw (1·30·36) 604

תֹּם innocence, simplicity (2·23) 1070

דֶּבֶק appendage, joining, soldering (1·3) 180

שִׁרְיוֹן body armor (1·8) 1056

רַכָּב charioteer (1·3) 939

מֶרְכָּבָה 35 chariot (5·44) 939

נֹכַח opposite to, in front of (2·22) 647

מַכָּה wound (2·48) 646

חֵיק bosom = interior (5·38) 300

רִנָּה 36 ringing cry (2·33) 943

שָׁטַף 38 to rinse, wash off (1·28·31) 1009

בְּרֵכָה pool, pond (1·17) 140

לקק to lick (3·5·7) 545

כֶּלֶב dog (7·32) 476

זוֹנָה harlot (2·33[?]) 275

קָדֵשׁ 47 temple prostitute [male] (3·11) 873

בָּעַר to consume, burn (4·26·28) 129

נִצָּב 48 deputy (6·7) 662

אֳנִיָּה ship (4·31) 58

אֳנִיָּה 50 ship (4·31) 58

בֵּרֵךְ* to bless; used here in the vulgar sense, it actually means "to curse," Piel (2·2), para. 5. 189

2 KINGS

Chapter 1

פָּשַׁע 1 to rebel, revolt (6·40·41) 833

שְׂבָכָה 2 [window] lattice (3·16) 959

עֲלִיָּה roof chamber (4·20) 751

זְבוּב flies; בעל ז׳ = lord of the flies (4·6) 256 and 127

חֳלִי sickness (4·24) 318

מִבְּלִי 3 on account of (3·25) 115

זְבוּב flies; see vs. 2 (4·6) 256 and 127

מִטָּה 4 bed (7·29) 641

מִבְּלִי 6 on account of (3·25) 115

זְבוּב flies; see vs. 2 (4·6) 256 and 127

מִטָּה bed (7·29) 641

שֵׂעָר 8 hair (1·28) 972

אֵזוֹר waist cloth (1·14) 25

אזר to gird on (1·6·16) 25

מָתְנַיִם loins (3·50) 608

כָּרַע 13 to bow (2·29·35) 502

בֶּרֶךְ knee (2·25) 139

לְנֶגֶד in front of, before (1·32) 617

יקר to be precious (2·9·11) 429

יקר 14 to be precious (2·9·11) 429

זְבוּב 16 flies; see vs. 2 (4·6) 256 and 127

מִבְּלִי on account of (3·25) 115

מִטָּה bed (2·29) 641

Chapter 2

סְעָרָה 1 tempest, storm-wind (2·15) 704

פֹּה 2 here, hither (8·44) 805

החשה 3 to be silent (3·9·16) 364

פֹּה 4 here, hither (8·44) 805

החשה 5 to be silent (3·9·16) 364

פֹּה 6 here, hither (8·44) 805

מִנֶּגֶד 7 opposite (4·26) 617

אַדֶּרֶת 8 cloak, mantle (3·12) 12

גלם to wrap up, fold, fold together (1·1·1) 166

נחצה to be divided (2·4·15) 345

הֵנָּה hither; ה׳ וה׳ = hither and thither (7·49) 244

חָרָבָה dry ground (1·8) 351

בְּטֶרֶם 9 before (2·39) 382

הִקְשָׁה 10 to make difficult (2·21·28) 904

הִפְרִיד 11 to make a division, separation (1·7·26) 825

סְעָרָה tempest, storm-wind (2·15) 704

קְרָעִים 12 torn piece, rag (1·4) 902

אַדֶּרֶת 13 cloak, mantle (3·12) 12

אַדֶּרֶת 14 cloak, mantle (3·12) 12

אַיֵּה where? (3·44) 32

נחצה to be divided (2·4·15) 345

הֵנָּה hither; ה׳ וה׳ = hither and thither (7·49) 244

מִנֶּגֶד 15 some way off from, at a distance (4·26) 617

גַּיְא 16 valley (3·48) 161

פצר 17 to urge (2·6·7) 823

מוֹשָׁב 19 situation (1·43) 444

שכל to make childless (2·18·24) 1013

צְלֹחִית 20 jar (1·1) 852

מֶלַח salt (3·28) 571

מוֹצָא 21 place of going forth (1·27) 425

מֶלַח salt (3·28) 571

שכל to make childless (2·18·24) 1013

קָטָן 23 small, young (4·47) 881

התקלס to scoff, mock, deride (1·3·4) 887

קֵרֵחַ bald (2·3) 901

דֹּב 24 bear (1·12) 179

Chapter 3

מַצֵּבָה 2 pillar (6·35) 663

נֹקֵד 4 sheep raiser (1·2) 667

כַּר he-lamb (1·11) 503

71

צֶמֶר wool (1·16) 856

פָּשַׁע 5 to rebel, revolt (6·40·41) 833

פָּשַׁע 7 to rebel, revolt (6·40·41) 833

אֵי 8 where? אֵי־זֶה = which? (2·39) 32

אֲהָהּ 10 alas! (3·15) 13

פֹּה 11 here, hither (8·44) 805

לוּלֵי 14 if not, unless (1·10) 530

נַגֵּן 15 to play [a stringed instrument] (3·14·15) 618

גֵּב 16 pit, ditch, trench (1·3[?]) 155

גֶּשֶׁם 17 rain, shower (1·35) 177

מִבְצָר 19 fortification (5·37) 131

מִבְחוֹר choice (2·2) 104

מַעְיָן spring (2·23) 745

סָתַם to stop up (2·10·13) 711

חֶלְקָה portion of ground (6·24) 324

הכאיב to mar (1·4·8) 456

חגר 21 to gird on (3·44·44) 291

חֲגֹרָה girdle, loin covering, belt (1·5) 292

זָרַח 22 to rise (1·18·18) 280

מִנֶּגֶד some way off from, at a distance (4·26) 617

אָדֹם red (1·9) 10

החרב 23 to attack one another (1·3·37[?]) 352

נחרב to fight together (1·1·3[?]) 352

הָרַס 25 to throw down, tear down (1·30·33) 248

חֶלְקָה portion of ground (6·24) 324

מַעְיָן spring (2·23) 745

סָתַם to stop up (2·10·13) 711

קַלָּע slinger (1·1) 887

שָׁלַף 26 to draw out (1·24·24) 1025

קֶצֶף 27 wrath (1·29) 893

Chapter 4

נֹשֶׁה 1 creditor (1·4) 674

אָסוּךְ 2 flask (1·1) 692

שֹׁכֵנֵךְ 3 K, שְׁכֵן Q, neighbor (1·20) 1015

רֵיק empty (1·14) 938

הַמְעִיט to make few (1·13·22) 589

נִשְׁיִ 7 debt (1·1) 674

מִדֵּי 8 out of the abundance of, i.e., as often as (1·15) 191

עֲלִיָּה 10 roof chamber (4·20) 751

קָטָן small (4·47) 881

מִטָּה bed (7·29) 641

מְנוֹרָה lampstand (1·39) 633

עֲלִיָּה 11 roof chamber (4·20) 751

חָרַד 13 to be anxiously careful (1·23·39) 353

חֲרָדָה anxious care (1·9) 353

עַם kinsman (1·34) 769

אֲבָל 14 verily, of a truth (1·11) 6

זָקֵן to be old, become old (1·25·27) 278

אַתְּי 16 you [2nd, fem.] (3·7) 61

חבק to embrace (1·3·13) 287

כָּזַב to tell a lie (1·12·16) 469

קֹצֵר 18 reaper (1·10[?]) 894

בֶּרֶךְ 20 knee (2·25) 139

צָהֳרַיִם midday, noon (1·23) 843

מִטָּה 21 bed (7·29) 641

אָתוֹן 22 she-ass (2·35) 87

אַתְּי 23 you [2nd, fem.] (3·7) 61

חרש 24 to bind on, i.e., to saddle (1·27·31) 289

אָתוֹן she-ass (2·35) 87

נָהַג to drive (2·20·30) 624

עָצַר to restrain, retain (4·36·46) 783

מִנֶּגֶד 25 some way off from, at a distance (4·26) 617

הַלָּז this (2·7) 229

הרף 27 to push away, thrust (1·11·11) 213

הרפה to refrain, let alone (1·21·44) 951

מָרַר to be bitter (1·6·14) 600

הֶעְלִים to conceal, hide (1·11·29) 761

הִשְׁלָה 28 to mislead [one] (1·1·7) 1017

חגר 29 to gird up (3·44·44) 291

מָתְנַיִם loins (3·50) 608

מִשְׁעֶנֶת staff (4·12) 1044

מִשְׁעֶנֶת 31 staff (4·12) 1044

קֶשֶׁב attentiveness (1·3) 904

הֵקִיץ to awake (1·22·23) 884

מִטָּה 32 bed (7·29) 641

גהר 34 to bend, crouch (2·3·3) 155

חמם to grow warm (1·23·26) 328

הֵנָּה 35 hither; ה' וה' hither and thither (7·49) 244

גהר to bend, crouch (2·3·3) 155

זרר to sneeze (1·1·1) 284

פָּקַח to open (6·17·20) 824

שפת 38 to set [on the fire] (1·4·4) 1046

סִיר pot (6·29) 696

בשל to boil (2·20·27) 143

נָזִיד pottage (3·6) 268

לקט 39 to gather (2·21·36) 544

אוֹרָה herb (1·2) 21

פַּקֻּעֹת gourds (1·1) 825

מְלֹא fullness (1·38) 571

פלח to cleave open, cleave through (1·4·5) 812

סִיר pot (6·29) 696

נָזִיד pottage (3·6) 268

נָזִיד 40 pottage (3·6) 268

סִיר pot (6·29) 696

קֶמַח 41 flour, meal (1·14) 887

סִיר pot (6·29) 696

בִּכּוּרִים 42 first fruits (1·17) 114

שְׂעֹרָה barley (4·34) 972

כַּרְמֶל fruit, garden growth (1·3[?]) 502

צִקְלֹן garment, wallet [dub.] (1·1) 862

מְשָׁרֵת 43 servant (2·20) 1058

Chapter 5

תְּשׁוּעָה 1 deliverance (3·34) 448

מְצֹרָע leprous (6·15) 863

גְּדוּד 2 band, troop (8·33) 151

שָׁבָה to take captive (2·29·37) 985

קָטֹן small, young (4·47) 881

גְּבֶרֶת 3 mistress over servants (2·15[?]) 150

אַחֲלֵי oh that! (1·2) 25

צָרַעַת leprosy (4·35) 863

חֲלִיפָה 5 change [of raiment] (3·12) 322

צָרַעַת 6 leprosy (4·35) 863

צָרַעַת 7 leprosy (4·35) 863

הִתְאַנָּה to seek an occasion (1·1·4) 58

קָצַף 11 to be angry (2·28·34) 893

הֵנִיף to wave (1·32·34[?]) 631

מְצֹרָע leprous (6·15) 863

טָבַל 14 to dip (2·15·16) 371

פָּצַר 16 to urge (2·6·7) 823

מֵאֵן to refuse (1·45·45) 549

מַשָּׂא 17 load (2·43) 672

צֶמֶד couple, pair (2·15) 855

פֶּרֶד mule (1·14) 825

סלח 18 to forgive (3·33·46) 699

נִשְׁעָן to lean, support oneself (3·22·22) 1043

כִּבְרָה 19 a distance (1·3) 460

חָשַׂךְ 20 to spare (1·26·28) 362

מְאוּמָה anything (1·32) 548

מֶרְכָּבָה 21 chariot (5·44) 939

חֲלִיפָה 22 change [of raiment] (3·12) 322

הוֹאִיל 23 to show willingness (2·18·18) 383

פָּרַץ to urge (2·46·49) 823

צור to confine, secure (8·31·31) 848

חָרִיט bag, purse (1·2) 355

חֲלִיפָה change [of raiment] (3·12) 322

עֹפֶל 24 mound, hill (1·8) 779

73

מֵאַן 25 whence? from where? (3·48[?]) 33

אָנָה where? אָנֶה וָאָנָה = anywhere (3·39) 33

מֶרְכָּבָה 26 chariot (5·44) 939

זַיִת olive tree, olive (2·38) 268

צָרַעַת 27 leprosy (4·35) 863

מְצֹרָע leprous (6·15) 863

שֶׁלֶג snow (1·20) 1017

Chapter 6

צַר 1 narrow, tight (1·20) 865

קוֹרָה 2 beam (2·5) 900

הוֹאִיל 3 to show willingness (2·18·18) 383

גזר 4 to cut down, cut, divide (1·6·12) 160

קוֹרָה 5 beam (2·5) 900

אֲהָהּ alas! (3·15) 13

אָנָה 6 whence? whither? (3·39) 33

קצב to cut off, shear (1·2) 891

הֵצִיף to cause to float (1·2·3) 847

פְּלֹנִי 8 a certain one; פ׳ אַלְמֹנִי = such a one (1·6) 811

אַלְמֹנִי someone, a certain one (1·3) 48

תַּחֲנוֹת encampment (1·1) 334

נָחַת 9 descending (1·1) 639

הִזְהִיר 10 to warn (1·13·21) 264

נסער 11 to be enraged (1·1·7) 704

מִשֶּׁלָּנוּ = מִן + שֶׁ + לְ + נוּ = of those that are ours 979 (שׁ, 4c)

חֶדֶר 12 chamber, room (3·37) 293

מִשְׁכָּב lying down (1·46) 1012

אֵיכָה 13 where? (2·18) 32

כָּבֵד 14 numerous (2·39) 458

הִקִּיף to surround (2·16·17) 668

מְשָׁרֵת 15 servant (2·20) 1058

אֲהָהּ alas! (3·15) 13

אֵיכָה what? in what manner? (2·18) 32

מֵאֲשֶׁר 16 than those who (1·17) 84

פָּקַח 17 to open (6·17·20) 824

סַנְוֵרִים 18 sudden blindness (2·3) 703

זֶה 19 this (1·11) 262

פָּקַח 20 to open (6·17·20) 824

שָׁבָה 22 to take captive (2·29·37) 985

כרה 23 to give a feast (1·1·1) 500

כֵּרָה feast (1·1) 500

גְּדוּד band, troop (8·33) 151

צוּר 24 to shut in, besiege (8·31·31) 848

צוּר 25 to shut in, besiege (8·31·31) 848

רֹבַע fourth part (1·1) 917

קַב kab [unit of dry measure] (1·1) 866

חֲרִי dung (2·3) 351

יוֹנָה dove (1·33) 401 [דִּבְיוֹנִים Q dove's dung (1·1) 179]

מֵאַיִן 27 whence? from where? (3·48[?]) 32

גֹּרֶן threshing floor (1·34) 175

יֶקֶב wine vat (1·16) 428

בִּשֵּׁל 29 to cook, boil (2·20·27) 143

הֶחְבִּיא to hide (1·6·34) 285

שַׂק 30 sackcloth (3·48) 974

בְּטֶרֶם 32 before (2·39) 382

מְרַצֵּחַ murderer (1·2) 954

לחץ to squeeze, press (3·14·15) 537

הוֹחִיל 33 to wait (1·15·42) 403

Chapter 7

סְאָה 1 a measure of grain (6·9) 684

שְׂעֹרָה barley (4·34) 972

שָׁלִישׁ 2 adjutant, officer (7·16) 1026

נִשְׁעַן to lean, support oneself (3·22·22) 1043

אֲרֻבָּה lattice, window (1·8) 70

הִנְּכָה = הִנֵּה + ךָ behold you!

מְצֹרָע 3 leprous (6·15) 865

פֹּה here, hither (8·44) 805

פֹּה 4 here, hither (8·44) 805

נֶשֶׁף 5 twilight (2·12) 676

שָׂכַר 6 to hire (1·17·20) 968

נֶשֶׁף 7 twilight (2·12) 676

מְצֹרָע 8 leprous (6·15) 865

הטמין to hide something (2·2·31) 380

בְּשֹׂרָה 9 good tidings (1·6) 142

החשה to be silent (3·9·16) 364

חכה to wait, tarry (2·13·14) 314

שֹׁעֵר 10 porter (2·37) 1045

שֹׁעֵר 11 porter (2·37) 1045

פְּנִימָה within (1·5) 819

רָעֵב 12 hungry (1·19) 944

נֶחְבָּה to withdraw, hide oneself (1·3·4) 285

בְּהִתְחָפְזָם 15 K, בְּחָפְזָם, Q, חפז to hurry away (1·6·9) 342

בָּזַז 16 to spoil, plunder (1·37·40) 102

סְאָה a measure of grain (6·9) 684

שְׂעֹרָה barley (4·34) 972

שָׁלִישׁ 17 adjutant, officer (7·16) 1026

נִשְׁעָן to lean, support oneself (3·22·22) 1043

רָמַס to trample (4·17·18) 942

סְאָה 18 a measure of grain (6·9) 684

שְׂעֹרָה barley (4·34) 972

שָׁלִישׁ 19 adjutant, officer (7·16) 1026

אֲרֻבָּה lattice, window (1·8) 70

רָמַס 20 to trample (4·17·18) 942

Chapter 8

אַתְּי 1 you [2nd, fem.] (3·7) 61

בַּאֲשֶׁר in where (1·19) 84

סָרִיס 6 eunuch (8·45) 710

תְּבוּאָה product, yield (1·43) 100

הֵנָּה 7 hither (7·49) 244

חֳלִי 8 sickness (4·24) 318

טוֹב 9 goods (1·32) 375

מַשָּׂא load (2·43) 672

חֳלִי sickness (4·24) 318

מִבְצָר 12 fortifications (5·37) 131

בָּחוּר young man (1·45) 104

עוֹלֵל child (1·11) 760

רטש to dash in pieces (1·2·4) 936

הָרָה pregnant (2·15[?]) 247

כֶּלֶב 13 dog (3·32) 476

מָחֳרָת 15 the morrow (1·32) 564

מַכְבֵּר a netted cloth or coverlet (1·1) 460

טָבַל to dip (2·15·16) 371

נִיר 19 lamp (2·5) 633

פָּשַׁע 20 to transgress (6·40·41) 833

פָּשַׁע 22 to transgress (6·40·41) 833

חָתָן 27 son-in-law, bridegroom (1·20) 368

מַכָּה 29 wound (2·48) 646

Chapter 9

חגר 1 to gird up (3·44·44) 291

מָתְנַיִם loins (3·50) 608

פַּךְ phial, flask (1·3) 810

חֶדֶר 2 chamber, room (3·37) 293

פַּךְ 3 phial, flask (1·3) 810

חכה to wait, tarry (2·13·14) 314

נקם 7 to avenge (1·2·34) 667

השתין 8 to urinate (1·6·6) 1010

עָצַר to restrain, retain (4·36·46) 783

כֶּלֶב 10 dog (3·32) 476

שגע 11 to be maddened (1·5·7) 993

שִׂיחַ the way in which he talks (1·14) 967

גֶּרֶם 13 self [dub.] המעלות ג׳ idiom for "the steps themselves" (1·5) 175

מַעֲלָה step (8·47[?]) 752

התקשר 14 to conspire (1·3·44) 905

מַכָּה 15 wound (2·48) 646

פָּלִיט fugitive (1·19) 812

צֹפֶה 17 watchman (3·19) 859

מִגְדָּל tower (3·49) 154

שִׁפְעָה multitude (2·6) 1051

רַכָּב horseman (1·3) 939

צֹפֶה 18 watchman (3·19) 859

צֹפֶה 20 watchman (3·19) 859

מִנְהָג driving (2·2) 624

שִׁגָּעוֹן madness (1·3) 993

נָהַג to drive (2·20·30) 624

חֶלְקָה 21 portion of ground (6·24) 324

זְנוּנִים 22 fornication [religious] (1·11) 276

כֶּשֶׁף sorcery (1·6) 506

מִרְמָה 23 treachery (1·39) 941

חֵצִי 24 arrow (1·4) 345

כָּרַע to bow down (2·29·35) 502

שָׁלִישׁ 25 adjutant, officer (7·16) 1026

חֶלְקָה portion of ground (6·24) 324

צֶמֶד couple, pair (2·15) 855

מַשָּׂא burden (2·43) 672

אֶמֶשׁ 26 yesterday (1·5) 57

חֶלְקָה portion of ground (6·24) 324

גַּן 27 garden (4·41) 171

מֶרְכָּבָה chariot (5·44) 939

מַעֲלֶה ascent (1·19) 751

קְבֻרָה 28 grave (3·14) 869

פּוּךְ 30 antimony, stibium (1·4) 806

הִשְׁקִיף to look down (2·12·22) 1054

חַלּוֹן window (3·30) 313

חַלּוֹן 32 window (3·30) 313

הִשְׁקִיף to look down (2·12·22) 1054

סָרִיס eunuch (8·45) 710

שמט 33 to let drop, let fall (2·7·9) 1030

נזה to spatter (1·4·24) 633

רָמַס to trample (4·17·18) 942

גֻּלְגֹּלֶת 35 skull, head (1·12) 166

כֶּלֶב 36 dog (3·32) 476

נְבֵלָה 37 corpse (1·48) 615

דֹּמֶן dung (1·6) 199

Chapter 10

אֹמֵן 1 nourisher, supporter (2·7[?]) 52

מִבְצָר 2 fortifications (5·37) 131

נֶשֶׁק weapons (1·10) 676

אֹמֵן 5 nourisher, supporter (2·7[?]) 52

דּוּד 7 basket, pot (1·7) 188

צִבּוּר 8 heap (1·1) 840

קָשַׁר 9 to conspire (9·36·44) 905

אֵפוֹא 10 then (1·15) 66

בִּלְתִּי 11 not, without (1·24) 116

שָׂרִיד survivor (1·28) 975

גְּבִירָה 13 queen mother, queen (2·15) 150

מֶרְכָּבָה 15 chariot (5·44) 939

קִנְאָה 16 zeal (2·43) 888

עָקְבָה 19 insidiousness (1·1) 784

עֲצָרָה 20 assembly (1·11) 783

לַאֲשֶׁר 22 to the one (1·38) 81

מֶלְתָּחָה wardrobe (1·1) 547

לְבוּשׁ raiment (1·31) 528

מַלְבּוּשׁ attire (1·8) 528

חפשׂ 23 to search through, search (1·8·23) 344

פֹּה here, hither (8·44) 805

רָץ 25 runner (8·25) 930

שָׁלִישׁ adjutant, officer (7·16) 1026

מַצֵּבָה 26 pillar (6·35) 663

נָתַץ 27 to pull down (8·31·42) 683

מַצֵּבָה pillar (6·35) 663

מַחֲרָאָה cesspool (1·1) 1123 n. 351a

חֲטָא 29 sin (2·33) 307

עֵגֶל calf (2·35) 722

הֵטִיב 30 to do well (1·3·20) 373

קצה 32 to cut off (1·2·5) 891

Chapter 11

גנב 2 to steal (1·30·39) 170

מֵינֶקֶת nurse (1·5) 413

חֶדֶר room, chamber (3·37) 293

מִטָּה bed (7·29) 641

התחבא 3 to hide oneself, draw back (1·10·34) 285

רָץ 4 runner (8·25) 930

רָץ 6 runner (8·25) 930

מַסָּח defense [dub.] (1·1) 587
הִקִּיף 8 to surround (2·16·17) 668
שְׂדֵרָה rows, ranks (2·4) 690
חֲנִית 10 spear (1·46) 333
שֶׁלֶט perh. shield (1·7) 1020
רָץ 11 runner (8·25) 930
שְׂמָאלִי left, on the left (1·9) 970
נֵזֶר 12 crown (1·24) 634
רָץ 13 runner (8·25) 930
חֲצֹצְרָה 14 clarion trumpet (3·29) 348
שָׂמֵחַ glad, joyful, merry (1·21) 970
קֶשֶׁר conspiracy (6·14) 905
שְׂדֵרָה 15 rows, ranks (2·4) 690
מָבוֹא 16 entrance (2·23) 99
נָתַץ 18 to pull down (8·31·42) 683
צֶלֶם image (1·17) 853
פְּקֻדָּה overseer (1·32) 824
רָץ 19 runner (8·25) 930
שָׁקַט 20 to be quiet, undisturbed (1·31·41) 1052

Chapter 12

הוֹרָה 3 to instruct (3·45·45[?]) 434
עֵרֶךְ estimate, valuation (2·33) 789
מַכָּר 6 acquaintance (2·2) 648
בֶּדֶק fissure, rent, breach (8·10) 96
בֶּדֶק 7 fissure, rent, breach (8·10) 96
בֶּדֶק 8 fissure, rent, breach (8·10) 96
מַכָּר acquaintance (2·2) 648
אוֹת 9 to consent, agree (1·4·4) 22
בֶּדֶק fissure, rent, breach (8·10) 96
נקב 10 to pierce (2·13·19) 666
חֹר hole (1·7) 359
סַף threshold (4·25) 706
צוּר 11 to confine, secure (8·31·31) 848
מָנָה to count (1·12·28) 584
תכן 12 to be measured out (1·1·18) 1067
חָרָשׁ artificer, engraver (4·38) 360

בֹּנֶה builder (2·9[?]) 124
גֹּדֵר 13 masons, wall builders (2·3[?]) 154
חֹצֵב hewer (1·8[?]) 345
מַחְצֵב hewing (2·3) 345
בֶּדֶק fissure, rent, breach (8·10) 96
חָזְקָה perh. repairing (1·6[?]) 306
סַף 14 bowl (1·6) 706
מְזַמֶּרֶת snuffers (1·5) 275
מִזְרָק basin (3·32) 284
חֲצֹצְרָה clarion trumpet (3·29) 348
אָשָׁם 17 guilt offering (1·46) 79
קָשַׁר 21 to conspire (9·36·44) 905
קֶשֶׁר conspiracy (6·14) 905

Chapter 13

לַחַץ 4 oppression (1·11) 537
לָחַץ to oppress (3·14·15) 537
מוֹשִׁיעַ 5 savior (1·27) 446
תְּמוֹל yesterday; כת׳ שלשום = as formerly (1·23) 1069
שִׁלְשׁוֹם three days ago (1·25) 1026
אֲשֵׁרָה 6 sacred tree or pole representing Canaanite goddess of fortune and happiness (11·40) 81
רַגְלִי 7 on foot (1·12) 920
דוּשׁ to tread, thresh (1·12·15) 190
חֳלִי 14 sickness (4·24) 318
חַלּוֹן 17 window (3·30) 319
קֶדֶם eastward (1·26) 870
יָרָה to shoot (1·13·25[?]) 434
הוֹרָה to shoot (2·11·25[?]) 434
תְּשׁוּעָה deliverance (3·34) 448
קָצַף 19 to be angry (2·28·34) 893
גְּדוּד 20 band, troop (8·33) 151
גְּדוּד 21 band, troop (8·33) 151
לָחַץ 22 to oppress (3·14·15) 537
רָחַם 23 to have compassion (1·41·46) 933

Chapter 14

חֵטְא 6 sin (2·33) 307

גַּיְא 7 valley (3·48) 161

מֶלַח salt (3·28) 571

חוֹחַ 9 brier, bramble (2·11[?]) 296

רָמַס to trample (4·17·18) 942

הִתְגָּרָה 10 to engage in strife (1·11·14) 173

נִגַּף 12 to be smitten (1·23·48) 619

פָּרַץ 13 to make a breach (2·46·49) 829

פִּנָּה corner (1·30) 819

תַּעֲרוּבָה 14 pledge; בני הת׳ = hostage (1·2) 787

קָשַׁר 19 to conspire (9·36·44) 905

קֶשֶׁר conspiracy (6·14) 905

עֳנִי 26 affliction (1·36) 777

מָרָה to be rebellious (1·21·43) 598

אֶפֶס [there is] no, i.e., an end of (2·43) 67

עָצַר to restrain, retain (4·36·46) 783

עֹזֵר help (1·19[?]) 740

מָחָה 27 to blot out (4·21·33) 562

Chapter 15

מְצֹרָע 5 leprous (6·15) 863

חָפְשִׁית freedom, separateness (1·2) 345

קָשַׁר 10 to conspire (9·36·44) 905

קָבֳל [cs. קֳבָל] before [dub.] (1·2[?]) 867

יֶרַח 13 month (1·12) 437

קֶשֶׁר 15 conspiracy (6·14) 905

קָשַׁר to conspire (9·36·44) 905

הָרָה 16 pregnant (2·15[?]) 247

קָשַׁר 25 to conspire (9·36·44) 905

שָׁלִישׁ adjutant, officer (7·16) 1026

אַרְמוֹן citadel, stronghold (1·33) 74

קָשַׁר 30 to conspire (9·36·44) 905

קֶשֶׁר conspiracy (6·14) 905

Chapter 16

רַעֲנָן 4 luxuriant, fresh (2·19) 947

צוּר 5 to shut in, besiege (8·31·31) 848

נָשַׁל 6 to clear out entirely (1·1·7) 675

שֹׁחַד 8 bribe (1·23) 1005

דְּמוּת 10 likeness (1·25) 198

תַּבְנִית pattern (1·20) 125

הִסִּיךְ 13 to pour out (1·13·24[?]) 650

זָרַק to throw, scatter abundantly (2·32·34) 284

מִבֵּין 14 from between (2·21) 107

יֶרֶךְ side (1·34) 437

זָרַק 15 to throw, scatter abundantly (2·32·34) 284

בִּקֵּר to consider, seek, inquire (1·7·7) 133

קִצֵּץ 17 to cut in pieces (3·9·14) 893

מִסְגֶּרֶת border (1·17) 689

מְכוֹנָה base (3·25) 467

כִּיּוֹר basin (1·23) 468

מַרְצֶפֶת pavement (1·1) 954

מוּסָךְ 18 architectural term of some covered structure (1·1) 697

מָבוֹא entrance (2·23) 99

חִיצוֹן outer, external (1·25) 300

Chapter 17

קֶשֶׁר 4 conspiracy (6·14) 905

עָצַר to shut up (4·36·46) 783

כֶּלֶא confinement (3·10) 476

צוּר 5 to shut in, besiege (8·31·31) 848

חִפֵּא 9 to do secretly (1·1·1) 341

מִגְדָּל tower (3·49) 159

מִבְצָר fortification (5·37) 131

מַצֵּבָה 10 pillar (6·35) 663

אֲשֵׁרָה sacred tree or pole representing Canaanite goddess of fortune and happiness (11·40) 81

גָּבֹהַּ high, exalted (1·41) 147

רַעֲנָן luxuriant, fresh (2·19) 947

גִּלּוּל 12 idol (4·48) 165

78

הֵעִיד 13 to exhort solemnly, admonish (2·39·44) 729

חֹזֶה seer (1·17) 302

הִקְשָׁה 14 to make stiff, stubborn (2·21·28) 904

עֹרֶף neck (2·33) 791

הֵעִיד 15 to enjoin solemnly (2·39·44) 729

הֶבֶל to become vain (1·4·5) 211

מַסֵּכָה 16 molten image (1·25) 651

עֵגֶל calf (2·35) 722

אֲשֵׁרָה sacred tree or pole representing Canaanite goddess of fortune and happiness (11·40) 81

קָסַם 17 to practice divination (1·11·11) 890

קֶסֶם divination (1·11) 890

נָחַשׁ to practice divination, observe signs (2·9·9) 638

הִתְאַנַּף 18 to be angry (1·6·14) 60

שֹׁסֶה 20 plunderers, spoilers (1·7) 1042

יַדָּא 21 K, יַדַּח Q, הִדִּיחַ to thrust away (1·27·43) 623

חֲטָאָה sin (1·8) 308

תְּחִלָּה 25 beginning (1·22) 321

אֲרִי lion (2·36) 71

אֲרִי 26 lion (2·36) 71

הוֹרָה 27 to teach (3·45·45[?]) 434

הוֹרָה 28 to teach (3·45·45[?]) 434

קָצָה 32 whole, מקצותם = from the whole of them, i.e., from among them (1·7) 892

פָּסִיל 41 idol, image (1·23) 820

Chapter 18

מַצֵּבָה 4 pillar (6·35) 663

אֲשֵׁרָה sacred tree or pole representing Canaanite goddess of fortune and happiness (11·40) 81

כָּתַת to crush (1·5·17) 510

נָחָשׁ serpent (1·31) 638

מָרַד 7 to rebel (4·25·25) 597

מִגְדָּל 8 tower (3·49) 154

מִבְצָר fortification (5·37) 131

צוּר 9 to shut in, besiege (8·31·31) 848

הנחה 11 to lead, guide (1·26·40) 634

בָּצוּר 13 fortified, made inaccessible (2·25[?]) 130

קָצַץ 16 to cut in pieces (3·9·14) 893

אֹמְנָה pillars, supporters of the door (1·1[?]) 52

צִפָּה to overlay, plate (1·44·46) 860

תַּרְתָּן 17 field marshal [title of Assyrian general] (1·2) 1077

כָּבֵד numerous (2·39) 458

תְּעָלָה conduit (2·9) 752

בְּרֵכָה pool, pond (2·17) 140

מְסִלָּה highway (1·27) 700

מַזְכִּיר 18 recorder (2·9) 271

בִּטָּחוֹן 19 trust (1·3) 105

מָרַד 20 to rebel (4·25·25) 597

מִשְׁעֶנֶת 21 staff (4·12) 1044

רָצַץ to crush (1·11·19) 954

נִסְמַךְ to support oneself (1·6·48) 701

נָקַב to pierce (2·13·19) 666

הִתְעָרֵב 23 to exchange pledges (1·2·17) 786

פֶּחָה 24 governor (1·28) 808

קָטָן small (4·47) 881

מִבַּלְעֲדֵי 25 apart from, without (1·12) 116

אֲרָמִית 26 in Aramaic (1·5) 74

יְהוּדִית in Jewish (2·6) 397

חֲרֵא 27 K, dung (2·3) 351 [צֹאָה Q, filth (1·5) 844]

שַׁיִן urine (1·2) 1010

יְהוּדִית 28 in Jewish (2·6) 397

הִשִּׁיא 29 to deceive (2·14·15) 674

תְּאֵנָה 31 fig, fig tree (2·39) 1061

דָּגָן 32 corn, grain (1·40) 186

תִּירוֹשׁ must, fresh or new wine (1·38) 440

זַיִת olive tree, olive (2·38) 268

יִצְהָר fresh oil, oil (1·23) 844

הֵסִית to instigate (1·18·18) 694

אַיֵּה 34 where? (3·44) 32

הֶחֱרִישׁ 36 to be silent (1·38·46) 361

מַזְכִּיר 37 recorder (2·9) 271

Chapter 19

שַׂק 1 sackcloth (3·48) 974

שַׂק 2 sackcloth (3·48) 974

תּוֹכֵחָה 3 rebuke, correction (1·4) 407

נְאָצָה contempt (1·2) 611

מַשְׁבֵּר breach (1·3) 991

אוּלַי 4 perhaps (1·45) 19

חֵרֵף to reproach (4·34·38) 357

גִּדֵּף 6 to revile, blaspheme (2·7·7) 154

שְׁמוּעָה 7 report (1·27) 1035

הִשִּׁיא 10 to deceive (2·14·15) 674

הֶחֱרִים 11 to destroy, devote to destruction (1·46·49) 355

אֵי 13 where? (2·39) 32

פָּקַח 16 to open (6·17·20) 824

חֵרֵף to reproach (4·34·38) 357

אָמְנָם 17 verily, truly (1·9) 53

הֶחֱרִיב to lay waste, make desolate (2·13·37[?]) 351

בּוּז 21 to despise (1·13·13) 100

לָעַג to mock, deride (1·12·18) 541

בְּתוּלָה virgin (1·50) 143

הֵנִיעַ to shake (2·14·38) 631

חֵרֵף 22 to reproach (4·34·38) 357

גִּדֵּף to blaspheme (2·7·7) 154

חֵרֵף 23 to reproach (4·34·38) 357

יַרְכָה extreme parts (1·28) 438

קוֹמָה height (3·45) 879

מִבְחוֹר choice (2·2) 104

בְּרוֹשׁ cypress, fir (1·20) 141

מָלוֹן lodging place (1·8) 533

כַּרְמֶל garden land; יער כ׳ = gardenlike forest (1·14[?]) 502

קוּר 24 to bore, dig (1·2·2) 881

הֶחֱרִיב to dry up (2·13·37[?]) 351

יָצַר 25 to preordain, plan (1·41·44) 427

הִשְׁאָה [Inf. cs. = לְהַשְׁאוֹת] to cause to crash (1·2·6) 980

גַּל heap, wave, billow (1·20) 164

נָצָה to be fallen in ruins (1·4·5) 663

בָּצוּר fortified, made inaccessible (2·25[?]) 131

קָצֵר 26 short (1·5) 894

עֵשֶׂב herb (1·33) 793

יָרָק green (1·8) 438

דֶּשֶׁא grass (1·14) 206

חָצִיר green grass, herbage (1·18[?]) 348

גָּג roof (2·29) 150

שְׁדֵפָה blighted or blasted thing (1·1) 995

קָמָה standing grain, i.e., maturity (1·10) 879

הִתְרַגֵּז 27 to excite oneself [to rage] (2·4·41) 919

הִתְרַגֵּז 28 to excite oneself [to rage] (2·4·41) 919

שַׁאֲנָן arrogance (1·11) 983

חָח hook, ring (1·7) 296

מֶתֶג bridle (1·5) 607

סָפִיחַ 29 growth from spilled kernels (1·4) 705

סָחִישׁ grain that shoots up of itself in the second year (1·2) 695

קָצַר to reap, harvest (1·24·24) 894

פְּלֵיטָה 30 escaped remnant (2·28) 812

שֹׁרֶשׁ root (1·33) 1057

לְמַטָּה downward (1·10) 641

לְמַעְלָה upward (1·34) 751

פְּלֵיטָה 31 escaped remnant (2·28) 812

קִנְאָה zeal (2·43) 888

הוֹרָה 32 to shoot (2·11·25[?]) 434

קְדֹם to meet, confront (1·24·26) 869

סֹלְלָה a mound (1·11) 700

גָּנַן 34 to defend, surround (2·8·8) 170

פֶּגֶר 35 corpse, carcass (1·22) 803

Chapter 20

אָנָּה 3 ah, now! I [or we] beseech thee! (1·6) 58 (אנא)

שָׁלֵם complete, perfect (1·28) 1023

בְּכִי weeping (1·30) 113

עִיר 4 K, חָצֵר Q, court 347

תִּיכוֹן middle (1·12) 1064

נָגִיד 5 ruler (1·44) 617

דִּמְעָה coll. tears [from eyes] (1·23) 199

גָּנַן 6 to defend (2·8·8) 170

דְּבֵלָה 7 pressed fig cake (1·5) 179

תְּאֵנָה fig, fig tree (2·39) 1061

שְׁחִין boil (1·13) 1006

מַעֲלָה 9 step (8·47[?]) 752

מַעֲלָה 10 step (8·47[?]) 752

אֲחֹרַנִּית backwards (2·7) 30

מַעֲלָה 11 step (8·47[?]) 752

אֲחֹרַנִּית backwards (2·7) 30

נכת 13 treasure (1·2) 649

בֹּשֶׂם spice, balsalm (1·30) 141

מֶמְשָׁלָה realm (1·17) 606

מֵאַיִן 14 whence? from where? (3·48[?]) 32

אצר 17 to store up, treasure (1·3·5) 69

סָרִיס 18 eunuch (8·45) 710

בְּרֵכָה 20 pool, pond (2·17) 140

תְּעָלָה conduit (2·9) 752

Chapter 21

אֲשֵׁרָה 3 sacred tree or pole representing Canaanite goddess of fortune and happiness (11·40) 81

עוֹנֵן 6 to practice soothsaying (1·10·11) 778

נָחַשׁ to practice divination (2·9·9) 638

אוֹב necromancer (2·16) 15

יִדְּעֹנִי familiar spirit (2·11) 396

פֶּסֶל 7 idol, image (1·31) 820

אֲשֵׁרָה sacred tree or pole representing Canaanite goddess of fortune and happiness (11·40) 81

הֵנִיד 8 to cause to wander (1·3·26) 626

הִתְעָה 9 to cause to err, to mislead (1·21·49) 1073

גִּלּוּל 11 idol (4·48) 165

צָלַל 12 to tingle (1·4·4) 852

קָו 13 line (1·17) 876

מִשְׁקֹלֶת leveling instrument (1·2) 1054

מָחָה to wipe (4·21·33) 562

צַלַּחַת dish (1·4) 852

נָטַשׁ 14 to abandon (1·33·40) 643

בַּז spoil, plunder (1·27) 103

מְשִׁסָּה plunder (1·6) 1042

נָקִי 16 innocent (3·43) 667

גַּן 18 garden (4·41) 171

גִּלּוּל 21 idol (4·48) 165

קָשַׁר 23 to conspire (9·36·44) 905

קָשַׁר 24 to conspire (9·36·44) 905

קְבֻרָה 26 grave (3·14) 869

גַּן garden (4·41) 171

Chapter 22

סַף 4 threshold (4·25) 706

בֶּדֶק 5 fissure, rent, breach (8·10) 96

חָרָשׁ 6 engraver, artificer (4·38) 360

גֹּדֵר masons, wall builders (2·3[?]) 154

מַחְצֵב hewing (2·3) 345

הִתִּיךְ 9 to pour out (1·5·21) 677

נִצַּת 13 to be kindled (2·6·27) 428

נְבִיאָה 14 prophetess (1·6) 612

מִשְׁנֶה second quarter, district (3·35) 1041

נִצַּת 17 to be kindled (2·6·27) 428

81

כבה		to be quenched (1·14·24) 459
רכך	19	to be softened, penitent (1·6·8) 939
נכנע		to humble oneself (1·25·36) 488
שַׁמָּה		horror, dismay (1·39) 1031
קְלָלָה		curse (1·33) 887

Chapter 23

עֵדָה	3	testimony (1·32) 730
מִשְׁנֶה	4	second (3·35) 1041
סַף		threshold (4·25) 706
אֲשֵׁרָה		sacred tree or pole representing Canaanite goddess of fortune and happiness (11·40) 81
שְׁדֵמָה		field (1·6) 995
כמר	5	priest (1·3) 485
מֵסַב		that which surrounds (1·5) 687
יָרֵחַ		moon (1·27) 437
מַזָּלוֹת		constellations (1·1) 561
אֲשֵׁרָה	6	sacred tree or pole representing Canaanite goddess of fortune and happiness (11·40) 81
הדקיק		to pulverize (2·8·13) 200
נָתַץ	7	to pull down (8·31·42) 683
קָדֵשׁ		temple prostitute [male] (1·11) 873
ארג		to weave (1·3·3) 70
אֲשֵׁרָה		sacred tree or pole representing Canaanite goddess of fortune and happiness (11·40) 81
נָתַץ	8	to pull down (8·31·42) 683
גַּיְא	10	valley (3·48) 161
לִשְׁכָּה	11	room, chamber (1·47) 545
סָרִיס		eunuch (8·45) 710
פַּרְוָרִים		structure (colonnade[?]) attached to west side of Solomon's temple (1·3) 826
מֶרְכָּבָה		chariot (5·44) 939
גָּג	12	roof (2·29) 150
עֲלִיָּה		roof chamber (4·20) 751

נָתַץ		to pull down (8·31·42) 683
מַשְׁחִית	13	corruption (1·19) 1008
שִׁקֻּץ		detested thing (3·28) 1055
מַצֵּבָה	14	pillar (6·35) 663
אֲשֵׁרָה		sacred tree or pole representing Canaanite goddess of fortune and happiness (11·40) 81
נָתַץ	15	to pull down (8·31·42) 683
הָדַק		to pulverize (2·8·13) 200
אֲשֵׁרָה		sacred tree or pole representing Canaanite goddess of fortune and happiness (11·40) 81
צִיּוּן	17	signpost, monument (1·3) 846
הַלָּז		this (2·7) 229
הניע	18	to shake (2·14·38) 631
פֶּסַח	21	passover (3·49) 820
פֶּסַח	22	passover (3·49) 820
פֶּסַח	23	passover (3·49) 820
אוֹב	24	necromancer (2·16) 15
יִדְּעֹנִי		familiar spirit (2·11) 396
תְּרָפִים		idol (1·15) 1076
גִּלּוּל		idol (4·48) 165
שִׁקֻּץ		detested thing (3·28) 1055
חָרוֹן	26	[burning of] anger (1·41) 354
כַּעַס		vexation, anger (1·25[?]) 495
קְבָרָה	30	grave (3·14) 869
עֹנֶשׁ	33	indemnity, fine (1·2) 778
עֵרֶךְ	35	estimate, valuation (2·33) 789
נגש		to exact (1·4·7) 620

Chapter 24

מָרַד	1	to rebel (4·25·25) 597
גְּדוּד	2	band, troop (8·33) 151
נָקִי	4	innocent (3·43) 667
סלח		to forgive (3·33·46) 699
מָצוֹר	10	siege (2·25) 848
צוּר	11	to shut in, besiege (8·31·31) 848
סָרִיס	12	eunuch (8·45) 710

קָצַץ 13 to cut in pieces (3·9·14) 893

חָרָשׁ 14 engraver, artificer (4·38) 360

מַסְגֵּר smiths (2·7) 689

זוּלָה except, besides (1·16) 265

דַּלָּה poor, weak, helpless one (2·5) 195

סָרִיס 15 eunuch (8·45) 710

אוּלֵי K, אֵילֵי Q, leading man (1·1) 17

גּוֹלָה exiles, exile (2·42) 163

חָרָשׁ 16 engraver, artificer (4·38) 360

מַסְגֵּר smiths (2·7) 689

גּוֹלָה exiles, exile (2·42) 163

מָרַד 20 to rebel (4·25·25) 597

Chapter 25

עָשׂוֹר 1 tenth day [of month] (1·15) 797

דָּיֵק bulwark, siege wall (1·6) 189

מָצוֹר 2 siege (2·25) 848

גַּן 4 garden (4·41) 171

הִשִּׂיג 5 to overtake (1·49·49) 673

עִוֵּר 7 to blind (1·5·5) 734

טַבָּח 8 guardsman (7·32) 371

נָתַץ 10 to pull down (8·31·42) 683

טַבָּח guardsman (7·32) 371

טַבָּח 11 guardsman (7·32) 371

דַּלָּה 12 poor, weak, helpless one (2·5) 195

טַבָּח guardsman (7·32) 371

כרם vinedresser (1·5) 501

יגב to be a husbandman (1·2·2) 387

מְכוֹנָה 13 base stand (3·25) 467

סִיר 14 pot (6·29) 696

יָע shovel (1·9) 418

מְזַמֶּרֶת snuffers (2·5) 275

מַחְתָּה 15 fire pan (1·21) 367

מִזְרָק basin (2·32) 284

טַבָּח guardsman (7·32) 371

מְכוֹנָה 16 base, stand (3·25) 467

מִשְׁקָל weight (1·48) 1054

קוֹמָה 17 height (3·45) 879

כֹּתֶרֶת capital of pillar (3·23) 509

שְׂבָכָה lattice work, network (3·16) 959

רִמּוֹן pomegranate (1·32) 941

טַבָּח 18 guardsman (7·32) 371

מִשְׁנֶה second (3·35) 1041

סַף threshold (4·25) 706

סָרִיס 19 eunuch (8·45) 710

פָּקִיד commissioner, deputy, overseer (1·13) 824

הצבא to muster [dub.] (1·2·14) 838

טַבָּח 20 guardsman (7·32) 371

מְלוּכָה 25 royalty (1·24) 574

גָּלוּת 27 exile, exiles (1·15) 163

כֶּלֶא imprisonment (3·10) 476

שָׁנָה 29 to change, alter (1·9·26) 1039

כֶּלֶא imprisonment (3·10) 476

אֲרֻחָה 30 meal, allowance (2·6) 73

APPENDIX

1. This list includes all words occurring over fifty times in the Old Testament, excluding proper nouns and numerals.

2. The number with the definition is the page number in BDB where the word occurs. E.g., "בְּאֵר well (24·38) 91" indicates that בְּאֵר can be found on page 91 of BDB.

3. The first definition listed for verbs is always the Qal meaning. E.g., אָבַד means "to perish" in the Qal stem.

4. Meanings for stems other than Qal are listed normally only if they differ from the following:

Niph.	=	passive of *Qal*
Piel	=	intensive of *Qal*
Pual	=	passive of *Piel*
Hiph.	=	causative of *Qal*
Hoph.	=	passive of *Hiph.*
Hithp.	=	reflexive of *Qal*

5. The occurrence of the stem with the meaning shown in item 4 above is indicated by an asterisk (*).

אָב	father 3	אַל	Adv. of negation 39
אָבַד	to perish 1	אֵל	god, God; power (5t) 42
	Pi. to cause to perish	אֶל	to, towards 39
	Hiph. to destroy, put to death	אֱלוֹהַּ	god, God 43
אָבָה	to be willing, consent 2	אַלּוּף	chief 49
אֶבְיוֹן	in want, needy, poor 2	אַלְמָנָה	widow 48
אֶבֶן	stone 6	אֶלֶף	thousand 48
אָדוֹן	lord (see BDB for explanation of	אִם	hypoth. part., interrog. part. 49
	אֲדֹנָי, אֲדֹנִי, אֲדֹנָי) 10	אֵם	mother 51
אָדָם	man, mankind 9	אָמָה	maid, hand maid 51
אֲדָמָה	ground, land 9	אַמָּה	cubit 52
אֶדֶן	base, pedestal 10	אֱמוּנָה	firmness, steadfastness, fidelity 53
אָהֵב	to love 12	אמן	to confirm, support 52
	Niph. ptc. =lovely, lovable 2 S 1:23		*Hiph.* to stand firm, to trust, believe
	Pi. ptc.=friends Zech. 13:6; lovers	אָמַר	to utter, say 55
אַהֲבָה	love 13		*Niph.* to be called
אֹהֶל	tent 13		*Hiph.* to avow Deut. 26:17, 18
אוֹ	or 14		*Hithp.* to act proudly, boast Ps. 94:4,
אָוֶן	trouble, sorrow, wickedness 19		Isa. 61:6
אוֹצָר	treasure, store, treasury, storehouse	אֱמֶת	firmness, faithfulness, truth 54
	69	אֲנַחְנוּ	we 59
אוֹר	light 21	אֲנִי	I 58
אוֹת	sign 16	אָנֹכִי	I 59
אָז	at that time, then 23	אָסַף	to gather, remove 62
אֹזֶן	ear 23		**Pi.* ptc. as subst.=rearguard, rearward
אָח	brother 26	אסר	to tie, bind, imprison, to harness 63
אָחוֹת	sister 27		*Pu.* to be taken prisoner Isa. 22:3
אחז	to grasp, take hold, take possession	אַף	nose, nostril, face, anger 60
	28	אַף	also, yea 64
	Pi. to enclose, overlay Job 26:9	אֵצֶל	in proximity to, beside 69
	Hoph. to be fastened to 2 Chron. 9:18	אָרוֹן	chest, ark 75
אֲחֻזָּה	possession 28	אֶרֶז	cedar 72
אַחַר	behind, after 29	אֹרַח	way, path 73
אַחֵר	another 29	אֹרֶךְ	length 73
אַחֲרוֹן	coming after, behind 30	אֶרֶץ	earth, land 75
אַחֲרִית	after-part, end 31	ארר	to curse 76
אֹיֵב	(ptc. of איב) enemy 33		*Hoph.* to be cursed Num. 22:6
אֵיךְ	how? how! 32	אֵשׁ	fire 77
אַיִל	ram 17	אִשָּׁה	woman, wife, female 61
אַיִן	subst., nothing, naught 34	אִשֶּׁה	an offering made by fire 77
	part of negation, is not, are not	אֲשֶׁר	part. of relation 81
אִישׁ	man 35	אֶת	mark of the accusative 84
אַךְ	surely, howbeit 36	אֵת	with 85
אָכַל	to eat 37	אַתְּ	you (sing. fem.) 61
		אַתָּה	you (sing. masc.) 61

Appendix

אַתֶּם	you (pl. masc.) 61		*Hoph.* to be broken into Jer. 39:2

אַתֶּם you (pl. masc.) 61

בְּ in, at, by, with 88

בֶּגֶד garment, covering 93

בְּהֵמָה beast, animal, cattle 96

בּוֹא to come in, come, go in, go 97

בּוֹר pit, cistern, well 92

בּוֹשׁ to be ashamed 101
Po'lel to delay Exod. 32:1 Judg. 5:28
Hithpo'l to be ashamed before one another Gen. 2:25

בָּחַר to choose 103
Pu. to be chosen, selected Eccl. 9:4

בֶּטֶן belly, body, womb 105

בָּטַח to trust 105

בִּין to discern, understand 106
Niph. to be intelligent, discerning, have understanding
Po'l. to attentively consider Deut. 32:10
*Hiph. to understand
Hithpo'l. to show oneself attentive, consider diligently
to get understanding Jer. 23:20; Job 26:14; Ps. 119:104
to show oneself to have understanding Ps. 119:100

בֵּין in the interval of, between 107

בַּיִת house, מִבַּיִת = on the inside, מִבֵּית = within 108

בָּכָה to weep, bewail 113
Pi. to lament Jer. 31:25
to bewail Ezek. 8:14

בְּכֹר, בְּכוֹר first born 114

בַּל Adv., not 115

בָּמָה high place 119

בֵּן son 119

בָּנָה to build 124

בַּעַד away from, behind, about, on behalf of 126

בַּעַל owner, lord, husband, citizens 127

בָּעַר to burn, consume 128
*Pi. to kindle, light
Pu. to burn Jer. 36:22

בָּקַע to cleave, break open or through 131
Pu. to be ripped open Josh. 9:4 Ezek. 26:10 Hos. 14:1

Hoph. to be broken into Jer. 39:2
Hithp. to burst (themselves) open Josh. 9:13
to cleave asunder Mic. 1:4

בָּקָר cattle, herd, ox 133

בֹּקֶר morning 133

בקשׁ *Pi.* to seek 134
Pu. to be sought Jer. 50:20 Esth. 2:23 Ezek. 26:21

בַּרְזֶל iron 137

בָּרַח to go through, flee 137
*Hiph. to pass through Ex. 26:28

בְּרִית covenant 136

ברך to kneel, bless 138
Niph. to bless oneself Gen. 12:3, 18:18, 28:14
Pi. to bless; to salute, greet
Pu. to be prospered
to have prosperity invoked Num. 22:6
Hiph. to cause to kneel Gen. 24:11

בְּרָכָה blessing 139

בָּשָׂר flesh 142

בַּת daughter 123

גָּאַל to redeem, act as kinsman 145
*Niph. to redeem oneself Lev. 25:49

גְּבוּל border, boundary, territory 147

גִּבּוֹר strong, mighty 150

גְּבוּרָה strength, might 150

גִּבְעָה hill 148

גֶּבֶר man 149

גָּדוֹל great 152

גָּדַל to grow up, become great 152
Pi. to cause to grow
to make great, powerful
to magnify
Pu. to be brought up Ps. 144:12
Hiph. to make great
to magnify
to do great things
Hithp. to magnify oneself Isa. 10:15 Ezek. 38:23 Dan. 11:36

גּוֹי nation, people 156

גּוּר to sojourn 157
Hithpo'l. to seek hospitality with 1 Kings 17:20 (Hos. 7:14 dub.)

גּוֹרָל   lot 174

גָּלָה   to uncover, remove 162
*Niph. to uncover oneself
*Pi. to disclose, lay bare
to make known, reveal
Hiph. to carry away into exile,
take into exile
Hithp. to be uncovered Gen. 9:21
to reveal oneself Prov. 18:2

גַּם   also, moreover, yea 168

גָּמָל   camel 168

גֶּפֶן   vine 172

גֵּר   sojourner 158

דָּבֵק   to cling, cleave, keep 179
Pu. to be joined together Job 38:38,
41:9
*Hiph. to pursue closely
to overtake
Hoph. to be made to cleave Ps. 22:16

דבר   to speak 180
Niph. to speak with one another
Hiph. to lead, or put to flight Ps. 18:48,
47:4
Hithp. to speak

דָּבָר   speech, word; saying, utterance;
matter, affair 182

דְּבַשׁ   honey 185

דּוֹד   beloved, love, uncle 187

דּוֹר   period, generation;
dwelling Isa. 38:12 Ps. 49:20 189

דֶּלֶת   door 195

דָּם   blood 196

דַּעַת   knowledge 395

דָּרַךְ   to tread, march
*Hiph. to tread, tread down 201

דֶּרֶךְ   way, road, distance, journey, manner 201

דָּרַשׁ   to resort to, seek 205
Niph. to let oneself be inquired of
to be required Gen. 42:22
to be sought out 1 Chron. 26:31

הַ, הָ, הֶ   (def. art.) the 206

הֲ, הַ, הֶ   interrog· part. 209

הֶבֶל   vapor, breath 210

הוּא   (3rd pers. sing. pron.) he, she (in Pent.), it; with art. = that 214–216

הוֹי   ah, alas, ha 222

הִיא   (3rd pers. sing. pron.) she, it; with art. = that 214–216

הָיָה   to be, become, come to pass, fall out 224

הֵיכָל   palace, temple 228

הָלַךְ   to go, come, walk 229
Niph. to be gone Ps. 109:23
Hithp. to walk, walk about, move to and fro

הלל   to be boastful 237
Pi. to praise
Hithpa. to make one's boast Ps. 10:3 44:9
Hithpa. to glory, boast, make one's boast
Po'el. to make fool of Isa. 44:25 Job 12:17 Eccl. 7:7
Po'al. to be mad Ps. 102:9, Eccl. 2:2
Hithpo. to act madly, like a madman

הֵם, הֵמָּה   (3rd pers. pl. masc. pron.; as neuter, rarely) they; with art=those (not defined in BDB) 241

הָמוֹן   sound, murmur, roar, crowd, abundance 242

הֵן   lo! behold! 243

הֵנָּה   fem. of הֵמָּה (see above) 241

הִנֵּה   lo! behold! 243

הָפַךְ   to turn, overturn 245
*Niph. to turn oneself, turn, turn back
Hithp. to turn this way and that Gen. 3:24 Judg. 7:13 Job 37:12
to transform oneself Job 38:14
Hoph. to be turned (upon) Job 30:15

הַר   mountain, hill, hill country 249

הָרַג   to kill, slay 246
Pu. to be slain Is. 27:7

וָ, וּ, וְ   (adv., conj.) so, then, and, and also, but, both . . . and (וְ . . . וְ), consecutive verb formations, (cohort.) so that (introduces apodosis after כִּ, אִם) then 251–255

זֹאת   fem. of זֶה (see below)

זָבַח   to slaughter for sacrifice 256

87

Pi. to sacrifice

זֶבַח   sacrifice 257

זֶה   (demonstr. sing. masc. pron. [fem., זֹאת] and adv.) this, here; also used idiomatically with prepositions 260–262

זָהָב   gold 262

זָכַר   to remember 269

זָכָר   male 271

זָנָה   to commit fornication, to be a harlot 275

Pu. Ezek. 16:34 ז׳ לֹא=fornication was not done

Hiph. to cause to commit fornication

to commit fornication

זעק   to cry, cry out, call 277

Niph. to be called together.

to assemble

to join

Hiph. to call, call out, or together

to make a crying Job 35:9 (וי ז׳ ויאמר)

to have proclamation made Jonah 3:7

to call out to, or at Zech. 6:8

זָקֵן   old 278

זָר   strange (adj.), stranger (noun) BDB under זור 266

זְרוֹעַ   arm, shoulder, strength 283

זָרַע   to sow, scatter seed 281

*Niph. to be made pregnant Num. 5:28

Pu. to be sown Isa. 40:24

Hiph. to produce seed Gen. 1:11, 12

to bear a child Lev. 12:2

זֶרַע   sowing, seed, offspring 282

חַג   festive-gathering, feast 290

חָדַל   to cease 292

Hoph. to be made to leave Judg. 9:9, 11, 13

חָדָשׁ   new 294

חֹדֶשׁ   new moon, month 294

חוֹמָה   wall 327

חוּץ   the outside, a street 299

חָזָה   to see, behold 302

חָזַק   to be or grow firm, strong, strengthen 304

Pi. to make strong, firm, hard

to strengthen

*Hiph. to prevail

to take or keep hold, seize, grasp

Hithp. to strengthen oneself

to put forth strength

to withstand 2 Chron. 13:7, 8

to hold strongly with

חָזָק   strong, stout, mighty 305

חָטָא   to miss, go wrong, sin 306

*Hiph. to miss the mark Judg. 20:16

to bring into guilt, condemnation

Hithp. to miss or lose oneself Job 41:17

to purify oneself

חַטָּאת   sin, sin offering 308

חַי   alive, living 311

חָיָה   to live 310

Pi. to preserve alive, let live

to give life Job 33:4

to quicken, revive, refresh

Hiph. to preserve alive, let live

to quicken, revive

חַיָּה   living thing, animal; life (some poetry); appetite Job 38:39; revival, renewal Isa. 57:10, 312

חַיִּים   life 313

חַיִל   strength, efficiency, wealth, army 298

חָכָם   wise 314

חָכְמָה   widsom 315

חֵלֶב   fat 316

חָלָה   to be weak, sick 317

Niph. to make oneself sick Jer. 12:13

to be made sick Dan. 8:27 Amos 6:6; Ptc.=diseased

Pi. to make sick Deut. 29:21 Ps. 77:11, to appease, entreat the favor of

Pu. to be made weak Isa. 14:10

Hithp. to make oneself sick 2 Sam. 13:2, 5, 6

*Hiph. to become sick Hos. 7:5

חֲלוֹם   dream 321

חלל   *Niph.* to pollute, defile oneself Lev. 21:4, 9, 320

to be polluted, defiled

Pi. to defile, pollute

to dishonor

to violate

to treat as common

Pu. to be profaned Ezek. 36:23

Hiph. to allow to be profaned Ezek. 39:7, 20:9

to begin

Hoph. to be begun Gen. 4:26

חָלָל   pierced 319

חָלַק   to divide, share 323

Niph. to divide oneself Gen. 14:15

to assign, distribute 1 Chron. 23:6, 24:3 (see Pi.)

Pi. to assign, distribute 1 Chron. 23:6, 24:3 (see Niph.)

to scatter Gen. 49:7 Lam. 4:16

Pu. to be divided Isa. 33:23 Amos 7:17 Zech. 14:1

Hiph. to receive a portion Jer. 37:12

Hithp. to divide among themselves Josh. 18:5

חֵלֶק   portion, tract, territory 324

חֵמָה   heat, rage 404

חֲמוֹר   he-ass, male donkey 331

חָמָס   violence, wrong 329

חֵן   favor, grace 336

חָנָה   to decline, bend down, encamp 333

חָנַן   to show favor, be gracious 335

Niph. to be pitied Jer. 22:23

Pi. to make gracious Jer. 26:25

Po'el to direct favor to Ps. 102:15 Prov. 14:21

Hoph. to be shown favor Isa. 26:10 Prov. 21:10

Hithp. to seek or implore favor

חֶסֶד   goodness, kindness 338

חָפֵץ   to delight in 342

חֵץ   arrow 346

חֲצִי   half 345

חָצֵר   enclosure, court 346

חֹק   something prescribed, a statute, decree, ordinance 349

חֻקָּה   something prescribed, enactment, statute 349

חֶרֶב   sword 352

חָרָה   to burn, be kindled (of anger) 354

Niph. to be angry Isa. 41:11, 45:24 Song of Sol. 1:6

Hiph. to be burned (?) Neh. 3:20

to cause to be kindled Job 19:11

Hithp. to heat oneself in vexation Ps. 37:1, 7, 8, Prov. 24:19

to hotly contend (dub.) Jer. 12:5

to strive eagerly (dub.) Jer. 22:15

חֶרְפָּה   reproach 357

חָשַׁב   to think, account, reckon 362

Hithp. to reckon oneself Num. 23:9

חֹשֶׁךְ   darkness, obscurity 365

חתת   to be shattered, dismayed 369

Niph. to be put in awe Mal. 2:5

Pi. to dismay, scare Job 7:14

to be shattered (?) Jer. 51:56

טָהוֹר   clean, pure 373

טָהֵר   to be clean, pure 372

Pi. to cleanse, purify

to pronounce clean *Pu.* to be cleansed 1 Sam. 20:26 Ezek. 22:24

Hithp. to purify oneself

to present oneself for purification

טוֹב   pleasant, agreeable, good 373

טָמֵא   to be, become unclean 379

Niph. to defile oneself, be defiled

to be regarded as unclean Job 18:3

Pi. to defile

to pronounce unclean

Hithp. to defile oneself

Hothp. to be defiled Deut. 24:4

טָמֵא   unclean 379

יְאֹר   stream, canal; stream of Nile 384

יָבֵשׁ   to be dry, dried up, withered 386

Pi. to make dry, dry up

Hiph. to exhibit dryness

יָד   hand 388

ידה   to shoot Jer. 50:14, 392

Pi. to cast Lam. 3:53 Zech. 2:4

Hiph. to give thanks, laud, praise

to confess

Hithp. to confess

to give thanks 2 Chron. 30:22

יָדַע   to know 393

Niph. to make oneself known

to be perceived Gen. 41:21 Ps. 74:5

to be instructed Jer. 31:19

Pi. to cause to know Job 38:12 Ps. 104:19(?)

Po. to cause to know 1 Sam. 21:3

Pu. ptc: known Isa. 12:5 as subst.=acquaintance (remaining Pu.)

Hithp. to make oneself known Gen. 45:1 Num. 12:6

יוֹם   day 398

יוֹמָם   daytime, by day 401

יַחְדָּו   together 403

יטב   to be good, well, glad, pleasing 405

יַיִן   wine 406

יכח   *Hiph.* to decide, adjudge, prove 406

Hoph. to be chastened Job. 33:19

Niph. to reason together Isa. 1:18

to reason Job 23:7

to be set right, justified Gen. 20:16

Hithp. to argue Mic. 6:2

יָכֹל   to be able, have power, prevail, endure 407

יָלַד   to bear, bring forth, beget 408

Pi. to cause (or help) to bring forth Exod. 1:16

Ptc. as subst. =midwife

Pu. to be born

Hiph. to beget

Hithp. to declare pedigree Num. 1:18

יֶלֶד   child, son, boy, youth 409

descendants Isa. 29:23

יָם   sea, freq. indicates western point of compass, west 410

יָמִין   right hand 411

יָסַף   to add 414

Niph. to join oneself to Exod. 1:10

יַעַן   on account of, because 774

יָעַץ   to advise, counsel 419

Niph. to consult together, exchange

counsel

Hithp. to conspire Ps. 83:4

יַעַר   wood, forest, thicket 420

יָצָא   to go or come out 422

יָצַק   to pour, cast, flow 427

Hiph. to pour out

Hoph. ptc.=cast, molten firmly established Job 11:15

יָרֵא   to fear 431

Pi. to make afraid, terrify

יָרַד   to come or go down, descend 432

יְרִיעָה   curtain 438

יָרַשׁ   take possession of, inherit, dispossess 439

Niph. to be impoverished

Pi. to take possession of, devour Deut. 28:42

Hiph. to take possession of Num. 14:24

יֵשׁ   is, are 441

יָשַׁב   to sit, remain, dwell 442

Pi. to set Ezek. 25:4

Hiph. to cause to be inhabited Ezek. 36:33 Isa. 54:3

to marry (only Ezra and Nehemiah)

Hoph. to be made to dwell Isa. 5:8

to be inhabited Isa. 44:26

יְשׁוּעָה   salvation; victory 447

ישׁע   *Hiph.* to deliver 446

Niph. to be liberated, saved

יָשָׁר   straight, right 449

יתר   *Qal* ptc. =remainder 1 Sam. 15:15, 45

Niph. to be left over, remain over

Hiph. to leave over, leave

to excel, show preeminence Gen. 49:4

to show excess=have more than enough Exod. 36:7

to make abundant Deut. 28:11; 30:9

יֶתֶר   remainder, excess, preeminence 451

כְּ   the like of, like, as 453

כַּאֲשֶׁר   according as, as, when 455

כָּבֵד   to be heavy, weighty, burdensome, honored 457

Niph. to be made heavy Prov. 8:24

to be honored, enjoy honor

to get oneself glory

Pi. to make heavy, insensible 1 Sam. 6:66

to make honorable

to honor, glorify

Pu. to be made honorable, honored Isa. 58:13 Pr. 13:18, 27:18

Hiph. to display honor

Hithp. to make oneself heavy Nah. 3:15

to honor oneself Prov. 12:9

כָּבוֹד   abundance, honor, glory 458

כבס   to wash, ptc. only = fuller, washer 460

Pu. to be washed Lev. 13:58, 15:17

Hothp. to be washed out Lev. 13:55, 56

כֶּבֶשׂ   lamb 461

כֹּה   thus, here 462

כֹּהֵן   priest 463

כּוּן   *Niph.* to be set up, established, fixed 465

to be directed aright

to be prepared, ready

Hiph. to establish, set up

to fix, make ready

to direct

to arrange, order 2 Chron. 29:19, 35:20

Po'lel to set up, establish

to constitute, make

to fix

to direct Job 8:8

Po'lal to be established Ps. 37:23

to be prepared Ezek. 28:13

Hithpo'l to be established

כֹּחַ   strength, power 470

כִּי   that, for, when, because, since 471

כִּכָּר   a round; hence

   1. a round district

   2. a round loaf

   3. a round weight, talent

כֹּל   whole, all 481

כָּלָה   to be complete, at an end, finished, accomplished, spent 477

Pi. to complete, bring to an end, finish

accomplish

to cause to cease Num. 17:25, Ps. 78:33

to exhaust, use up

to consume Lev. 26:16

to destroy

Pu. to be finished, ended Ps. 72:20

to be complete Gen. 2:1

כְּלִי   article, utensil, vessel 479

כְּמוֹ   like, as, when 455

כֵּן   so, thus 485

כָּנָף   wing, extremity 489

כִּסֵּא (כִּסֵּה)   seat of honor, throne 490

כסה   to conceal, cover, ptc. only: Act.= to conceal Prov. 12:16, 23 491

Pass.="covered" Ps. 32:1

Niph. to be covered Jer. 51:42 Ezek. 24:8

Pual to be clothed 1 Chron. 21:16 Eccl. 6:4

כְּסִיל   stupid fellow, fool 493

כֶּסֶף   silver, money 494

כָּעַס   to be vexed, angry 494

Pi. to be angered 1 Sam. 1:6 Deut. 32:21

כַּף   hollow, flat of hand, palm, sole, pan 496

כְּפִי   according to the command of, according to the mouth of, in proportion to (of, that) 805

כָּפַר   *Pi.* to cover over, pacify, make propitiation, atone 497

Hithp. to be covered 1 Sam. 3:14

Nithp. to be covered Deut. 21:8

כְּרוּב   cherub 500

כֶּרֶם   vineyard 501

כָּרַת   to cut off, cut down 503

Niph. to be chewed Num. 11:33

Pual to be cut off Ezek. 16:4

to be cut down Judg. 6:28

Hiph. to take away 1 Sam. 20:15

to permit to perish 1 Kings 18:5

כָּשַׁל   to stumble, stagger, totter 505

Niph. (= Qal)

to be tottering, feeble Isa. 40:30, 1 Sam.

2:4. Zech. 12:8

Pi. Ezek. 36:14 only (but see BDB)

*Hiph. to make feeble, weak Lam. 1:14

Hoph. ptc. only=the ones who have stumbled Jer. 18:23 Ezek. 21:20(?)

כָּתַב   to write 507

Pi. to write Isa. 10:1

כָּתֵף   shoulder, shoulder-blade; side; support 1 Kings 7:30, 34 509

לְ   to, for, in regard to 510

לֹא, לוֹא   Adv., not 518

לֵב   inner man, mind, will, heart 524

לֵבָב   inner man, mind, will, heart 523

לְבַד   in a state of separation, alone, by itself 94

לְבַד מִן   besides, apart from 94

לְבִלְתִּי   so as not, in order not (to) 116

לָבַשׁ   to put on, wear, clothe, be clothed 527

Pu. ptc. only=arrayed

לחם   to fight, do battle Ps. 35:1, 56:2, 3 535

Niph. to engage in battle, wage war

לֶחֶם   bread, food 536

לַיִל, לַיְלָה   night 538

לוּן, לִין   to lodge, pass the night 533

Hiph. to cause to rest, lodge 2 Sam. 17:8

Hithpo'l to dwell, abide Job 39:28 Ps. 91:1

לָכַד   to capture, seize, take 539

Hithp. to grasp each other Job 41:9 to compact Job 38:30

לָכֵן   therefore 486

לָמַד   to exercise in, learn 540

Pi. to teach

לָמָה, לָמֶה   why? 554

לְמַעַן   for the sake of, on account of, to the intent that, in order that 775

לְפִי   according to (as) 805

לִפְנֵי   at the face of or front of, in the presence of, before 816

לָקַח   to take 542

Pu. to be taken Gen. 2:23 3:19, 23 Jer. 29:22

to be stolen Judg. 17:2

to be taken captive Jer. 48:46

to be taken away, removed 2 Kings 2:10 Isa. 53:8

Hoph. to be taken, brought

Hithp. to take hold of oneself Exod. 9:24 Ezek. 1:4

לָשׁוֹן   tongue 546

מְאֹד   muchness, force, abundance, exceedingly 547

מֵאַחַר   from after 29

מָאַס   to reject, refuse, despise 549

מָגֵן   shield 171

מִגְרָשׁ   common, common land, open land 177

מִדְבָּר   wilderness 184

מָדַד   to measure 551

Pi. to extend, continue Job 7:4

to measure, measure off 2 Sam. 8:2 Ps. 60:8, 108:8

Po. to be measured Hab. 3:6

Hithpo. to measure himself 1 Kings 17:21

מִדָּה   measure, measurement 551

garment Ps. 133:2

size Jer. 22:14

stature 1 Chron. 11:23, 20:6

מַדּוּעַ   wherefore? on what account? 396

מְדִינָה   province 193

מֶה, מָה   what? how? aught? 552

מהר   *Niph.* to be hurried, hasty 554

Pi. to hasten, make haste

Inf. Abs. מַהֵר quickly, speedily

מַהֵר   quickly, speedily 555

מוֹעֵד   appointed time, place, meeting 417

מוּת   to die 559

Po'lel to kill, put to death

*Hoph. to die prematurely Prov. 19:16

מָוֶת   death 560

מִזְבֵּחַ   altar 258

מִזְמוֹר   melody 274

מִזְרָח   place of sunrise, east 280

מַחֲנֶה encampment, camp 334

מָחָר tomorrow, in time to come 563

מַחֲשָׁבָה thought, device 364

מַטֶּה staff, rod, shaft; tribe, branch Ezek. 19:11, 12, 14 641

מִי who? 566

מַיִם (pl. of מַי) pl. only; water, waters 565

מָכַר to sell 569

*Niph. to sell oneself

מָלֵא to be full, fill 569

*Niph. to be accomplished, ended Exod. 7:25 Job 15:32

*Pi. to confirm 1 Kings 1:14

Pu. ptc.=set Song of Sol. 5:14

Hithp. to mass oneself Job 16:10

מָלֵא full 570

מַלְאָךְ messenger 521

מְלָאכָה occupation, work; workmanship; property; service, use; public business 521

מִלְחָמָה battle, war 536

מלט Niph. to slip away 1 Sam. 20:29 2 Sam. 4:6 572

to escape

to be delivered

Pi. to lay (eggs) Isa. 34:15

to let escape 2 Kings 23:18

to deliver

Hiph. to give birth to Isa. 66:7

to deliver Isa. 31:5

Hithp. to slip forth, escape Job 41:11

to escape Job 19:20

מָלַךְ to be, become, king or queen, to reign 573

Hoph. to be made king Dan. 9:1

מֶלֶךְ king 572

מַלְכוּת royalty, royal power, reign, kingdom 574

מִלִּפְנֵי from before, because 817

מַמְלָכָה kingdom, sovereignty, dominion, reign 575

מִן out of, from, on account of, off, on the side of, since, above, than, so that not 577

מִנְחָה gift, tribute, offering 585

מְנַצֵּחַ Pi. ptc. of נצח; in Psalms=perh. musical director, choir master; elsewhere=director 663

מִסְפָּר number; recounting Judg. 7:15 708

מְעַט a little, fewness, a few 589

מַעַל above, upwards 751

מֵעַל from upon, from over, from by (beside) 758–759

מַעֲלָה upwards 751

מֵעִם from with or beside; away from, from 768

מַעֲשֶׂה deed, work 795

מִפְּנֵי from the face or presence of, from before, because 818

מָצָא to attain to, find 592

to learn, devise Eccl. 7:27, 27, 29

to experience Ps. 116:3 Eccl. 7:14

to find out

to come upon, light upon

to hit Deut. 19:5 1 Sam. 31:3 1 Chron. 10:3

*Niph. to be gained; secured Ho. 14:9

to be left

to be present

to prove to be 1 Chron. 24:4 2 Chron. 2:16

to be sufficient Josh. 17:16

*Hiph. to cause to encounter 2 Sam. 3:8 Zech. 11:6

to present Lev. 9:12, 13, 18

מַצָּה unleavened bread or cake(s) 595

מִצְוָה commandment 846

מִקְדָּשׁ sacred place, sanctuary 874

מָקוֹם standing place, place 879

מִקְנֶה cattle 889

מַרְאֶה sight, appearance, vision 909

מָרוֹם height 928

מָשַׁח to smear, anoint 602

מִשְׁכָּן dwelling place, 'tabernacle' 1015

מָשַׁל to rule, have dominion, reign 605

Hiph. to cause to rule Ps. 8:7 Dan. 11:39

to exercise dominion Job 25:2

מִשְׁמֶרֶת guard, watch; charge, function 1038
מִשְׁפָּחָה clan 1046
מִשְׁפָּט judgment, justice, right manner, fitting 1 Kings 5:8; fitness Isa. 28:26; 40:14 1048
מֵת dead one, corpse 559 (מוּת)
מִתַּחַת from under, from beneath, from 1066
נָא part. of entreaty of exhortation, I pray, now 609
נְאֻם utterance, declaration 610
נבא *Niph.* to prophesy 612
Hithp. to prophesy
נבט *Pi.* to look Isa. 5:30 613
Hiph. to look
to regard, show regard
נָבִיא spokesman, speaker, prophet 611
נֶגֶב south country, Negeb, south 616
נגד *Hiph.* to declare, tell 616
to avow, acknowledge, confess Isa. 3:9 Ps. 38:19
Hoph. to be told, announced, reported
נֶגֶד in front of, in sight of, opposite to 617
נָגַע to touch, reach, strike 619
Niph. to be stricken, defeated Josh. 8:15
Pi. to strike Gen. 12:17 2 Kings 15:5 2 Chron. 26:20
Pu. to be stricken Ps. 73:5
Hiph. to reach, extend
to approach
to befall
נֶגַע stroke, plague, mark 619
נגש to draw near, approach 620
Niph. (as Qal)
Hoph. to be brought near 2 Sam. 3:34 Mal. 1:11
Hithp. to draw near Isa. 45:20
נֶדֶר vow 623
נָהָר stream, river 625
נוּח to rest 628
Hiph. to leave
to abandon Jer. 14:9 Ps. 119:121
to permit

Hoph. to be caused to rest La. 5:5 Zech. 5:11
ptc. as subst=space left, open space Ezek. 41:9, 11
נוס to flee, escape 630
Po'lel to cause to flee, to drive Isa. 59:19
Hithpo'l to take flight Ps. 60:6
Hiph. to put to flight Deut. 32:30
to drive hastily Exod. 9:20
to cause to disappear, hide Judg. 6:11
נָחַל to get or take as a possession 635
Pi. to divide for a possession
נַחַל torrent, torrent valley, wady 636
נַחֲלָה possession, property, inheritance 635
נחם *Niph.* to be sorry 636
to comfort oneself
Pi. to comfort, console
Pual to be relieved, consoled Isa. 54:11, 66:13
Hithp. to be sorry, have compassion Deut. 32:36 Ps. 135:14
to rue Num. 23:19
to comfort oneself, be relieved Gen. 37:35 Ps. 119:52
to ease oneself Ezek. 5:13 Gen. 27:42
נְחֹשֶׁת copper, bronze, (dual) fetter of copper or bronze 638
נָטָה to stretch out, spread out, extend, incline, bend 639
Niph. to be stretched out Num. 24:6 Zech. 1:16
to stretch themselves out Jer. 6:4
Hiph. to stretch out Isa. 31:3 Jer. 6:12, 15:6
to spread out 2 Sam. 16:22, 21:10 Isa. 54:2
to turn, incline
נטע to plant 642
Niph. to be planted Isa. 40:24
נכה *Niph.* to be smitten 2 Sam. 11:15 645
Pu. to be smitten Exod. 9:31, 32
Hiph. to smite, strike

נֶסֶךְ drink-offering; molten images 651

נָסַע to pull out or up, set out, journey 652

Niph. to be pulled up Isa. 38:12 Job 4:21

נַעַר boy, lad, youth; servant 654

נַעֲרָה girl, damsel 655

נָפַל to fall, lie 656

Pi'lel Ezek. 28:23 But BDB="rd. וְנִפַּל"

נֶפֶשׁ soul, living being, life, self, person, desire, appetite, emotion, passion 659

נצב *Niph.* to take one's stand, stand 662
Hiph. to station, set, set up
Hoph. to be fixed, determined Gen. 28:12 Judg. 9:6 Nah. 2:8

נצל *Niph.* to deliver oneself, be delivered 664
*Pi.*to strip off, spoil 2 Chron. 20:25 Exod. 3:22, 12:36
to deliver Ezek. 14:14
Hiph. to snatch away, deliver
Hoph. to be plucked out Amos. 4:11 Zech. 3:2
Hithp. to strip oneself Exod. 33:6

נצר to watch, guard, keep 665

נָשָׂא to lift, carry, take 669

נָשִׂיא a chief, prince 672

נָתַן to give, put, set 678
Hoph. (as *Niph.*)

סָבַב to turn about, go around, surround 685
Niph. to turn oneself
to be turned over Jer. 6:12
Pi. to change 2 Sam. 14:20
Po. to encompass, surround

סָבִיב circuit, round about 686

סָגַר to shut, close 688
Pi. to deliver up
Pu. to be shut up
Hiph. to deliver up
to shut up

סוּס horse 692

סֹפֵר secretary, muster officer, scribe 708

סוּר to turn aside 693

Po'lel to turn aside Lam. 3:11

*Hiph. to put aside

סָלָה (a benediction[?]) see BDB 699

סֶלַע crag, cliff 700

סֹלֶת fine flour 701

סָפַר to count 707
Pi. to recount, rehearse, declare

סֵפֶר document, writing, book 706

סָתַר *Niph.* to hide oneself 711
to be hid, concealed
Pi. to carefully hide Isa. 16:3
Pu. to be carefully concealed Prov. 27:5
Hithp. to hide oneself
Hiph. to conceal, hide

עָבַד to work, serve 712
Niph. to be tilled Deut. 21:4 Ezek. 36:9, 34
ptc.=cultivated Eccl. 5:8 (dub.)
Pu. to be worked Deut. 21:3 Isa. 14:3

עֶבֶד servant, slave, subject 713

עֲבֹדָה labor, service 715

עָבַר to pass over, through, by, on 716
Niph. to be forded Ezek. 47:5
Pi. to impregnate Job 21:10
to cause to pass across 1 Kings 6:21

עֵבֶר region across or beyond, side 719

עַד as far as, even to, up to, until, while 723

עֵד witness 729

עֵדָה congregation 417

עֵדוּת testimony 730

עוֹד still, yet, again, besides 728

עוֹלָם forever, always, everlasting; ancient, old; age 761

עָוֹן iniquity, guilt; punishment of iniquity 730

עוֹף coll. birds, fowl; flying insects 733

עוּר to rouse oneself, awake 734
Po'l to rouse, incite
Pilp. to rouse, (raise?) Isa. 15:5
Hithpo'l to be excited Job 31:29, 17:8
to rouse oneself Isa. 64:6
Hiph. to rouse
to act aroused Ps. 35:23, 73:20

עוֹר   skin, hide 736

עֵז   she-goat; pl. subst.=goat's hair 777

עֹז   strength, might 738

עָזַב   to leave, forsake, loose 736
Pu. to be deserted Isa. 32:14 Jer. 49:25

עזר   to help 740
Hiph. (dub.) as Qal 2 Sam. 18:3 2 Chron. 28:23

עַיִן   eye; surface Exod. 10:5, 15 Num. 22:5, 11
appearance Lev. 13:5, 37, 55 Num. 11:7 1 Sam. 16:7(?), gleam, sparkle Ezek. 1 (5t), 8:2, 10:9 Dan. 10:6 Prov. 23:31 744

עִיר   city, town; fortress 746

עַל   on, on the ground of, according to, on account of, on behalf of, concerning, besides, in addition to, together with, beyond, above, over, by, onto, toward, to, against 752–759

עָלָה   to go up, ascend, climb 748
Niph. to take oneself away 2 Sam. 2:27
to be exalted Ps. 47:10, 97:9
Hiph. to take away Ps. 102:25 Job 36:20
Hoph. to be carried away Nah. 2:8
to be taken up 2 Chron. 20:34
to be offered Judg. 6:23
Hithp. to lift oneself Jer. 51:3

עֹלָה   whole burnt offering 750

עֶלְיוֹן   upper, high, highest 751

עַם, עָם   people, nation 766

עִם   with 767

עָמַד   to take one's stand, stand; to arise, appear
to be appointed Ezek. 10:14
to grow flat, insipid Jer. 48:11 763
Hiph. to station, set
to have a fixed look ע׳ אֶת-פָּנָיו 2 Kings 8:11
to restore Ezra 9.9
to raise Dan. 11:11, 13

עַמּוּד   pillar, column 765

עָמָל   trouble, mischief, toil 765

עֵמֶק   valley, lowland 770

עָנָה   to answer, respond 772
Niph. to make answer Ezra 14:4, 7
Hiph. ptc. Eccl. 5:19 (dub.) See BDB

ענה   to be put down or become low Isa. 25:5 776
to be depressed, down cast Isa. 31:4
to be afflicted Ps. 116:10, 119:67 Zech. 10:2
Niph. to humble oneself Exod. 10:3
to be afflicted Isa. 53:7, 58:10 Ps. 119:107
Pi. to humble, afflict
Pu. to be afflicted Ps. 119:71, 132:1 Isa. 53:4
to be humbled Lev. 23:29
Hiph. to afflict 1 Kings 8:35 2 Chon. 6:26
Hithp. to humble oneself Gen. 16:9 Ezek. 8:21 Dan. 10:12
to be afflicted 1 Kings 2:26 Ps. 107:17

עָנִי   poor, afflicted, humble 776

עָנָן   cloudmass, cloud 777

עָפָר   dry earth, dust; ore Job 28:2 779

עֵץ   tree, trees, wood 781

עֵצָה   counsel, advice 420

עֶצֶם   bone, substance; self (same) 782

עֶרֶב   evening; night Job 7:4 787

עֲרָבָה   desert plain, steppe 787

עֶרְוָה   nakedness, pudenda 788

עָרַךְ   to arrange, set in order
to compare Isa. 40:18 Ps. 40:6
to be comparable Ps. 89:7 Job 28:17, 19 789
Hiph. to value, tax

עָשָׂה   to do, work
to make
to acquire
to use 1 Sam. 8:16 Exod. 38:24
to spend, pass. Eccl. 6:12 793
Pu. to be made Ps. 139:15

עֵת   time; experiences, fortunes Isa. 33:6 Ps. 31:16 1 Chron. 29:30 773

עַתָּה now 773

פֵּאָה corner, side 802

פָּדָה to ransom 804

פֶּה mouth; end 2 Kings 10:21, 21:16 Ezra. 9:11
portion Deut. 21:17 2 Kings 2:9 Zech. 13:8 804

פוּץ to be dispersed, scattered 806
Niph. (as Qal)

פָּלַל *Pi.* to mediate, arbitrate, interpose 813
Hithp. to pray, intercede

פֶּן lest 814

פָּנָה to turn, turn and look, look 815
Pi. to turn away, put out of the way
Hiph. to turn Judg. 15:4 1 Sam. 10:9 Jer. 48:39
to make a turn
Hoph. to be turned Jer. 49:8 Ezek. 9:2

פָּנֶה face 815

פָּעַל to do, make 821

פַּעַם once, time, step, now; anvil 821

פָּקַד to attend to, visit, muster, appoint 823
Niph. to be missed, lacking
Pi. to muster Isa. 13:4
Pu. to be passed in review Exod. 38:21
to be caused to miss Isa. 38:10
Hithp. to be mustered Judg. 20:15, 17, 21:9
Hothp. (as Hithp.)
Hiph. to set, make overseer
to commit, entrust
to deposit
Hoph. to be visited Jer. 6:6
to be deposited Lev. 5:23
to be made overseer

פַּר young bull, steer 830

פְּרִי fruit 826

פַּרְעֹה Pharaoh 829

פָּרַשׂ to spread out, spread 831
Niph. to be scattered Ezek. 17:21, 34:12

פָּרָשׁ horseman; horse 832

פֶּשַׁע transgression; guilt of transgression; punishment for transgression; Dan. 8:12, 13, 9:24; offering for transgression Mic. 6:7 833

פָּתַח to open 834

פֶּתַח doorway, opening, entrance 835

צֹאן (coll.) small cattle, sheep and goats, flock, flocks 838

צָבָא army, host; war, warfare, service 838

צַדִּיק just, righteous 843

צֶדֶק rightness, righteousness 841

צְדָקָה righteousness 842

צָוָה *Pi.* to lay charge (upon), give charge (to), charge, command, order 845

צוּר rock, cliff 849

צֵל shadow, shade 853

צָלַח to rush
to be successful, prosper 852
Hiph. to show experience, prosperity

צָעַק to cry, cry out 858
Niph. to be summoned
Hiph. to call together 1 Sam. 10:17
Pi. to cry aloud 2 Kings 2:12

צָפוֹן north 860

צַר adversary, foe 865

צָרָה straits, distress 865

צָרַר to bind, tie up
to be scant, cramped 864
Pu. to be tied up Josh. 9:4
Hiph. to make narrow, press hard, cause distress

קָבַץ to gather, collect, assemble 867
Niph. (as Qal)
Hithp. to gather together, be gathered together

קָבַר to bury 868

קֶבֶר grave, tomb 868

קָדוֹשׁ sacred, holy 872

קָדִים East, east wind 870

קֶדֶם front, east; ancient, of old; beginning Prov. 8:22, 23 869

קָדַשׁ to be set apart, consecrated 872
Niph. to show oneself sacred, majestic

to be honored

to be consecrated Exod. 29:43

Pi. to consecrate, dedicate;

to keep sacred

to honor as sacred, hallow

Hiph. (as *Pi.*)

Hithp. to be observed as holy Isa. 30:29

to consecrate oneself

קֹדֶשׁ   apartness, sacredness 871

קָהָל   assembly, company, congregation 874

קוֹל   sound, voice 876

קוּם   to arise, stand up, stand

to be fulfilled 877

Pi. to fulfil Ezek. 13:6 Ps. 119:106

to confirm, ratify Ruth 4:7

to establish Ps. 119:28

to impose Esth. 9 (7 times)

Po'l. to raise up

Hithpo'l to rise up

*Hiph. to raise, set up

קָטֹן   small, insignificant 882

קטר   *Pi.* to make sacrifices smoke 882

Pu. to be fumigated Song of Sol. 3:6

Hiph. to make (sacrifices) smoke

Hoph. to be made to smoke Lev. 6:15 Mal. 1:11

קְטֹרֶת   incense, sweet smoke of sacrifice 1 Sam. 2:28 (?) Isa. 1:13 Ps. 66: 15, 141:2 882

קִיר   wall 885

קָלַל   to be slight, swift, trifling 886

Niph. to show oneself swift Isa. 30:16

to be, appear trifling

to be lightly esteemed 2 Sam. 6:22

Pi. to curse

Hiph. to make light, lighten

to treat with contempt

Pilp. to shake Ezek. 21:26

to whet Eccl. 10:10

Hithpalp. to shake oneself Jer. 4:24

קָנָה   to get, acquire; buy 888

קָנֶה   stalk, reed; shoulder joint Job 31:22 889

קֵץ   end 893

קָצֶה   end; border, outskirts 892

קָרָא   to call, proclaim, read 894

*Niph. to call oneself Isa. 48:2

קרא   to encounter, befall, often

with ל (לִקְרַאת) = toward, against

Niph. to meet unexpectedly Exod. 5:3 Deut. 22:6 2 Sam. 18:9, 20:1

Hiph. to cause to befall Jer. 32:23

קָרַב   to approach, come near 897

Niph. to be brought Exod. 22:7 Josh. 7:14

Pi. to cause to approach, bring near

קֶרֶב   inward part, midst 899

קָרְבָּן   offering, oblation 898

קָרוֹב   near 898

קֶרֶן   horn; hill Isa. 5:1; rays Hab. 3:4 901

קָרַע   to tear 902

קֶרֶשׁ   board, coll. boards Ezek. 27:6 903

קֶשֶׁת   bow 905

רָאָה   to see 906

to select 2 Kings 10:3 1 Sam. 16:1

to provide, furnish Deut. 33:21 Gen. 22:8, 14

to consider, reflect Eccl. 7:14

*Niph. to appear

Pu. to be seen, detected Job 33:21

*Hiph. to cause to experience Hab. 1:3 Ps. 60:5 71:20 85:8

Hithp. = reciprocal

רֹאשׁ   head, top; beginning, first; chief; sum 910

רִאשׁוֹן   former, first, chief; before, formerly 911

רֵאשִׁית   beginning, first, chief 912

רַב   much, many, great, chief 912

רֹב   multitiude, abundance 913

רבה   to be, become, much, many, great 915

Pi. to increase, enlarge Judg. 9:29 P 44:13

to bring up, rear Lam. 2:22 Ezek. 19:2

*Hiph. הַרְבֵּה greatly, exceedingly

רֶגֶל   foot 919

רָדַף   to pursue, chase, persecute 922
Hiph. to chase Judg. 20:43

רוּחַ   breath, wind, spirit; quarter, side Ezek. 42:16, 17, 18, 19, 20 1 Chron. 9:24 Jer. 52:23 924

רוּם   to be high, exalted, rise 926
Po'lel to cause to rise
to erect, raise, exalt
Hoph. to be taken off Lev. 4:10
be abolished Dan. 8:11
Hithpo'l to exalt oneself Isa. 33:10 Dan. 11:36

רוּץ   to run 930
Po'lel to run swiftly, dart Nah. 2:5

רֹחַב   breadth, width 931

רָחוֹק   distant, far; distance 935

רָחַץ   to wash 934
Pu. to be washed Prov. 30:12 Ezek. 16:4
Hithp. to wash oneself Job 9:30

רָחַק   to be or become far, distant 934
Pi. to send far away

רִיב   to strive, contend 936
Hiph. ptc.=displaying contention 1 Sam. 2:10 Hos. 4:4

רִיב   strife, dispute 936

רֵיחַ   scent, odor 926

רָכַב   to ride, mount and ride 938

רֶכֶב   chariots; upper millstone Deut. 24:6 Judg. 9:53 2 Sam. 11:21 riders, troop 2 Kings 7:14 Isa. 21:7, 9, 22:6 939

רָנַן   to give ringing cry 943
Pu. "no ringing cry shall be given" Isa. 16:10

רַע   bad, evil; distress, misery, injury, calamity 948

רֵעַ   friend, companion, fellow 945

רָעָב   famine, hunger 944

רָעָה   to pasture, tend, graze 944

רָעָה   evil, misery, distress, injury 949

רֹעֶה   shepherd, herdsman 945 (רָעָה)

רעע   to be evil, bad 949
Niph. to suffer hurt Prov. 11:15, 13:20

Hiph. to do an injury, hurt to do evil, wickedly

רָפָא   to heal 950
Hithp. Inf. cstr. to get healed 2 Kings 8:29, 9:15 2 Chron. 22:6

רצה   to be pleased with, to accept 953
to be pleased Ps. 40:14 1 Chron. 28:4
to make acceptable
Niph. to be accepted
Pi. to seek favor Job 20:10
Hiph. to pay off Lev. 25:34
Hithp. to make oneself acceptable 1 Sam. 29:4

רָצוֹן   goodwill, favor, acceptance, will 953

רַק   only, altogether, surely 956

רָשָׁע   wicked, criminal; guilty 957

שָׂבַע   to be sated, satisfied, surfeited 959
Niph. ptc. sated Job 31:31
Pi. to satisfy Ezek. 7:19 Ps. 90:14

שָׂדֶה   field, land 961

שִׂים, שׂוּם   to put, place, set 962
Hiph. (see BDB) Ezek. 14:8, 21:21 Job 4:20
Hoph. to be set Gen. 24:33

שָׂכַל   to be prudent 1 Sam. 18:30 968
Hiph. to look at Gen. 3:6
to consider, ponder
to have insight
to cause to consider
to give insight
to act prudently
to prosper
to cause to prosper Deut. 29:8 1 Kings 2:3

שְׂמֹאל   the left 969

שָׂמַח   to rejoice, be glad 970
Pi. to cause to rejoice
Hiph. (=*Pi.*) Ps. 89:43

שִׂמְחָה   joy, gladness, mirth 970

שָׂנֵא   to hate 971
Niph. to be hated Prov. 14:17, 20
Pi. ptc. only, enemy

שָׂעִיר   he-goat, buck 972

שָׂפָה   lip, speech, edge 973

שַׂר   chief, ruler, official, captain, prince 978

שָׂרַף   to burn 976

Pi. ptc. one burning Amos 6:10

Pu. to be burnt up Lev. 10:16

שֶׁ ,שַׁ ,שֲׁ   who, which, that 979

שְׁאוֹל   sheol, hades 982

שָׁאַל   to ask, inquire 981

Niph. to ask for oneself 1 Sam. 20:6, 28 Neh. 13:6

Pi. to inquire carefully 2 Sam. 20:18 to beg Ps. 109:10

Hiph. to grant, make over to 1 Sam. 1:28, 2:20(?) Exod. 12:36

שָׁאַר   to remain, be left over 1 Sam. 16:11 983

Niph. (as Qal)

שְׁאֵרִית   rest, residue, remnant, remainder 984

שֵׁבֶט   rod, staff, club, sceptre; tribe 986

שבע   *Qal* ptc. pass. those sworn Ezek. 21:28 989

Niph. to swear

Hiph. to cause to swear

to adjure

שָׁבַר   to break, break in pieces 990

Hiph. to cause to break out Isa. 66:9

Hoph. to be broken, shattered Jer. 8:21

שָׁבַת   to cease, desist, rest 991

Niph. to cease

Hiph. to cause to fail Lev. 2:13 Jer. 48:35 Ruth 4:14

שַׁבָּת   Sabbath 992

שדד   to deal violently with, despoil, devastate, ruin 994

Niph. to be utterly ruined Mic. 2:4

Pi. to assault Prov. 24:15, 19:26

Pu. to be devastated

Po'el to violently destroy Hos. 10:2

Hoph. to be devastated Hos. 10:14 Isa. 33:1

שָׁוְא   emptiness, vanity 996

שׁוּב   to turn back, return 996

Po'l. to bring back

to restore Ps. 23:3 Isa. 58:12

to lead away Ezek. 38:4, 39:2 Isa. 47:10

to apostatize Jer. 8:5

Pu. to be restored Ezek. 38:8

שׁוֹפָר   horn 1051

שׁוֹר   a head of cattle (without reference to sex); bullock, ox 1004

שׁחה   to bow down Isa. 51:23 1005

Hiph. to depress Prov. 12:25

Hithpa'lel to bow down, prostrate oneself

שָׁחַט   to slaughter, beat 1006

Niph. to be slaughtered Num. 11:22 Lev. 6:18

שחת   *Niph.* to be marred, spoiled Jer. 13:7, 18:4 1007

to be injured Exod. 8:20

to be corrupted, corrupt Gen. 6:11, 12 Ezek. 20:44

Pi. to spoil, ruin

to pervert, corrupt

Hiph. (=*Pi.*)

Hoph. ptc. spoiled, ruined Prov. 25:26 Mal. 1:14

שׁיר   to sing 1010

Po'l. to sing

Hoph. to be sung Isa. 26:1

שִׁיר   song 1010

שִׁית   to put, set

to make 1011

Hoph. to be imposed Exod. 21:30

שָׁכַב   to lie down 1011

שָׁכַח   to forget 1013

Pi. to cause to forget Lam. 2:6

Hiph. (=*Pi.*) Jer. 23:27

Hithp. to be forgotten Eccl. 8:10

שכם   *Hiph.* to start early, rise early 1014

שָׁכֵן   to settle down, abide, dwell 1014

Pi. to make settle down, establish

to make to dwell Num. 14:30 Jer. 7:3, 7

Hiph. to lay Ps. 7:6

to place, set, establish Gen. 3:24 Josh. 18:1

to cause to settle Ezek. 32:4

to cause to dwell Ps. 78:55

שָׁלוֹם peace, completeness, soundness, welfare 1022

שָׁלַח to send, stretch out

to let loose Ps. 50:19 1018

Pi. to send away

to let go, set free

to shoot forth

to let down Jer. 38:6, 11

to shoot 1 Sam. 20:20

Hiph. to send

שֻׁלְחָן table 1020

שָׁלַךְ *Hiph.* to throw, fling, cast 1020

שָׁלָל prey, spoil, plunder, booty 1021

שלם to be complete, sound Job 9:4 1022

Pi. to complete, finish 1 Kings 9:25

to make whole

to make safe Job 8:6

to make good

to reward, recompense

Pu. to be performed Ps. 65:2

to be repaid, requited Jer. 18:20 Prov. 11:31, 13:13

Hiph. to make and end of Isa. 38:12, 13

to complete, perform Job 23:14 Isa. 44:26, 28

שֶׁלֶם peace offering; sacrifice for alliance or friend 1023

שָׁם there, thither 1027

שֵׁם name 1027

שמד *Niph.* to be exterminated, destroyed 1029

Hiph. to annihilate, exterminate to destroy

שָׁמַיִם heavens, sky 1029

שמם to be desolated, appalled 1030

Niph. (as Qal)

Po'. to be appalled Ezra 9:3, 4

to be appalling, causing horror

Hithpo. to be appalled

to cause oneself desolation, ruin Eccl. 7:16

שְׁמָמָה devastation, waste 1031

שֶׁמֶן fat, oil 1032

שָׁמַע to hear 1033

Niph. to grant hearing 2 Chron. 30:27

Pi. to cause to hear 1 Sam. 15:4, 23:8

שָׁמַר to keep, watch, preserve 1036

Niph. to be on one's guard

to keep oneself, refrain 1 Sam. 21:5

to be kept, guarded Hos. 12:14 Ps. 37:28

Pi. to pay regard Jonah 2:9

Hithp. to keep oneself from Ps. 18:24 2 Sam. 22:24 Mic. 6:16

שֹׁמֵר watchman 1036 (שָׁמַר)

שֶׁמֶשׁ sun; pinnacle, battlement 1039

שֵׁן tooth, ivory 1042

שָׁנָה year 1040

שַׁעַר gate 1044

שִׁפְחָה maid, maid-servant 1046

שָׁפַט to judge, govern 1047

Niph. to enter into controversy, plead

to be judged Ps. 9:20, 37:33, 109:7

Po'el ptc. opponent-at-law Job 9:15 Zeph. 3:15 Ps. 109:31

שֹׁפֵט judge 1047 (שָׁפַט)

שָׁפַךְ to pour out, pour 1049

Pu. to be poured out, shed Zeph. 1:17 Num. 35:33

to be caused to slip Ps. 73:2

Hithp. to pour oneself out Job 30:16 Lam. 4:1, 2:12

שקה *Hiph.* to cause to drink, give to drink 1052

Pu. to be watered Job 21:24

שֶׁקֶל shekel 1053

שֶׁקֶר deception, falsehood 1055

שרת *Pi.* to minister, serve 1058

שָׁתָה to drink 1059

Niph. to be drunk Lev. 11:34

תְּהִלָּה praise, song of praise; renown, fame 239

תָּוֶךְ midst 1063

תּוֹעֵבָה   abomination 1072

תּוֹרָה   direction, instruction, law; custom, manner 2 Sam. 7:19 435

תַּחַת   underneath, below, instead of 1065

מִתַּחַת   from under, from beneath 1066

תָּמִיד   continually, continuity 556

תָּמִים   complete, whole, sound, healthful, wholesome, innocent 1071

תמם   to be complete, finished 1070

תִּפְאָרָה   beauty, glory 802

תְּפִלָּה   prayer 813

תָּפַשׂ   to lay hold of, seize, grasp 1074
Pi. to grasp Prov. 30:28

תָּקַע   to thrust, clap, give a blow 1075
Niph. to be blown Amos. 3:6 Isa. 27:13
to strike oneself into (pledge oneself) Job 17:3

תְּרוּמָה   contribution, offering 929